PLANECRAFT

HAND PLANING
by
MODERN   METHODS

•

COMPLETELY REVISED & ENLARGED

WOODCRAFT SUPPLY CORP.
Woburn, Mass. 01888

First published 1934
Revised and Enlarged 1950
Revised and Enlarged 1959
Tenth Printing 1980
Eleventh Printing 1982

This edition is reprinted by permission
of Record Ridgway Tools, Limited

Manufactured in the United States of America

Woodcraft Supply Corp.
41 Atlantic Ave.
P.O. Box 4000
Woburn, Massachusetts 01888
1982

ISBN 0-918036-00-3

LC #79-57129

PREFACE

The pride of Craftsmanship which has distinguished all woodworkers since the birth of the Craft is undoubtedly traceable in a great measure to the intimacy which must necessarily exist between the craftsman, the tool, and the material. That intimacy is responsible for the critical attitude which every woodworker assumes in the choice of his tools, and for the opinion held generally by all woodworkers, professional and amateur, that good work can only be done with good tools which respond to the skill of the user. Such tools are a constant delight to use, and because of their beauty and finish are a joy to possess.

It has been the aim of the authors to produce a workshop companion which will be of some real service to the craftsman who earns his bread and butter by his craft, and to the amateur who finds enjoyment in his leisure by the exercise of his craft. They crave indulgence from those readers to whom certain portions of this book may be elementary, but they believe that even to them the record of improvements and of recent research herein presented will prove of value.

The authors would like to acknowledge the help they have received from the British Museum; Reading Museum; Sheffield Public Library; Dr. C. H. Mercer (Ancient Carpenters' Tools);—Batchelder, Esq. (Design in Theory and Practice); and A. H. Collins, Esq., in the research involved in tracing the history of the Plane; from Messrs. Macmillan for the loan of blocks of sash windows; and from Messrs. Evans Bros., in their very helpful "Woodworker" series of books.

In the following pages the authors have endeavoured to outline for the benefit of the reader the results of long and varied experience as craftsmen in both the making and using of the tools described in this book, and their aim and object will have been achieved if they have been of some service to the Ancient and Honourable Craft of Woodworking.

C. W. HAMPTON,
E. CLIFFORD.

PUBLISHER'S PREFACE

Since its publication in 1934, Planecraft has continued to fill the void in woodworking tool literature concerning the use of bench and specialty planes. This edition is an (exact) reprint of the original, although several of the products such as the "Stay-Set" cap iron and Fibreboard planes have been either replaced or discontinued.

We wish to thank Record Ridgway Tools Ltd., successors to the C. & J. Hampton, Ltd., for allowing us to reprint this book.

We suggest the following titles for their historical or technical significance regarding hand planes.

W.L. Goodman, British Planemakers from 1700, Needham Market (England) 1978.

Henry Mercer, Ancient Carpenters Tools, Doylestown (Pennsylvania) 1929

R.A. Salaman, Dictionary of Tools, London 1975

Alvin Sellens, The Stanley Plane, S. Burlington (Vermont) 1975

Alvin Sellens, Woodworking Planes, Augusta (Kansas) 1978

CONTENTS

Fig. 1.—Erecting a Timber Framed House about 1420 A.D.
(MS 18850, fol. 15b, British Museum)

Chapter 1

The History of the Plane

In tracing the story of the Carpenter's Plane through the ages, one has to rely mainly on the work of the archeologists to shed some light on the past, and although their researches have revealed something about early craftsmanship, very little has come to light about the tools used in early days. This may be explained to some extent by the fact that until recent times the craftsman working in wood received very little recognition for his contribution to the amenities of civilization or to the treasures of Art, so many examples of which still exist as monuments to his skill in craftsmanship and design, for in earlier times the worker was often his own designer.

Then also, the lack of documentary evidence on craftsmanship and woodworking tools in early days may be due to the social gap which separated those who were learned enough to compile written works and those who worked with their hands, one class having little in common with the other, the result being that one has to rely on other evidence than that of the written word. Furthermore, in the days of the Guilds, the "mistery" of the craft was taught in the workshop by example and the spoken word, and manuals of craftsmanship only appeared a comparatively short time ago.

In ancient Egypt the craft of the woodworker was on a high level —work that has been buried in tombs shows such accepted constructions as mortise and tenon joints, and in one tomb a model of a contemporary carpenter's shop has been found. This is now in the Metropolitan Museum of New York, to the authorities of which we are indebted for the reproduction of a photograph of the model (Fig. 2). It is interesting because, whilst it shows several carpenters busily employed at their trade, and some of the partly-finished work, not one of the carpenters is using a plane but they are trimming their boards with an adze, and smoothing them after the manner of the stone-mason, by scouring them with a stone. The mummy cases in the British Museum, and others, show evidence of this method of finish. It would be a fairly safe assumption that in those days the plane was quite unknown, although iron was well known and widely used.

Although it is a natural assumption that the first plane was a chisel fixed in a block of wood, as the chisel was known in the early days (the

Fig. 2

mortising in Fig. 2 is in principle the same as modern practice and the chisel is similar to modern chisels) who first tried it and by whom it was copied and improved is still one of the hidden mysteries of the past which will probably never be solved.*   What is certain, however, is that by the time of the Roman civilization the plane was in a very advanced stage.   Between the time of the Ancient Egyptians and the Romans,

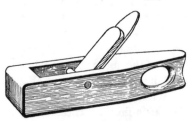

Fig. 3.   Roman Plane (Pompeii).

considerable development had taken place, and the carpenter's plane had become a highly-specialised tool.   No specimen of a Roman wooden plane has so far been traced, though doubtless such were used, but Flinders Petrie discovered in Pompeii planes which have a wood core

---

* Modern research is leaning towards the restriction of the cut of the adze—possibly by the attachment of a block or blocks of wood to the blade—resulting in a shaving rather than a chip (*vide* W. L. Goodman, Practical Education and School Crafts, Feb. 1957).

Fig. 4.—Roman Plane (Reading Museum).

sheathed in iron plate (Fig. 3). The excavations at Silchester yielded an iron plane (Fig. 4) of much sturdier construction, and of a very different pattern, though still probably having a wood core also. Excavations on the Continent have yielded Roman planes of Bronze, one of which, at Cologne, is all metal with no wood core. This era of development presents a remarkable similarity with the subsequent development of the plane from 1800 onwards as may be seen later.

The Pompeii planes are remarkable in several ways. There was evidently a desire on the part of the worker for a more permanently accurate sole, hence the metal sheathing. This sheathing passes round the plane, top, nose and sole, and holes are cut in the sole and top for the mouth and escapement. The hand hole is pierced in a workmanlike way, in such a position as to get a maximum result for the effort expended, and actually follows modern practice in some respect, though we do not close the top of the handle as is done here. In common with the Silchester Plane, the cutter or iron is secured by a wedge, holding against a strong rivet which passes through the centre of the plane. This method is still employed by the Chinese, who use a piece of iron roughly resembling a cut nail, as a wedge.* It is not certain of what material the Roman wedge was made, but it was probably wood. The position of the handle leaves little to be desired, and it has been suggested that the central rivet and wedge are superior to the channel and wedge which are to be found on the present planes, but it may be that the rivet and wedge method is more prone to chatter.

The iron plane from Silchester offers a remarkable resemblance in its main lines of design to the most up-to-date planes of to-day. This may best be demonstrated by comparing a modern metal Jack Plane with the Roman plane (Fig. 4) which is 13¼ in. long, 2¼ in. wide, the cutter is 4¼ in. long and has a pitch of 65 degrees.

Both the planes illustrated have single irons, and it has always been assumed that the invention of the cap iron came early in the 19th

---

* c.f. also Fig. 20, page 20

9

century, the need for it being strongly felt with the increased use of mahogany so popular at that period. It is, therefore, interesting to find that among the iron tools which were found in the excavations at the Roman border fortress of Newstead, was what appeared to be a Roman

Fig. 5

double plane iron (Fig. 5) which is similar to the cap iron in principle This double iron appears to be unique, the only specimen until the cap iron appeared early in the nineteenth century. It may indeed not be a plane iron at all; there were no planes found with it, but its form and design are such that they are very suggestive of an early attempt at a cap iron. The two irons are welded together at the top. The same "smith's hoard" of tools yielded several chisels, tanged and socketed, quite equal in design and workmanship to modern tools, and also, curiously enough, a moulding plane iron which will cut a moulding about an inch wide. This, like the cap ironed cutter, appears to be the only one of its kind that has been found, and Flinders Petrie wondered at this, as mouldings were in great favour by the Roman carpenters. A possible explanation is that most of these mouldings were made with a scratch stock, the blades of which, being small, would be easily lost. The two cutters discussed here, the chisels, and actual examples of Roman craftsmanship which are fine examples of the wheelwright's art, may be seen in the National Museum of Antiquities, in Edinburgh.

It is interesting to speculate at this point as to what degree the native craftsman of Britain contributed to the improvement of the plane, but there is little evidence to guide us. Julius Caesar has given vivid descriptions of the chariots used by the Ancient Britons. After he had defeated them, they retreated with some 4,000 chariots. He also makes a point of the greatness of the fleet which he had to conquer and its superior seaworthiness to his own. If we allow for a pardonable exaggeration on the general's part, we are forced to the conclusion that both the smith's and the carpenter's art (and the smith and the carpenter may have been one and the same person) were more advanced than we have usually assumed, and after the Roman conquest there must have been a fusion of the craft knowledge of both peoples—the Newstead Cap Iron may indeed have been the work of a British or Pict craftsman. However that may be, after the end of the Roman period it is extremely difficult to trace anything at all connected with the plane for several centuries. Yet the invaders of England came over in wooden ships;

they lived in houses made of wood; they had wooden pails, one of which, an excellent example of workmanship, still survives; so the craft of the woodworker must have existed and continued even in those perilous times and on through the Norman Conquest. The Norman castles and churches could not have been built without the prior constructions of the carpenter for the stone-mason to use, though again, the stone-mason may have been his own carpenter; yet not a vestige of evidence seemingly can be found of the tools used. It may be that with the incursion of the Northmen the plane was lost, and its work done with the axe and the adze, for when in later times the carpenter is depicted in illuminated manuscripts he is as often as not using an axe or an adze (c.f. also Fig. 1), whilst the few remaining 13th century chests show by the texture of their surfaces that they were worked by the adze; yet by the 14th century the carpenter had a kit of tools very much the same in content as he carries now, and it included a "pleyn"; for a 14th century poem, anonymous, rendered into modern English by Mr. A. H. Collins, records a humorous and very human conversation in which (in the characteristic style of those days) all the tools speak for themselves and take a part, and from which we extract:—

> "What, Sir Rule?" then said the plane—
> "My master shall not want for gain.
> I'll work for him, both day and night
> To get him good with all my might.
> I'll cleanse the wood on every side
> To help my master in his pride."

The type of "pleyn" would most probably be somewhat like the plane which appears in Fig. 1, which is from a manuscript in the British Museum. Apart from the wide variety of tools here depicted, the picture is of value in that it shows a long plane was then in use. Some of the other manuscripts of the period show only a shorter plane, and that has led some to wonder whether or not the longer plane as used in Roman times had been lost. The evidence of the picture is that the

Fig. 7.—Plane of date c. 1514.

Fig. 6. — Early 15th Century Plane (French) British Museum. MSS 4431, fol. 196.

11

mediaeval carpenter was fully aware of the use of the longer plane as well as the shorter one, for at his feet lies a small smoothing plane also, very similar to another one (Fig. 6) which appears on a French manuscript, also in the British Museum. It will be noted that the plane which is in use has two handles, horizontally fixed, though the carpenter is only using the back one. Does this indicate that on occasion a helper was pressed into service to pull at the fore-end—as we shall see later was done with some planes of a later date? Or is it merely that at times the plane was pushed and at other times pulled? Or is it that the iron may be set either way? The horizontally-placed handle probably persisted for some time, as a variant of it will be seen in a later plane (Fig. 13).

From this time onward, evidence, though still scanty, allows us to follow the trend of the design of the tool a little better. Dürer's famous picture, "Melancholia", gives us a vivid impression of the Smoothing Plane (Fig. 7) of his time for, whilst the minute correctness of the detail of his pictures may not always satisfy the art critic, it admirably conveys to us what the plane was like—the shapeliness of the body, the rounded end, the shaping of the forward horn—that fitness for purpose which becomes a craftsman making a tool when he knows from practical

Fig. 8.—Plane of 16th Century.

12

experience precisely what is required. The detail of the picture is such that we can see from it the method even of fitting the horn into the body. The pictures of the "Swan" Planes (Figs. 1 and 6) are not so abundantly full of detail, but there also we may see how carefully the tool was designed for comfortable handling.

The planes of the 15th, 16th, and 17th centuries are almost invariably fitted with a forward horn. This disappeared in England, if indeed it was ever very common, but it has persisted on the Continent until the present day and almost all the planes of Northern Europe are so fitted. The woodcut of Jost Ammon (photographed by Mr. A. H. Collins from a book published in 1574, now in Frankfurt), (Fig. 8), shows a chestmaker at work using a horned plane very similar to that of the Melancholia Plane. The chestmakers were, of course, pioneers in the craft of the cabinet-maker, and they "builded better than they knew".

The forward horn presented an opportunity for a good deal of variation and individuality. It is a product of an age when time, in terms of hurry and bustle, did not count for much. It was an age when men expressed themselves very freely in their craft—"designers" in the modern sense had not appeared. It was natural that a man who was making his own tools should make them primarily to serve his purpose efficiently, but having completed a sound "utilitarian" tool, he frequently satisfied an innate aesthetic urge by incorporating carved decoration in the design. Not only so, they were also open to inspection and undoubtedly sound criticism by fellow members of the Guild. It is not unlikely indeed that in many cases they were made so as to invite criticism. So long then, as the horn served its primary purpose efficiently—the only excuse that it had for being there—that it was comfortable for the hand and not likely to produce blisters and kindred troubles—it could be, and was, treated in a host of ways.

Fig. 9.—Early German Plane (probably 16th Century).

A scroll was a natural suggestion, and the scroll appears very frequently (Fig. 9). It was not always an elegant scroll, some are better than others, but all show a healthy individuality of treatment, and one may read into them apprentice struggles towards a mastery of a manly craft, for it must be assumed that, much as the apprentice of forty or fifty years ago made his own tool chest as a triumph (or otherwise!) over his craft, the earlier apprentice must have spent the majority of his spare time in making his tools, the very instruments of his craft. But when we come across a plane of the type shown in Fig. 10, it would not seem that we have the work of an apprentice hand—that, surely, is the product of a master craftsman. The scrolls are finished work—the toe and heel

Fig. 10.—Cabinet Maker's Plane of 17th Century.
(Batchelder: Design in Theory and Practice.)

are so designed that it is impossible to trap the fingers, yet this design is cleverly hidden in the decoration—the decoration *is* the design. There is little wonder that the saying was handed down generation by generation to the present day, that a craftsman is known by his tools.

It was the custom at one time to incorporate in the carved decoration the owner's initials and the date of manufacture, and several planes thus decorated have survived. Of such, it is often noticed that they do not

Fig. 11

14

carry evidence of excessive wear; they must have been veritable treasures. Often they are wide Rabbet Planes or Moulding Planes which would not, of course, be subject to as much wear as a Jack or Smooth. Fig. 11 shows a late example of one of these dated planes, the reproduction of which is inserted by courtesy of the South Kensington Museum, where two similar planes are preserved. One, dated 1688, with the initials P F was at one time in the Museum of Antiquities at Edinburgh. This was 21 inches long but, falling to pieces through decay, it was destroyed, and as, unfortunately, no photograph of it was taken, we are unable to include a pictorial representation.

(It is a pity that there have been in the past so few museums like the two we mention; our task would have been much simplified, but whilst museums are teeming with flints and armour, the tools of war, few have any of the craftsman's tools of peace. It is even on record that a well-known museum refused a large collection of Greek tools on the grounds that they had no aesthetic attraction. South Kensington and Edinburgh have appreciated the craftsman's point of view, but against centuries of academic tradition their task has not been easy. With a modern trend towards industrial and folk museums, the position has recently improved. Craftsmen can make a valuable contribution to this effort by presenting to museums, specimens of tools which have become obsolete though their historical value may be considerable.)

The Smooth Plane of the Nova Zembla expedition, left by ship's carpenters in 1596 (Rijks Museum, Amsterdam) has a simpler variant of the forward horn, but its principal interest for us is its iron, not shown

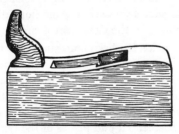

Fig. 12.—Smoothing Plane of 1596 (Rijks Museum, Amsterdam).

in the sketch (Fig. 12). This, both in shape and bevel edge, closely resembles a modern iron, but there is no slot or other provision for a cap iron; it was a single iron plane. The time of the double-iron had not yet arrived.

Hibben shows (The Carpenter's Tool Chest) two English Planes of the 17th century—a smooth and a jack—which call for passing comment. The jack is provided with a forward horn reminiscent of the hooked horn of the "swan" type plane of the 15th century. The handle or toat (the derivation of this word is obscure—has it any connection with O.E. totian in the sense of sticking out, protruding?) is of very unusual form

Fig. 13.—English: 17th Century Plane.   Fig. 14.—English: 17th Century Plane.

(Fig. 13)—a more decorative form perhaps of the flat handles of the 15th century plane noted above (Fig. 1). The Smooth Plane has neither forward horn nor backward handle, but fore and aft the shape is ogee, thus leaving enough protection against trapped fingers (Fig. 14). Was the horn discarded because the workman found it in the way when he wished to dislodge the iron by rapping the forward part of the plane on the bench top? On discarding it did he still continue to grasp his plane round the front of the nose, as when he had the horn, until the later method of holding the plane fingers across the top, thumb down, was adopted? A projecting toe was certainly very much in favour about this time, and it continued until well into the early part of the 19th century.

Except as regards the toat and the horn, the form of the 17th century planes differed very little from the form of the wood planes of the 18th and 19th centuries, some of which still linger amongst us. The hollow toat appeared in the later 18th century; the horn disappeared—at any rate in England—though on the Continent it survives.

An interesting variation has been noted in one or two survivals where a plane has been fitted with two blades, sometimes these being on adjacent faces. The purpose of this is not quite clear, though a possible explanation is that one of the irons was ground slightly round, and used as a jack, whilst the other was ground as a try plane, dead straight. An illustration is not available, but odd planes of the type may be met with occasionally in private collections.

Many craftsmen using modern planes, during a comparatively long spell of planing, frequently adopt a pull on the knob for a time as a relief from a push on the handle. This raises the point as to whether or not planes were always pushed, and it may explain in part the reason for the horn. "Nouveau Manuel Complet du Charpentier" (Biston Boutereau at Hanus, Paris, 1848) shows a Galère, or Demi-varlope, an organ builder's plane (Fig. 15) through which two handles pass, fore and aft, and the accompanying instructions indicate how the plane is pulled by one man and pushed by another at the same time. Hibben shows a

16

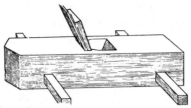

Fig. 15.—French Galère (Demi Varlope) 1848.

similar plane as a 17th century plane. The Chinese Plane is fitted with a similar crossbar, and this is definitely pulled and not pushed; and some Japanese Planes follow the same lines and method of working. There are men who are still at the bench who can remember wide architrave moulding planes being used that were bored with a hole in the fore part. The craftsman pushed the plane in the ordinary way whilst the apprentice assisted by standing at the other end of the work hauling on a cord attached to the plane through the hole. It has been very difficult to trace one of these "holed" Moulding Planes; they called for laborious work, and with the general adoption of the Spindle Machine

Fig. 16.—"Holed" Moulding Plane.

they were gladly lost or forgotten by their owners. Fig. 16 shows one of these planes. It had two irons (one of which is missing) and was discovered in Gloucester Technical College. The cooper has yet another variation. His plane is neither pulled nor pushed; he works to-day exactly as he did in the 16th century (Fig. 17).

Fig. 17.—Cooper's Jointer Plane (from Jost Amman, 1539-1591)
(length about 5 ft. 6 in.)

But to return to the main story. We have reached a time when the art of the cabinet-maker was approaching a very high level, a time when craftsmanship was at its best, and when new and strange woods were being imported plentifully from distant lands which had figure and grain calling for greater and still greater skill in their mastery, and the wood-worker responded with more efficient tools. The demand for a finer finish and greater accuracy of work meant much experimenting with planes to achieve this object. It is a remarkable fact that, except for the lower pitch of the iron, development now offers a close parallel with that of Roman times. It started with an iron sheathing, like that of the Pompeii Planes (discovered at a later date). Fig. 18 shows such a plane

Fig. 18.—Ironplated Plane of date about 1800.

discovered in the United States of America, dating from about 1800. It is virtually a wooden plane, with a sheathing of iron, a low set cutting-iron and a very narrow mouth, ideal for the shooting of mitres and end grain and for smooth finish to difficult grained wood. It is said that this plane was made in England, and it was destined to be the forerunner of many similar types. The fixing of the blade is by wedge, the wedge being of such a form that the iron can be withdrawn without rapping the plane on the bench, and it has a protruding toe! Belonging to approximately the same time, Fig. 19 (top) shows a similar plane discovered in Norwich, England. In this case the sole is made in two parts, one of them notched so as to form an extremely narrow mouth.

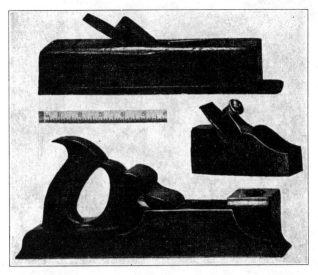

Fig. 19

Countersunk screws attach the sole to the wood core of the body. A striking knob is let into the fore part, and the plane bears evidence of adjustment at the rear in many hammer marks. On the side of the plane are two well-worn ebony strips, indicating that it has seen much service on the shooting-board. The low pitch of the irons of these two planes would necessitate the use of single irons with which they are fitted. The Norwich Plane has no sheathing on the sides or ends.

The difficulty of assigning a definite date to such planes as the foregoing iron ones will be at once appreciated by the reader, and in days when communication and transport were vastly inferior to modern times, it will not be surprising to discover that one part of the world was more forward than another, and the evidence of the iron plane shown in Fig. 20 indicates that this type of plane was in an advanced stage as early as 1719 in France. The plane, approximately $8\frac{1}{2}$ in. long and accommodating a $1\frac{1}{2}$ in. cutter (which has disappeared), is made of plate about $\frac{1}{8}$ in. thick, sides being brazed to the sole, which projects fore and aft. Presumably the lining was of wood, and the riveted crossbar held the wedge and cutter. The pitch is about 30 degrees. A bent-over projection at the fore-end is carved or filed into the form of a shell, giving a comfortable fore grip, whilst the rounding of the back would afford a comfortable hold for the right hand. The edges are highly ornate, and suggest that the upper surfaces of the wood filling may

19

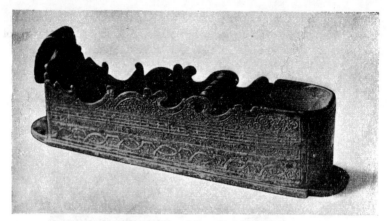

Fig. 20.—French Iron Plane, 1719.

have been equally decorative in keeping. Sides and end are completely covered with decoration which is probably etched, though it may have been carved, when one recalls the high degree of skill that the French locksmiths exhibited nearly two centuries prior to this. The name of the owner, Jaques Boquay; his address, Rue d'Argenteuil, Paris; and the date, 1719 appear in the decoration of the rounded after-end and, as befits such a famous violin maker, the fore-end is decorated with a trophy of musical instruments. Midway around the sides runs a musical air, with the love song:—

> Je dors du moment que je suis à table,
>> Je ne puis dormir, quand je suis seul au lit,
> Sans toi, ma cherie, tout m'est insupportable,
>> Et tout à mes yeux par toi est embelli.

This is translated by D. F. Duce thus:—

> Sleep holds me when I'm left alone at table,
>> Yet comes not, when alone in bed I lie;
> Without you, dear, to live I am not able,
>> I need you near, the world to beautify.

The plane is in the possession of Messrs. Wm. E. Hill & Sons, violin makers, by whose courtesy permission was given to photograph it.

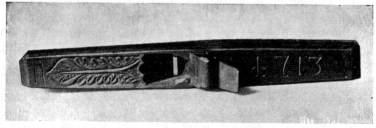

Fig. 21.

A beech Try Plane of approximately the same period (1713), Fig. 21, also in the possession of Messrs. Hill, bears the initials I.B. and the date 1713, and is carved on the fore part of the top, the escapement being neatly and cleanly finished with three gouge cuts. This plane

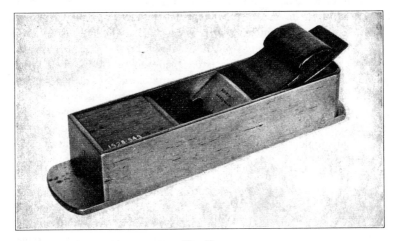

Fig. 22.

is remarkable in having neither handle nor fore grip, but running the whole length of the plane on both sides is a gouged groove, about half an inch from the bottom, into which fingers and thumb may fit as the hand is stretched over the plane. Another unusual feature is the

Fig. 23.

21

tapering from centre to front and back, this giving an easier grip, especially when the hand is rather small.

Other planes of the early years of the 19th century have survived in which a sheathing or plating of iron is employed, and in some cases this sheathing is dovetailed together as in the examples shown in Figs. 22 and 23, the first of which is shown by courtesy of the South Kensington Museum, the second being from East Anglia, possibly a "gain" from a shipwreck. The plates of this latter plane are not dovetailed in the strict sense of the word, but are rather notched into each other and brazed. After the fashion of the Roman development, however unwittingly, this plane shows the central rivet and not side channels for the blade and wedge, the rivet being rectangular in section and set at the appropriate angle in the body, parallel with the line of the cutter. The wood core still persisted; considering the technique of the time it was easier to make the plane so, and tradition ever dies hard. Even when later the wedge is made of brass, and is centrally pivoted, and the hold maintained by a screw, lever fashion (Fig. 19 centre), the body core is still of wood. This is a plane of mid-19th century, probably "home made" but typical of many of that time and later, which was retrieved from an attic in Dundee where it had lain for many years. By this time the craft of the toolmaker had developed, and many planes from 1800 onwards trace their origin to Sheffield and London. The plane shown in Fig. 22 was made by Nelson, of Edgware Road, London, about 1820, whose business was taken over in 1824 by J. Buck, the maker of the beautiful Panel Plane shown in Fig. 19 (bottom). The sole and sides of this plane are made very solidly of one piece of iron; the filling is of rosewood; the wedge is shaped for easy removal and a striking knob is provided in the usual forward position.

As if to follow the Roman precedent still more closely, bronze was often used by the craftsmen of yesterday for their plane bodies, but usually only in the smaller planes such as bull nose and shoulder planes. Behind all these searchings and experiments was a desire for more permanent accuracy of the sole and mouth, and the advantages of metal for this purpose having been demonstrated in practice, it was not long before cast iron was exploited to further this end. Knowles, in 1827, took out a patent for a cast iron plane which required no wood filling. The fitting of the iron was by wedge, with the usual side channels, and therein lay its weakness, for adjustment by hammer on a cast iron tool is asking for trouble. Hence, inventive minds set about to minimise this defect, and in a year or two there appeared a plane on similar lines, still using a wedge, but in this new pattern adjustment was arranged by forming in the fore part of the sole a square hole, through which projected a block of wood. This block could be raised or lowered at will by a screw adjustment on the top of the plane—thus, the blade being fixed initially by the wedge, the effective amount of cut and the thickness of the shaving were dependent upon the position of the block. This meant that the major part of the sole was not in use, so it was really no

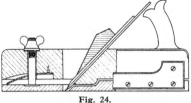

Fig. 24.

solution, and the plane had no longer life than the plane with a similar aim (Fig. 24) which appears in "Spon's Mechanic's Own Book" (second edition, 1886). In this case, the plane, a Wood Jack of conventional pattern, is sawn through horizontally. The two parts are joined by a long hinge plate, pivoted on the upper half. The upper part also retains, by wedge, the cutting iron, By means of a screw stop and spring the amount of available "iron" is controlled, and on the return stroke, the pressure naturally being relieved over the nose, the blade does not draw along the work, but rides above it.

About the middle of the 19th century inventors concentrated more on the elimination of the wedge and finding a more satisfactory way of adjusting the iron. In 1844 Sandford patented a screw adjustment of the iron, the top of the iron being turned over at right angles to form a nut for the adjustment. It was, however, Bailey of the United States of America who later introduced the lever cam to replace the wedge and also the screw adjustment operating through a Y lever. To Bailey also must be given the credit of seeing the advantage of a thin cutter in that grinding and honing were reduced to a minimum.

These improvements came gradually, and at first, carpenters were reluctant to discard the wood body entirely—some of the earlier improvements were fitted to planes on which the upper part resembled a modern iron plane whilst the lower half was of wood. About seventy years ago, G. A. Warren had added the eccentric cam method of lateral adjustment; had re-introduced the forward horn in the form of a knob, and had invented the separable frog. Other details have been added later, both in the U.S.A. and England.

The last improvement is due to the makers of Record Iron Planes, and consists of a separable cap iron (Fig. 25), the effect of which is entirely to eliminate any possibility of chatter. It simplifies grinding and honing, and ensures that the cap iron shall return to the exact setting. It increases efficiency and also saves the time of the user.

Thus, steadily improving through the ages, the modern plane, accurately made and capable of accurate and easy work, is not the

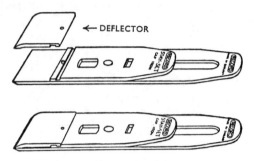

Fig. 25.—Record "STAY-SET" Cap Iron.

invention of any one man, but embodies in itself the work and thought of many, and though the machine plane is with us, the hand plane will never leave us. Its present form is more efficient than ever it has been;

Fig. 26.—Modern Record Plane.

its materials, thanks to modern research, were never better. But, is the present form the ultimate one?

Thus far, our survey of the plane has in the main been concerned with the form of the plane, important in that it naturally affects the "feel" and the handling of the tool, but we have considered very little the material of which the various planes were made, nor have we discussed the character of that most vital part the cutter or "iron" as it is frequently called by the craftsman. As regards the material of the body of the wooden planes, there is no record of course of what timber those appearing in the early manuscripts were made; of the rest, the favourite wood was red beech, in England at any rate. On the Continent, white beech and birch have both been used, as is the case at the present day. With the arrival of the iron-cased planes, mahogany was a favourite wood, later giving way to rosewood.

The original "irons" of the historical planes have mostly disappeared, for in the nature of things the iron is ground away with sharpening, and another iron replaces that originally installed. Most of the planes we have illustrated have seen many years of service, and the irons that have been found in them are often much more modern than are the bodies. A thicker iron than is at present used was characteristic of the older planes. Some experiment had been made with thinner irons about a century ago, even in wood planes, the irons of the cased mitre planes being usually of a thinner gauge. A tapered iron was at one time in favour, but it gradually gave way to the parallel iron. Steel facings on iron backs have been standard practice, but it is not easy to discover when this welded or composite cutter was first introduced.

To those accustomed to think of engineering as a modern science, and the use of tool steel as a nineteenth century innovation, it is a puzzle how good carpentry and cabinet-making was done with the material available for cutters to the earlier workers. We have already hinted at the high degree of skill that must have existed in Britain long before the Christian era, but when we read in Homer that the hissing of the stake which Ulysses drove into the eye of Polyphemus was like that of the steel quenched in water—an account that was written not later than the ninth century B.C., we are bound to realise that the hardening and tempering of steel, a delicate art at any time, was a familiar process at a very remote time, and to have been so familiar as to have been used in such a simile, it must have been practised in Homer's time for many years. That steel should have been in common use is not so remarkable—it is most likely that most of the iron in use in early times was really steel—it is not unlikely that most of the so-called iron in use in early times contained sufficient carbon which, together with a good deal of hammering by the blacksmith, would enable it to be hardened.

Jas. Napier ("Manufacturing Arts of Ancient Times", pp. 213 *et seq.*) suggests that bronze was tipped with steel or iron. Iron tools were used by the Ancient Egyptians and the Hebrews; an iron tool was found embedded in one of the tombs dating back to somewhere about 3,500 B.C.; Tubal Cain, the blacksmith, was the sixth in descent from Adam; but there is a suggestion that the Egyptians considered iron an impure metal—they preferred bronze. That the Ancients had a method of hardening copper and bronze, which is now a forgotten art, is not borne out by the facts. If it were, the bronze that is found would be hard, and that is not so—unless it has passed through a normalization due to time. Hard edges could be obtained by hammering, and the Romans had certainly small field anvils on which such hammering was done, as when sharpening a scythe. In any case, although bronze was used for a plane body by the Romans, there is no indication that they used bronze for the blades. Those which have survived are of iron or steel.

The steel of which the blades were then made was "natural" steel, the carbon content of which was accidental, subject to many variations, and the cutting and edge-keeping qualities of these blades would vary accordingly. This would be the case until the fifteenth and sixteenth centuries, the methods of the ironfounders having varied but little except in the magnitude of their output until these times. Metallurgy is a comparatively new science, and in spite of the work of Huntsman in the mid-18th century; of Bessemer a century later, and of many others, the variation of the qualities of plane irons has persisted almost up to the present day. Within living memory, indeed, the purchase of a satisfactory plane iron was largely a matter of luck. It might be too hard or too soft; it might hold its edge or it might not.

The contribution of Huntsman to the development of the plane was an indirect one, but important in that it very materially improved the qualities of the steels available for the cutting irons. It was about 1740 that he introduced the "Crucible Process" of melting steel in small crucibles. The effect of this was that the slag, or rich iron silicate which was present, mechanically mixed with the steel, could be freed readily. The removal of this cinder greatly improves the steel. The process was costly then, and it remains costly to-day, but the quality of the steel is so suitable for plane blades, and so incomparably better than the cheaper-produced Bessemer open-hearth steel of later introduction, that Record plane cutters are always made from best crucible cast steel, further improved through the application of modern scientific knowledge, advanced metallurgical research and wide practical experience. The details of this laboratory research and workshop experiment need not be traced here; it will be sufficient to note that the main lines of the research were devoted to careful analysis and accurate heat treatment, the ultimate result being the well-known and proved Tungsten steel cutter, fitted to all Record Planes. This forms the latest and most far-reaching development of the plane up to the present time. The design, material and performance of Record Tools are always under close scrutiny and where improvements are found necessary to meet modern conditions, our experience and facilities enable us to introduce new features to meet these demands. Improvements in both design and performance of Tools are accepted by the user as a matter of course, and he is unaware of the amount of time, energy and work put in for such developments. Our three Factories are equipped with up-to-date plant for the specialised production of Record Tools.

The reader will naturally ask: "Why is this Tungsten steel better than ordinary steel?" There are two reasons which stand out most clearly. The first is that Tungsten has the property of uniting with the Carbon in the steel and forming Tungsten Carbide. Tungsten

Carbide is the main constituent of all high speed cutting materials as used in modern machine tools for metal working, turning lathes, boring machines, milling machines, gear-cutting machines, etc.

This material will cut at tremendous speeds, even when working on hard steel. In fact, its introduction a few years ago caused great changes in the design of machines on account of its capacity to cut at very high speeds. It is therefore logical that a plane iron containing the correct amount of Tungsten is harder and more resistant to wear, and will take a keener cutting edge, **and hold it** for a longer period than would an ordinary steel. This has been proved beyond doubt in the use of Record Irons.

Secondly, the correct and proper introduction of Tungsten is greatly beneficial in steel for plane irons as it prevents grain growth in the steel. This means that in the fully hardened cutter the steel is of very small grain size, which is immediately obvious when a blade is fractured. Because the grain size is small, the steel is more resistant to shock, and therefore the keen edge will suffer less damage when cutting than any other steel. (Fig. 27 and Fig. 28).

 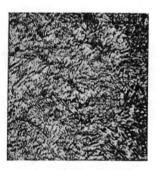

Fig. 27.—Ordinary Cast Steel under Microscope.   Fig. 28.—Tungsten Steel under Microscope.

(Both on the same Magnifications.)

Modern Science has brought engineering aids to the help of the Plane Maker which were not available a few years ago, enabling the maximum grade of skill to be employed on every operation. Thus, by using skilled engineering, not only is the bevel of the cutter correctly ground, but a uniform thickness and parallelism are attained in every blade (a factor which has so much to do with the efficiency of the whole assembly), and the elimination of looseness and chatter when the plane is in service.

The whole of the heat treatment (Annealing, Hardening, Tempering) is in like manner controlled scientifically by delicate pyrometric instruments which are so sensitive as to record the slightest variation of temperature, eliminating all "hit or miss" methods and discounting human error.

Fig. 29.—Testing Record Plane Irons.

Finally, every Record Tungsten Steel Cutting Iron is tested on a Hardness Testing Machine which inexorably and unrelentingly speaks the truth. Consequently, the makers of Record Planes have not the slightest hesitation in guaranteeing to be right every individual blade that leaves the works. Never in the history of tools was the craftsman able to command a better plane than he can to-day.

For allied reading on the subject of this Chapter:—
Mercer: "Ancient Carpenter's Tools."
Flinders Petrie: "Ancient Tools and Weapons."
Hibben: "The Carpenter's Tool Chest."

W. L. Goodman: "The History of Woodworkers' Tools". (Practical Education and School Crafts, 1957-8.)

Chapter 2

Bench Planes, Block Planes

On account of their more frequent use, three planes have by common usage acquired the description "Bench Planes". Taken in order of their size, they are the Smooth, the Jack, and the Trying Plane. Of the latter variety, the shorter ones are sometimes called "Fore" planes. In recent years, another plane, the smallest of all, the Block Plane, has come to stay with us as a Bench Plane.

Fig. 30.—Record Jack Plane.

Of the Bench planes, the Jack, No. 05 and No. 05½, 14 in. and 15 in. long, respectively, is the first to be used, and is called into action more frequently than any other. It is used in the preliminary cleaning and squaring of timber, and it can be used also for accurate shooting of moderately long edges, provided the iron is suitably ground and honed for that purpose. (See Chapters 4 and 5.)

Fig. 31.—Record Jointer Plane.

For shooting long edges, however, the Fore or Jointer Plane should be used. No. 06 has a cutter 2⅜ in. wide, and a length of 18 in.; No. 07 has a similar cutter, with an increased length of 22 in., and will be found equal to most of the work occurring in joiners' and cabinet-makers' shops. When extra long lengths have frequently to be jointed, the

No. 08, having a $2\frac{5}{8}$ in. cutter, and a sole length of 24 in. is strongly recommended. In spite of its length and its 9 lb. weight, this plane is exceedingly pleasant to handle. Its weight keeps it well down to its job, and the position of the knob and handle, well down to their work, makes control quite easy, and accurate work a regular feature.

Fig. 32.—Record Smooth Plane.

The Smooth Plane, as its name indicates, is used for smoothing up any irregularities that are present after the Jack Plane has been used, and for smoothing over joints after glueing so that all presents a clean and smooth finish, free from blemishes. It is made in three sizes, No. 03, cutter $1\frac{3}{4}$ in., length 8 in.; No. 04, cutter 2 in., length 9 in.; No. 04$\frac{1}{2}$, cutter $2\frac{3}{8}$ in., length 10 in. The choice of size depends a great deal on the class of work that predominates. In a general workshop where a Jack is also used, No. 03 or 04 will be found most suitable. No. 04$\frac{1}{2}$ is extremely useful in smoothing up longer lengths, but not so handy for skimming over joints. In an amateur's workshop it might serve as a Jack, whilst many professionals use it as a general purpose plane.

BLOCK PLANES

The Block Plane is so called from the fact that it was originally brought into being for the making and re-trimming of Butchers' Blocks which, to better withstand the constant wear due to chopping, were made of hardwood—usually sycamore or maple, these being white in colour—with the end grain upwards. The pitch of the smoothing plane was too high to do this work without the danger of splitting off much of the fibre; so a lower pitched plane, made of wood, was devised for the purpose. Lowering the pitch of the cutter naturally necessitated making the grinding angle more acute, and it was found to be impossible to lower the pitch to any appreciable extent without making the grinding angle so acute as to make it too weak. Consequently it was found that the only practicable way of lowering the pitch was to reverse the blade, so that the ground side was uppermost. This meant, of course, that there was no need for a cap iron on a block plane. For a long time the only woodworker who possessed a block plane was the man engaged on butchers' blocks. In due course with the introduction of iron planes, the wood-bodied block plane gave way to the iron-bodied one, which was much superior. Nowadays the use of the block plane is almost universal, and there is a large variety of detail in their design and a constantly expanding demand for them, yet it is quite certain that only a small proportion of those used ever come into contact with a butcher's block.

To understand how this has come about, it will be necessary to digress a little and to examine a part of the history of the craft. Fifteenth century woodwork owes a good deal of its charm to its simplicity and to the frankness of its construction. Its mortise and tenon joints are straight through and there is no attempt to hide them. Later they are still openly shown, and further secured with "Trenails"—wooden round pegs—these pegs forming decorative spots by virtue of their careful placing, yet primarily they are essential parts of the construction. But by the end of the eighteenth century, the woodworker's skill had so far advanced that he was able to make good and sound joints which were hidden away out of sight. His tenons were curtailed so that they did not project through. There was good enough reason for it—the shrinkage of the stiles due to the natural drying out of the wood, resulted in the ends of the tenons projecting. With a contemporary advance in the art of polishing, this projection became a very noticeable blemish. Thus, open and frank dovetail box joints gave way to secret dovetails, and it was traditional in the workshops, even within living memory, never to leave end grain exposed if there was any possible way of preventing it.

With such conditions, it is quite easy to see that there was a grand opening for the unscrupulous worker—if a joint was hidden from sight and no one was ever to see it—why worry to be honest about it? Good joints call for careful workmanship and time expended on them. The unscrupulous just dodged it, and spent time only on those parts which were to be seen. The result was a very widespread decline in craftsmanship, for the honest man cannot compete under such conditions.

A return to sound ideas had to come sooner or later, and the main credit for its return must be given to Ernest Gimson and his immediate followers. He broke away boldly from the hidden constructions and the superfluous ornament of the Victorian Period, and designed and executed his work on the lines of simplicity, good proportion and decoration based in the main on the essential constructions he employed. It is to the school of craftsmen that he founded that posterity will look for the characteristic expression of the cabinet-maker of the present day. The secret dovetail gave way to the open box dovetail, the arrangement frequently decorative (Fig. 33); the stub tenon gave way to the through tenon, often left deliberately projecting, the edges being bevelled off as a decoration (Fig. 34), or it was wedged with wood of a different colour from the tenon, and so on.

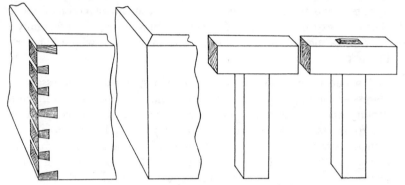

Figs. 33 and 34.—New and old treatment of Joints.

It is this extended use of end grain that has called for the expansion of the need for the block plane to such an extent that practically every woodworker to-day finds it impossible to get on satisfactorily without one, and it also explains the reason for the constant improvements in the design, embracing refinements which a few years ago would not have been dreamed of, until to-day some of the block planes are highly efficient precision tools, able in ordinary daily work to leave clean surfaces by the removal of shavings the thickness of which is in the neighbourhood of .001 in.; for whilst it is admitted that there is a good deal of shoddy work turned out to-day, the claim that woodwork is being done of a higher grade than ever before in history is easy to sustain, and the number of men, both professional and amateur whose ideals are in this manner fashioned, is legion.

The Record Block Planes are designed according to the demand of the worker for a simple and economical tool without any refinements on the one hand, and for the demand for a highly-finished tool with every refinement of accurate and quick adjustment on the other. In the first class should be placed No. 0110, and No. 0130.

Fig. .35—Record Block Plane, No. 0110.

Fig. 36.—Record Block Plane which may be used for bull nose work also. No. 0130.

These two planes are quite efficient in practice. The cutters are rigidly held with a knurled wheel and screw. The base and sides are accurately ground and polished, and are square to each other. Whilst

0110 is just a block plane pure and simple, 0130 is so designed that the blade may be used in another position, so that it may be used as a bull-nosed plane. This plane is a deservedly popular one with the joiners, who find that they can use it in places difficult of access, and with one hand if the work calls for that.

Fig. 37.—RECORD Block Plane No. 0120.

Fig. 38.—RECORD Block Plane No. 0220.

A slight disadvantage of the previous two planes is that owing to their very economical price, they are not fitted with any screw adjustment to the cutter. No. 0120, whilst being still economical in price, is fitted with a screw adjustment for regulating the depth of the cut; an addition that is well worth the little extra initial cost, as adjustment of the cut is both positive and speedy. No. 0220 is similarly furnished as regards adjustment, but differs in design in that instead of the cutter being secured with a knurled wheel and screw, it is secured with a plated lever and cam which, being on the top is slightly more easy of access. The cost of these two planes is the same.

Fig. 39.—RECORD Block Plane No. 09½.

Further refinements of the block plane have been made, which still further extend their usefulness, enabling them to clean up to a fine finish the most difficult of woods, in that adjustment of the mouth has been fitted in addition to cutter adjustment. This is arranged by having the forward part of the sole to slide in an accurately-machined groove, it being secured in any position by the knurled screw which replaces the hardwood knob that is fitted to those block planes which have no mouth adjustment. Thus it is but a matter of a few seconds to alter the width of the mouth to suit the varying conditions that are met with as the work proceeds; the knurled screw is given a turn to slacken it, the lever is moved to open or close the mouth to any desired position, and the screw tightened up again. In general design, No. 09½ follows No. 0220, Fig. 38. It is six inches long, cutter 1⅝ in. wide, and has thumb recesses. Sides and base are accurately ground and polished.

33

Fig. 40.—RECORD Block Plane, No. 018.

The most refined plane in the range of block planes, a plane which cannot be too highly recommended as being equal to any demand of the craftsman who is fastidious about his tools, is here shown. No. 018 is six inches long, with $1\frac{5}{8}$ in. wide cutter. The blade is secured with an ingeniously designed knuckle-joint lever cap, made of steel and plated. This enables the cutter to be firmly locked in a moment and at the same time forms a very comfortable hold for the palm of the hand. In general design it closely follows No. 09½ described on page 33, as it is also fitted with the adjustable mouth. It has screw adjustment for depth of cut and lever for sideways adjustment of the cutter, and recesses for finger and thumb. Sides and sole are accurately ground and polished, and the whole tool carries a high-grade finish. A craftsman possessing this tool need have no fear whatever of cleanly finishing any work from the plane, end grain or long grain, easy timber or difficult.

It will be convenient here to mention a small plane which, whilst not ordinarily appealing to the joiner or cabinet-maker, have appeal to those engaged in small woodwork such as the making of models. This is a craft which can call at times for a high grade of skill, though of a different type from that of the general woodworker, and can excite quite as high a degree of pride of craftsmanship. Each one indeed of the foregoing block planes has its interest for the worker in miniature, though it will readily be seen that their prime purpose is that of the full scale worker, and the model enthusiast also frequently requires tools which are on a smaller scale. No. 0102 is a block plane $5\frac{1}{2}$ in. long, with a $1\frac{3}{8}$ in. cutter which is reduced to bare essentials, and very low in price. The cutter is held in position by a plated knurled wheel and screw, and the sole and sides are ground and polished. There is no adjustment to the cutter.

Fig. 41.—RECORD Block Plane No. 0102.

Chapter 3

Record Technical Jack Plane No. T5

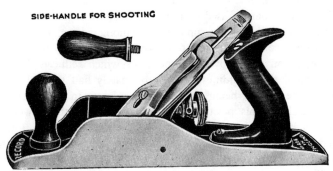

SIDE-HANDLE FOR SHOOTING

Fig. 42.

Record Technical Jack Plane, No. T5 (Fig. 42) although primarily designed to simplify and expedite training of boys and youths in Schools and Technical Institutions, embodies important improvements which will amply repay the attention, not only of instructors in the wood-working trades, but also of the craftsman and the serious amateur. Proved over a long period in actual school practice under modern conditions, it has been noticed invariably that boys learn to plane much more quickly with it; that they turn out accurate work from a very early stage, and that they are able to do more work in a given time, being much less subject to fatigue. It can be used from the commencement of training and is highly recommended for use in Central, Secondary, Junior and Senior Technical Schools and Colleges, and it will be appreciated by any serious craftsman. It must in no way be regarded as merely a junior's tool which must be discarded as soon as the adult stage is approached. It is a plane which has retained all those features which have made Record Planes standard in all parts of the world, but in addition, its improved design has made it more suitable for its particular purpose, *i.e.*, for use in Schools.

The length of the sole (13 in.) and the width of the cutter (2 in.) have been so arranged that they will cover the whole range of work attempted in day and evening schools and yet be within the capacity of the youngest to operate; whilst the skilled amateur whose work does not embrace the truing up of very long lengths will also find these proportions suitable for his work.

In view of the immature physical development of some of the pupils in Modern Secondary Schools, it might be thought that the weight (5 lbs.) is too heavy; this judgment being based on previous experience with the more clumsy wooden jack. Yet actual working observations have shown without doubt that the Record Jack Plane, T5, produces less fatigue and is considerably easier for all pupils than a wood jack plane of somewhat less weight. In the very early days of school wood-working, it was soon realised by the pioneer instructors that a deviation from the wood jack (then in common use among craftsmen) would have to be made if young boys were to do any planing at all, and the result was a reduction of the overall dimensions which reduced the weight and increased the "handiness". Approximately half the tail end was removed, the handle being thus set much lower in the stock. The natural result of this position was an easier push, the power being applied in better relation to the work. In Record Planes it will be noticed that the lowest possible position for the handle, immediately behind the cutting edge, is chosen, this resulting naturally in the expenditure of minimum effort.

The knob on the fore part of the plane is likewise set low on the plane, and is much more naturally grasped by a beginner than is the fore part of a wood jack. It is a case of a natural grasp against an unnatural grasp; the former is instinctive, the latter has to be learned by long practice. Hence, arising out of the design and the positioning of the handles there comes an advantage in ease of operation which, combined with the advantages accruing from the general constructional features noted below, quickly disposes of the fallacy that the slightly heavier tool may cause accelerated fatigue. Observation of half a day's practice in any school workshop will easily demonstrate the immeasurable superiority of the Record T5 Jack Plane over any others at present in use.

An experienced teacher of woodwork may be apprehensive of the danger of broken bodies when iron planes are in use, especially if his experience has been mainly or wholly with a set of wood planes. Those who have had some years of experience with iron jacks, whether in industry or in schools, have discovered that this fear of broken bodies is more apparent than real. Broken bodies do not occur anything like so frequently as they are reputed to; indeed, with ordinary supervision, they are of extremely rare occurrence.

It was a frank recognition of the fact, however, that conditions in a school workshop are in many ways different from those that hold in industry that led to the design of the body of the Record Technical Jack Plane No. T5; for whilst there is no appreciable increase in weight, there is a considerable increase in strength. Actually the sole is thinner than usual in an iron jack, thus minimising the total weight, but beads fore and aft together with cross ribbing give the whole of the sole an immense strength and resistance to sudden shock; whilst the enlarged wings (see Fig. 42) are amply supported by sturdy internal ribs which are also carried as an enlarged web across the sole. Careful observation and wide enquiry have established the fact that body breakage is more a bogey to be feared than a danger to be faced, and that handle breakage is very considerably less than that experienced with a batch of wooden planes.

The improved design of the wings gives a wide and steady bearing on the shooting-board, thus minimising the tendency of the beginner to cant the plane over. The plane is supplied with an extra detachable

Fig. 43.—Shooting with Record School Jack Plane, No. T5.

side handle which can be screwed into either side of the plane (Fig. 44). Boys (and men) are quick to appreciate the assistance this handle gives when the plane is used for shooting with the hand either low down as shown in Fig. 43, or with the hand grasping it more fully; the former method of handling giving the best results. On the shooting-board the T5 settles down steadily and easily to its work, and pupils need but the slightest demonstration to master the operation.

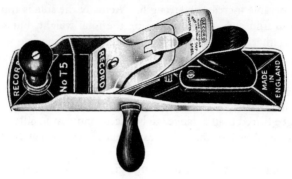

Fig. 44.—Side Handle attached for Shooting.

In general construction the Record Plane T5 has all the well-known and appreciated features of the other planes in the Record range. Nothing has been sacrificed in the sturdiness or the workmanship of the frog, which is fully adjustable.   A movement forward gives an effective smaller mouth; a movement backward a wider mouth.   To adjust, slacken the two screws A (Fig. 45); draw the frog backward or forward by turning the screw B; tighten screws A when the desired adjustment

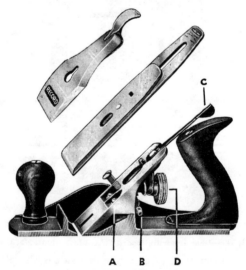

Fig. 45.—Frog Adjustment.

is secured.   Once the adjustment is made, the blade covers up the tightened screws A; so that the pupils are not likely to interfere with them.

In all school workshops that are used for younger pupils in the day time and for older pupils in the evening, it is found that the evening students demand a coarser shaving than is desirable for the younger ones, and in this respect the Record T5 is admirable in that cutter adjustment, both vertical and lateral, is instantaneous—by means of the usual adjustments as fitted to all Record Smooth, Jack and Try Planes.

The cutters are of high-grade Crucible Cast Tungsten Steel, a steel which takes an ultra fine edge and retains it for a long period. The heat treatment of this steel throughout is carefully and scientifically controlled. In service they are superior, whilst in maintenance they save time in sharpening and grinding. Either the standard cap iron or the Stay-Set Cap Iron may be used with this plane. The Stay-Set Cap Iron (described on page 45) is recommended.

General maintenance of a set of Record T5 Planes will take up much less time than that expended on a set of wood planes. In common with many other tools, Record Technical Jack Planes improve with use, and lubrication of the sole eases the work and improves the working qualities. If the frog is set too far forward with a very fine setting of the cap iron, it may be found that a "choke" can be induced if too coarse a feed is given. The remedy is to draw the frog back slightly. Spare parts are readily available and are standardised. When ordering the Record Technical Jack Plane, it should be specified by number. Thus, if the ordinary cap iron is required, order Record Plane T5; if Stay-Set Cap Iron, Record Plane T5-SS.

T5 is used in so many schools and kindred establishments throughout the world that it may be considered the standard jack plane for this purpose. Many teachers of woodwork using it exclusively keep about half a dozen blades in reserve ready sharpened for use; and change a blade that is going "off" at once—the dull blade only taking a moment or two to re-service and be returned to the "reserve". In conjunction with the "one-bevel" method of sharpening (see page 58) maintenance time for planes is so reduced in this way as to become negligible.

SUMMARY OF ADVANTAGES

1 Boys can handle the plane more easily; can do better and more accurate work, and more of it.

2 Instructor's time spent in maintenance is considerably reduced; time spent on grinding, sharpening and setting is but a fraction of that spent on wood jack planes.

3 Soles are permanently true. No shooting or truing-up of sole is called for periodically, no wear on soles; no time wasted on re-mouthing.

4 Keen and lasting sharpness of cutters.

5 Choice of standard or Stay-Set Cap Iron.

6 Shooting is improved and simplified.

7 Instant adjustment from coarse mouth to fine and vice versa, or any intermediate position.

8 Modern conditions are more closely approached. More and more craftsmen are using iron jacks in place of wood planes.

9 All parts interchangeable; spare parts available.

Chapter 4

Adjustment of the Plane

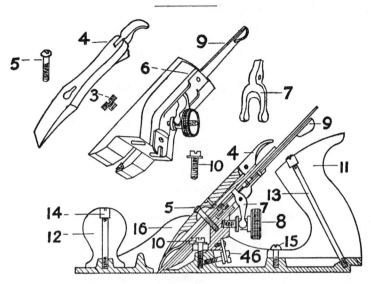

Fig. 46.—Parts of Record Planes.

3—Cap Screw.   4—Lever Cap.   5—Lever Cap Screw.   6—Frog, complete.
7—"Y" Adjusting Lever.   8—Adjusting Nut.   9—Lateral Adjusting Lever.
10—Frog Screw.   11—Plane Handle.   12—Plane Knob.   13—Handle Bolt and Nut.
14—Knob Bolt and Nut.   15—Handle Toe Screw.   16—Plane Body.
46—Frog Adjusting Screw.

The first introduction to a modern plane suggests complication which is really non-existent.   A few minutes of intelligent examination will quickly reveal an amazing simplicity which is combined with an efficiency that is an utter impossibility with the older wooden planes even when the latter are used with that ultra skill which only a minority of workers attain even in a lifetime of practice.

Study the section view in Fig. 46 and note the names of the parts, a few of which, of course, correspond with those of the older planes. The new names will be those of the parts which allow the more accurate, yet simple adjustments impossible with the slot and wedge method.

Take up your plane and remove the lever cap by lifting the cam and raising the lever cap.   You can now remove in its entirety the double plane iron.*   With a screwdriver slacken the screw which holds the two together.   (Some workers use the lever cap for this purpose: this is not a wise practice, as the lever cap is not intended as a screwdriver.)   Slide

---

* See Page 45 for description of "STAY-SET" Cap Iron.

the cap iron back, half-way up the slot, from the cutting edge, and turn it at right angles. In doing this, there is a possibility (if you do not slide fully half-way up) of rubbing or knocking the cutting edge with the cap iron, but once you have performed the operation, you will notice how to keep the cap iron from damaging the edge.

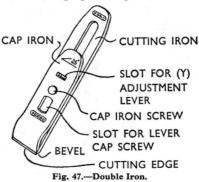

CAP IRON

CUTTING IRON

SLOT FOR (Y) ADJUSTMENT LEVER

CAP IRON SCREW

SLOT FOR LEVER CAP SCREW

BEVEL

CUTTING EDGE

Fig. 47.—Double Iron.

Slide the cap iron down and so disengage the screw head through the hole in the cutting iron. The sequence is just the reverse of Fig. 48, *i.e.*, d, c, b, a; and quickly becomes an automatic movement. Now examine the cutting edge. If it is not sharp (see Grinding and Honing, Chapters 5 and 6, which show you how to tell at a glance if the edge is sharp), it must be sharpened, and you will do that according to the instruction given.

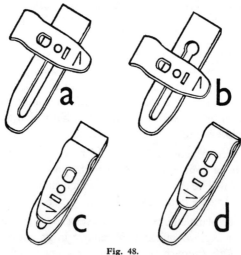

Fig. 48.

Some users have wondered why the cap iron screw hole is placed at the bottom of the slot rather than at the top, as it is in the old fashion wooden plane, where fewer movements of the cap iron are needed before it can be screwed tight. If the hole were made at the top of the slot there would be a danger, when the blade was nearly worn out, that the hole would rest opposite the roller of the lateral adjustment, which would then become ineffective. So, in order that the blade can be used right to the end, the hole is put at the bottom.

If, however, the plane iron is sharp, we can assemble the plane ready for work. To fix the cap iron, the sequence is as in Fig. 48, *i.e.*, exactly the reverse of what we have already done. With the cutting iron face side (*i.e.*, the flat, unbevelled side) upwards, place the screw of the cap iron, which has the round side up, in the hole, cap iron at right angles to blade (or cutting iron) as at "a". Keeping the cap iron at right angles, slide it up the slot fully half-way as at "b". Now turn the cap iron to bring it lying along the cutting iron in the position shown at "c". Now slide the cap iron down to its working position as at "d", for the work it is about to do.

For Rough Work .	Cap Iron $\frac{1}{32}$ in. to $\frac{1}{16}$ in. from edge.	
For Finishing Work .	,, $\frac{1}{64}$ in.	,, ,,
For Hard Woods with irregular grain	,, as close as you can get it to cutting edge.	

Tighten the screw, preferably resting the whole on the bench in case the screwdriver slips.

The double iron must now be put into the plane. The ground or bevelled side of the cutting iron goes downwards. Place the cutting end of the iron into the mouth first and then lay the iron back on to the

Fig. 49.—Sighting the Plane: adjusting for depth of cut.

43

frog so that the end of the Y adjusting lever fits into the small slot on the cap iron and so that the roller which gives lateral adjustment fits into the slot of the plane iron.

The plane iron should now feel nicely bedded down. Replace the Lever Cap by sliding down under the Lever Cap Screw, and snap down the cam lever. The Lever Cap should snap smartly and easily into place. If it is too easy, tighten the lever cap screw. If it goes too hard, slacken the lever cap screw a little.

The cutting iron may now project too far, or it may not project at all. Holding the plane upside down, as in Fig. 49, turn the brass nut until you can just see the blade project through. It may project more on the right than it does on the left, or vice versa. Adjust this by means of the lateral adjusting lever, sighting it as in Fig. 49. Some workers will prefer to "feel" the adjustment with the finger tips instead of sighting.

Now try a cut with it on your wood. If it cuts too much or too little, make the necessary adjustment with the nut as just described. You can adjust the plane to cut the thinnest tissue paper shavings (.001 in.) if you wish, by just a turn of the nut. **Always let the last adjustment be a forward one,** *i.e.*, **one that pushes the blade down, as this takes up any back lash that may develop in the adjustment.**

The Iron Plane offers a major advantage over any wood plane in that the effective width of the mouth can be varied to suit the particular type of work which is being undertaken. Thus, when coarse "hogging" work is the order of the day, a wide mouth can be used: when fine, accurate, finished work on hard or soft woods with awkward grain has to be done, the closest mouth can be used, giving a mere tissue shaving.

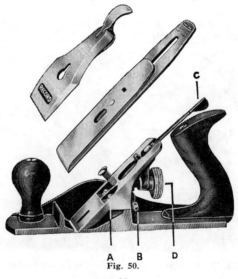

A　B　　D

Fig. 50.

The width of the mouth is adjusted by loosening the two frog screws A (Fig. 50) and by turning the adjusting screw B until the desired setting is obtained. Then tighten up the two frog screws A again. A fine mouth in conjunction with a close-set cap iron will give the very finest shaving; a coarse shaving can be removed by a combination of a wide mouth and a coarsely set cap iron.

Observation over a wide field tends to indicate that users generally do not make enough use of this frog adjustment to get the full use they might out of the planes. When adjusting a fine set cap iron to a very narrow mouth, it must be remembered that the plane is set for the finest shaving, and consequently it will not do to have too much iron. On a slightly uneven surface, it is quite possible, having in mind that the sole of the plane is so true, that a fine set plane will take off a shaving in one place and refuse to do so in another; this can happen when the unevenness is very slight indeed. The remedy is not more iron, but the planing off of the high spots until all is true. If a coarse shaving is required, then the mouth must be adjusted accordingly. A fine mouth and a closely-set cap iron will give a fine shaving, but if the iron is adjusted too far out at the same time, there will not be room for the shavings to get away, and there will be a choke. A very little experiment will soon show the worker how to gain the very real advantages that the frog adjustment carries. It is emphasised that this adjustment is a very delicate one, a small turn of the screw having a large effect. Hence, work gently. It is important that the screws A should be tightened after every adjustment.

RECORD "STAY-SET" CAP IRON

The foregoing description has dealt with the Cap Iron as it has been known for many years, and which is still available. The most recent and far-reaching improvement in Plane development is in the Record

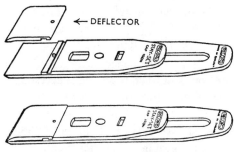

Fig. 51.—Record "STAY-SET" Cap Iron.

"Stay-Set" Cap Iron (Fig. 51) which is made in two parts, the upper, or main part and the lower, or deflector. In adjusting this cap iron the sequence shown in Fig. 54 is quite unnecessary, as the deflector is merely lifted off, and seldom will it be necessary to move the upper part. Once the deflector is set at the required distance (See Table, p. 43), the cutter may be honed many times and the deflector put back in exactly the same place as it occupied before. There is no need to remove the upper portion, even for grinding. It will at once be appreciated that the "Stay-Set" Cap Iron is a great time saver. (Woodworkers generally do not appreciate the total time taken up in sharpening and setting tools.) The saving of time, however important, is not the main advantage of the "Stay-Set" Cap Iron. The one bugbear of fine work with planes has hitherto been the tendency some of them had to "chatter". "Chattering" with the "Stay-Set" Cap Iron is an impossibility. Probably the best description of the "Stay-Set" Cap Iron would be summarised thus (See Figures 51 and 52):

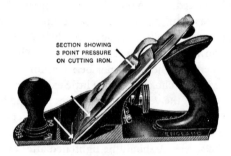

SECTION SHOWING 3 POINT PRESSURE ON CUTTING IRON.

Fig. 52.—Double Iron with "STAY-SET" Cap Iron and Lever Cap assembled, showing 3 point pressure.

1. The Cutting Iron can be honed or sharpened without removing the Cap Iron.

2. The Record "Stay-Set" Cap Iron stays set. The deflector, which fits into a slot on the Cap Iron, can be lifted clear when released from the plane. After honing it is only necessary to replace the deflector in the slot. No unscrewing or tightening is required.

3. The Cutting Iron can be honed many times before it is necessary to re-set the Cap Iron; and when re-setting is necessary, the operation is identical with that of re-setting the old type.

4. The application of pressure at three points (instead of two as in the old type) has at last eliminated all possibility of chatter; the "Stay-Set" Cap Iron is guaranteed chatter proof.

5. The "Stay-Set" Cap Iron has been increased in thickness and is in close pressure contact with the cutting iron for the whole of its length, which greatly increases the rigidity of the entire cutting unit.

6. The extra thickness of the Cap Iron and deflector not only gives greater rigidity, but it is more robust, and allows a longer thread for the Cap Screw, lessening the need for complete removal of Cap Screw with possible loss in the shavings on the floor.

7. On account of the parallelism of the top face of the deflector with the cutting iron, the pressure exerted by the lever cap is always constant, throughout the entire length of adjusment of the cutter. In the old type, the convexity of the Cap Iron caused a variation of pressure of the Lever Cap, according to the position of the latter on the Cap Iron.

When ordering a plane with a "Stay-Set" Cap Iron, order the number followed by the letters SS; *e.g.*, Record Jack Plane $05\frac{1}{2}$-SS.

Chapter 5

Grinding the Iron

As the plane is sent out from the makers, it has a perfectly ground edge, thanks to modern machinery, a close application of scientific methods, and a live spirit of deep research. (This edge, of course, must be whetted or honed before use. See Chapter 6.) In the course of use, however, it requires to be reground from time to time. When does a

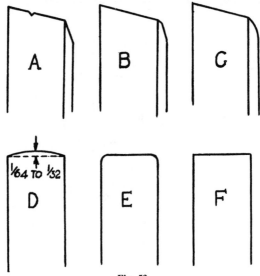

Fig. 53.

plane iron require regrinding? Fig. 53 shows clearly when grinding is necessary. At A we see an iron that has "snicked", due generally to topping a nail in the work, to catching the ironwork of the vice, or to some other careless handling, a frequent cause for grinding with beginners, but not very frequent with the craftsman who avoids trouble that way. B shows an edge that with frequent whetting has become "thick", the most general cause. C shows an edge that is "rounded", due to inexperienced whetting, and caused by rocking the iron on the oilstone (see Whetting the Iron).

The shape of the cutting edge. According to the work in hand, the shape of the cutting edge may vary. If coarse and rough work is in hand, the blade may be ground as at D (Fig. 53), but this will result in a series of corrugations on the work that must later be removed for a nice finish. For general work, and in a general way, the edge shown at E is to be preferred, where the edge is straight except that the sharpness is just rounded off the corners. For jointing (as described on page 76 *et seq.*) there is no compromise at all. The edge must be dead straight and square.

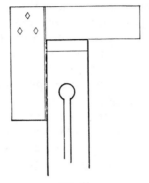

Fig. 54.

In every case the edge must be at right angles to the side of the iron. These sides are dead straight and parallel as they leave the works, a vast improvement on the old irons, which might be, but seldom are, either straight or parallel. A try square may be used to check squareness (Fig. 54) or the cap iron itself may be used as a guide, as all cap irons are machined square with the sides before they leave the works. The cap iron can therefore be screwed into position and left there while grinding, as a guide to squareness of the cutting iron.

Fig. 55.—A Typical power-driven Wet Grindstone

49

Should grinding be wet or dry? The answer to this question depends upon the facilities available. There is no doubt that a good natural stone, used under water is by far the safer method. The stone may be turned by hand (with the aid of a helper—and it is not so laborious as is generally supposed; the pressure should not be too heavy) or it may be treadled (the advantage here is that an assistant is not required); or it may be power driven. In the first two methods it will be found better for the stone to revolve towards the edge being ground; when the stone is power driven it may revolve either way.

The water dripping on to the stone whilst grinding keeps the edge cool so that there is no danger of drawing the temper; and it washes away the "grindings" so that the stone is always cutting. If the stone became clogged with particles of steel there would arise a burnishing of the cutter rather than a removal of metal, and there would almost certainly be a rise in temperature at the edge of the cutter, leading to a loss of temper.

But with a fast revolving artificial stone, cooling presents a difficulty. Water is out of the question; and soaking with paraffin is not always safe, owing to the possible disintegration of the stone. So one is compelled (a) to use a very light touch indeed and (b) to quench frequently. There is nearly always the temptation to bear a little heavier on the cutter, to speed up the work, which means a drawing of the temper due to the heat generated. The result of this is a cutter which can be sharpened to a keen enough edge, but an edge which has far too short a working life. Hard bearing will almost certainly result in the edge turning blue—a "burnt" cutter which is then useless for its purpose. In mild cases there may only be $\frac{1}{8}$ in. or $\frac{3}{16}$ in. of the cutter affected by the "burning": the rest of it **may** not have been hot enough to be spoilt. In this case careful grinding in expert hands might cut away the affected part and leave the rest in good order; **the moral is to keep the cutter cold so that the temper cannot be drawn.**

It seems to be increasingly difficult for many craftsmen as well as amateurs to have a wet grindstone available and in this case we would strongly recommend the "one-bevel" method of sharpening (see page 58). The cut will not suffer, and the great advantage is that there is never any need to grind at all. Any joiner who has occasion to work away from the workshop for considerable periods will immediately appreciate what this means.

First, then, we must shape the edge as in Fig. 54. The blade, held on the rest, must approach the wheel radially as in Fig. 56, and with gentle pressure be passed to and from across the face of the stone as

shown by the arrows, until the desired shape is attained, ensuring all
the time, by constant reference to the try square or by comparing with

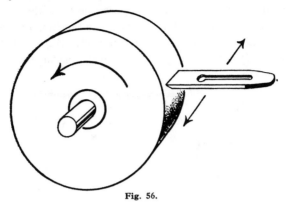

Fig. 56.

the cap iron, as indicated above, that the edge is "square" with the side.
If any "snicks" are present (as at A, Fig. 53) they must be ground right
out, so that they do not show on the "face" (or flat) side of the blade.
They will disappear first on the ground side, but if they are not taken
right off the face side they will be in evidence again when the bevel is
taken off.

Now for the bevel. If your stone has an adjustable rest you can set
it so that the bevel will be 25°. If not, you must, by skill, grind off the
blade to that angle. Use a motion right and left, parallel with the axis of
the grindstone (Fig. 59) and avoid working in an arc of a circle, or using
more pressure on one side than the other. Don't allow the slightest
roundness to creep in as at C (Fig. 57).

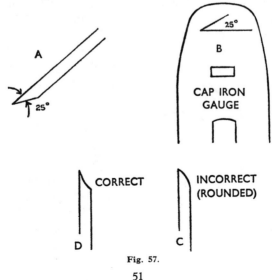

Fig. 57.

51

A slight concavity as at D is admissible: in fact the shape of the stone will give this, but on no account must a convexity be allowed, or even a series of flats.   Both of these faults are due to holding the blade at varying angles to the stone, and by dipping and rocking the blade whilst grinding.   The correct angle for grinding is marked on the cap iron (Fig. 58), and reference to this should be made, placing the blade on the

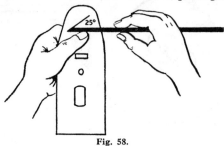

Fig. 58.

gauge and grinding accurately to the mark.   The ground surface should present one continuous face.   You can see how the grinding is progressing by holding up the edge to the light and sighting along it.   So long as any "flat" remains, it will reflect the light, and as you sharpen this reflected light will gradually diminish.   In grinding, however, it may not entirely disappear, owing to a certain amount of burr that is present.   You will be finally rid of the reflected light when you whet the iron.

Finally, use light pressure: keep square and steady, and when using an emery or carborundum or other artificial stone, quench the cutter frequently.   If at the first attempt you find you haven't ground correctly, do not be discouraged.   Thousands of others have had similar initial failures, and the knack is one which is quickly learned.   When you have realised what you are after and have found the action of the stone, you

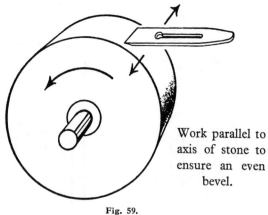

Work parallel to axis of stone to ensure an even bevel.

Fig. 59.

52

will no longer fear to grind: and you will have no patience with the needless extra labour always caused by a "thick" edge. Good work cannot be done, even by an expert, with a blunt tool. The expert knows it and never tries.

The expert may grind a bevel slightly less than 25° on occasion. This edge will work very nicely on soft wood, but it is too thin to stand up to work on hardwoods.

You cannot grind a plane iron unless you have a true surface on the grindstone. If irregularities have appeared, or channels have been cut, the stone must be trued up. On an artificial stone you can use the cutter specially made for the purpose. A natural stone can be trued up by grinding it level with the end of a piece of iron pipe. With a natural stone use plenty of water, but do not allow the stone, or part of it, to stand in water, as this softens it. Allowing a grindstone to stand in the sun hardens it. A grindstone may crack in frosty weather if left in the open.

Chapter 6

Whetting (or Honing) the Cutting Iron

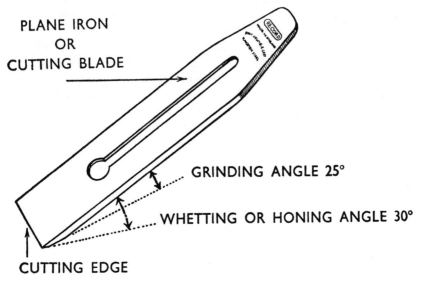

PLANE IRON
OR
CUTTING BLADE

GRINDING ANGLE 25°

WHETTING OR HONING ANGLE 30°

CUTTING EDGE

Fig. 60.

The cutting edge as left from the grindstone, whilst of the correct bevel, is far too coarse to do the fine work a woodworker requires. The craftsman knows that a keen edge is not only productive of better results, but that those results are more quickly obtained with less expenditure of energy, so he never begrudges the time taken up in sharpening. Whetting or honing the edge is undertaken much more frequently than grinding, and results in a little bit being honed off the blade each time until the blade assumes a shape such as that of a "thick" blade, Fig. 53, B. Then the blade is ready for grinding once again. It must not be assumed that the oilstone merely burnishes or presses the edge of the blade. The oilstone has a true cutting action like that of the grindstone, but it cuts more slowly and leaves a keener edge. The question arises as to which type of stone is best suited for Plane Cutting Irons. It is an important point, for, taking two extremes, a scythe and a razor blade, you obviously would not sharpen your razor with the same stone as you would sharpen your scythe.

The best kind of stone for planes, chisels, and other carpenter's tools is a medium or fine cutting grit, which may be either natural or artificial, i.e., manufactured. Natural stones, unfortunately, are becoming increasingly difficult to procure; and although there is still an element of luck in the behaviour of any given natural stone, those who are fortunate enough to obtain a Washita (Lily white) stone, will seldom have cause to grumble; whilst those who are fortunate enough to possess an Arkansas stone will have a veritable de luxe stone—the price will certainly be high, yet it will prove to be worth all it costs. Neither of these two stones could be described as quick cutting, but slow cutting on an oilstone is more a virtue than otherwise; and the slower the cut generally speaking the better the edge. Manufactured stones tend as a rule to quicker cutting, although there is a fairly wide choice of grit (e.g. the Carborundum No. 200 is very slow cutting, but it makes a very satisfactory cutting edge—if you have the time and patience to spare; whilst others of the same make are almost as quick as a grindstone—and correspondingly quicker in wearing away). There is much to be said in favour of a combination stone, medium and fine, as such a stone may be used for the preliminary shaping of the angle on the medium side, and the finishing touches can be done on the fine side. Boxing them calls for a little more care, as they must be a push fit but not so tight that the stone cannot be turned over. The method shown in Fig. 69 is advisable provided the end blocks are not a slack fit; whilst a two-lidded box would not be too difficult to design. India and Aloxite have proved very satisfactory stones for Record blades. And for a finish we have yet to find a better stone than the above mentioned Arkansas (natural) stone. It is our experience that most new stones will take a lot of oil before they give

Fig. 61.—Position of Hands in Honing (or Whetting).

their best performance, and this indicates that one must not be too niggardly with oil: most of them will stand soaking with oil for a few days, though India stones are oil filled as sold.

The process of whetting is simply rubbing the bevelled edge of the blade on the face of the oilstone. There are one or two things that must be observed in doing this, or the desired result will not appear.

First put a few drops of oil on the stone and wipe the stone thoroughly clean *with a rag*. Many carpenters are in the habit of cleaning the stone with a handful of shavings, but this so often results in filling the pores of the stone with dust and grit, that it is not a practice to be commended. A clean rag or cotton waste is much to be preferred.

Having cleaned the stone and put some fresh oil on it, take up the blade in the hands as indicated in Fig. 61. Bring the blade into contact with the stone, noting Fig. 62. Feel the bevel in contact throughout, and then raise the back slightly so that you will work on the front, i.e. the

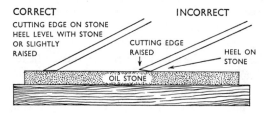

CORRECT INCORRECT

CUTTING EDGE ON STONE
HEEL LEVEL WITH STONE
OR SLIGHTLY
RAISED

CUTTING EDGE
RAISED

HEEL ON
STONE

OIL STONE

Fig. 62.

cutting edge. The best motion is to and fro, though some craftsmen use a figure of 8 motion. The latter in inexperienced hands is apt to produce an alteration of bevel. Its possible advantage is that there is a certain amount of oblique cut which is supposed to clear the "grindings" away. As, however, the particles of steel float on the oil and so are carried away, the advantage of the figure of 8 motion (see Fig. 63) is a little doubtful.

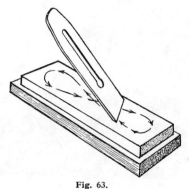

Fig. 63.

Do not be too sparing with the oil: lack of oil will result in "glazing" —i.e. the pores of the stone are clogged with steel, and the stone assumes a polished appearance: and it will then cut but poorly if at all. The condition can be remedied by cleaning with paraffin and re-truing as described below. Often the application of paraffin tends to make the stone cut more quickly; and this is not always an advantage. A soaking with melted vaseline will usually slow a stone that is too fast.

For an initial attempt use the to and fro motion as in Fig. 61. Use as much of the flat surface of the stone as possible, for in this way the wear on the stone is more evenly spread, and you will delay the time when your stone becomes "hollow" and needs truing up. Do not allow the iron to "rock" as this must inevitably result in a curved surface that cannot produce an edge that will cut well: and it will almost certainly call for a re-grind. Keep the angle of the iron to the stone constant. This will mean that the wrists must be kept rigid but it does not call for a vice-like grip. Apply moderate pressure and keep on whetting until the line of reflected light on the edge disappears.

There will be a certain amount of wire edge rubbed away, and this will hang on at the extreme edge. The amount varies somewhat with the type of stone in use. To remove it, turn the blade flat side down on to the oilstone and right across the stone, and draw the blade with a wiping motion over the stone. This will remove the wire edge without making a bevel; any bevel on the flat side is undesirable as the cut is not so good, and there is a risk that the fit of the cap iron may be spoiled, in which case shavings could lodge between cutting iron and cap iron and so cause a choke. If the oil stone is at all hollow (and many oilstones are slightly hollow due to sharpening narrow chisels) there is a tendency for the operator to raise the top end of the cutting iron to remove the wire edge; thus causing an unwanted bevel. The placing of the iron fully across the stone, wiping the wire edge off on the boundary of the stone farthest away from the operator, prevents this happening.

The line of light on the edge should now have disappeared completely and you should have a sharp edge. For an ultra-keen edge, just before you have finished on the medium (Washita or India) whet on an Arkansas stone.

The effectiveness of the edge will depend upon the accuracy with which you have kept the two faces truly flat and free from curve: the meeting of these two faces in a sharp keen angle: and also the "polish" which you will have put on with the oilstone. A coarse stone will not give this polish—the surface will be covered with scratches: it is these scratches which must be removed—that is why an Arkansas stone and a very fine artificial stone give an edge that is better; and moreover a

57

scratch-free sharpening will have a longer working life than a sharpening which is indifferently finished. Record blades are not only made of the finest steel for their particular purpose; but the face side of the iron is finished smoothly so that the operator can work up the type of surface required in a reasonable time. Good honing is an art worth taking considerable trouble to perfect, and it goes a long way towards explaining the old craftsman's tradition that you don't really get the best out of a blade until you have been using it some time.

There is much to be said in favour of the method of honing which is employed by many experienced craftsmen, in which the **whole** of the surface of the 25° bevel is honed to a keen edge, thus using one bevel instead of two. For fine finishing work this method gives a very pleasing and satisfactory cut, and in fact with most timbers the cut is better than with two bevels. The time taken up in honing is not very much more than that taken up in the two-bevel method, owing to the structure of the blade (see page 25). Exponents of the two-bevel method claim (a) the time taken in sharpening is slightly less (b) the edge is slightly stronger because the "thicker" angle results in more metal behind the edge. (The latter point may be realised more clearly by comparing a paring chisel edge with a mortice chisel edge: it is not so certain that its advantage is so marked with a plane blade, the action of which is very dissimilar to that of a mortice chisel.) Moreover there is a definite advantage in that one never has a thick edge, and so one can always get a workable, satisfactorily honed edge even (a) when one is working on a site away from the workshop and grindstone or (b) when one (as is the case with most amateurs) does not possess a wet grindstone.

Fig. 64.—Record Edge Tool Honer No. 161.

The amateur (and the younger professional) who finds difficulty in mastering the art of sharpening, will find Record No. 161 Edge Tool Honer of great value for honing not only plane irons (and plough irons) but also spokeshave irons and chisels. The iron to be sharpened is

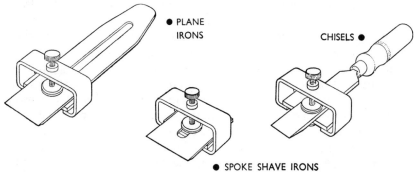

● PLANE IRONS

CHISELS ●

● SPOKE SHAVE IRONS

Fig. 65.

passed, bevel side towards the ball, through the frame and secured by the holding screw in such a position that, for the second bevel method, for a plane iron the edge projects 1 in. from the frame. (Plough, Combination and Multiplane irons will project $\frac{3}{4}$ in. If the one-bevel method of sharpening is preferred, the edge will project about $1\frac{1}{4}$ in.).

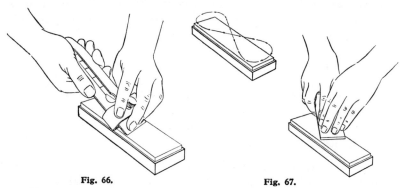

Fig. 66.   Fig. 67.

Having put some oil on the clean stone, not being niggardly but at the same time not flooding it, take a comfortable hold on the honer (Fig. 66) in such a way that slight pressure can be exerted on the edge

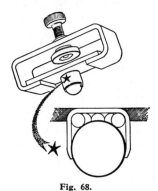

Fig. 68.

59

which is being sharpened. The honer will be resting on the stainless steel ball—which runs on a concealed ball bearing (see Fig. 68) but it is on the edge that attention should be focused—you can forget about the ball, so long as it is running on the stone and you don't let it drop over the edge of the stone—this could bend the casing and cause a jamming of the ball. A somewhat oblique position of the blade to the stone will probably be found preferable, and it has the advantage that all, or most, of the edge is on the stone. A series of circular movements should be made (similar to the method employed by a French polisher); or a figure of 8 movement may be made, but a direct, up-and-down the stone motion is best avoided. As soon as the angle is clearly defined and the edge sharp and clean, the wire edge can be taken off in the manner already described, keeping the face side of the iron dead flat on the stone so as not to make a bevel on the flat side of the iron. It will be found easier to wipe the wire edge off if the iron is removed from the honer first.

If the ball should stick, it should be freed immediately to prevent any flat forming on the surface of the ball—and this can usually be done by flushing fresh oil into the bearing from underneath and working the ball free with the fingers. If the ball is not free, a flat or series of flats will form on the surface of the ball; the ball cannot then work efficiently, and there is a danger of ploughing grooves in the stone.

The honer should not be used as a jig for grinding, nor should it be used on a stone, which, however quick cutting it may be, is quick wearing, as the abrasive sludge mixture will be carried into the bearing and will clog it.

The veriest tyro will be able to get a satisfactory edge on his tools with this No. 161 Honer: and the "feel" of the constant angle will come with practice.

The final touch can now be put on with a strop. For this purpose you require a piece of leather (preferably Buff, but Kip will serve if you use the smooth side). Dress it with a little tallow (Russian, not town) and a little of the finest flour emery. Work this well into the strop and have the strop flat on the bench. Work as if you were whetting on the oilstone, but not in a forward direction as this would cut the strop; work only backwards. If you carry out these instructions you will have an edge that woodworkers in bygone days would have given half their lives to secure. Many experienced men strop on the fleshy part of the palm of the hand, but a strop as indicated gives better results. The wire edge should be taken off on the stone, and not on the strop. Steel particles embedded in the strop will prevent the strop from doing its job; and they are much easier put in than got out.

Any thin oil will do. A good mixture is half machine oil and half paraffin. Cycle lubricating oil will do. A favourite oil for oilstones is neatsfoot oil, (get it from a saddler or leather merchant) which has the advantage of not drying out quickly, and of staying on the top of the stone. It may get thick in very cold weather, but that will not detract from its use, as it can be put on with a stick. Indeed the old carpenters used to keep a bottle of neatsfoot oil with a stick in it always hanging near the bench. Water will not be suitable as it is not thick enough to float the particles of steel, but soap suds will serve. Keep your oilstone clean and wipe it after use every time. Do not use it dry, and do not allow it to "glaze". If there is any tendency to glaze, wash it well in paraffin.

When the oilstone becomes hollow it will not give you efficient service. You can true it up on the flat side of the grindstone. Another way of truing a worn oilstone is to grind it on a flat stone "flag", using water and a little fine sand as grit. It pays to keep your stone flat. Whenever possible, use the edge of the stone for honing small and narrow cutters, and the wide face for broad cutters like plane irons. This will save a lot of "hollowing" due to uneven wear.

If when fitting the stone into its box, two pieces of wood, end grain upwards, are inserted as shown in Fig. 69 the oilstone will tend to

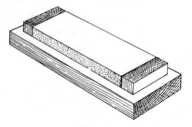

Fig. 69.

remain straight and true longer, as a longer stroke can be made without fear of overrunning the edge. The ends must of course make a tight fit.

Keep your oilstone covered when not in use. In a very dry room, or one subject to sunshine, oilstones are apt to harden. In a warm shop it is a good plan to keep the oilstone cover on with a few drops of clean oil on the surface of the stone.

If by mischance you should break your oilstone, this need not affect its service, as if the two parts are tightly put together in their place correctly it can be used as before. Boxing oilstones is not only better for the stones, it saves accidents caused by dropping.

The tendency of the oilstone box to slip on the bench can be prevented by driving two nails in the bottom, towards one end, cutting off the nail heads in such a way as to leave slight projections, which get a grip on the bench face.

In many instructional workshops, a separate strongly framed table is used for oilstones only; the surface being covered with zinc or some other material from which the oil can be easily wiped: the oilstone cases being screwed to the table top to prevent them moving. This practice keeps the dirty oil away from the working benches where there is always a chance of it getting on to the work in hand. When, however, for one reason or another, a separate table is out of the question, it is a good plan to screw the oilstone boxes on to the base of a shallow box: one lid can cover all the stones; and a batten screwed on to the underside of the base can be held in the vice. The oilstones will be held rigidly and there is no marking or defacing of the bench top. When honing is finished, the stones in their container can be stored in a rack or cupboard underneath the bench.

The lone worker will prefer the slightly projecting two-nail method as above, or may even be happy securing his oilstone box in the vice. In any case whatever method is used, it is wise to have the oilstone always at a constant height, this tending to keep the angle constant and uniform.

When one is in the middle of an interesting construction, there is a natural inclination to put off grinding a plane blade, though sooner or later this must be done. As soon as the honed bevel is the least bit long, the blade should be ground, and it is much more satisfactory to keep it properly ground and ready for any emergency than to have to break off to do it. A makeshift grind can be done with a coarse artificial oilstone, but it is not so good as a proper grind on a natural revolving stone, which leaves a slightly hollow face which is best for the honing process. It is a very good plan to keep handy, as many experienced workers do, two or three spare blades which are ready sharpened; so that when a blade begins to go "off" a new one can be inserted straight away, the work thus not being delayed; and the dull blades can be sharpened again quite quickly at some convenient time, preferably before leaving the bench at the end of the session. In this way not only will a sharpened iron always be at hand, but the life of the irons will be increased; and moreover the time spent on actual maintenance is at a minimum. You cannot do good work unless your plane irons are sharp. Treat your oilstone as your best friend, and as your plane's best friend too.

Sharpening for Plastics. Plastics, Perspex, Formica, plywood having resin type cements and so on are notorious for their quick blunting of plane blades. Where only small amounts are to be planed, or when this type of work occurs only infrequently, the ordinary sharpening can be used, the quicker blunting of the blade being accepted as a necessary nuisance. If the work comes frequently, however, it is worth while keeping a blade specially for that work, grinding and sharpening it at a blunt angle somewhere near 80°-85°. An edge of this type will last sharp longer than a normally sharpened one. Special steels have been tried for the work but they are relatively expensive and cannot ordinarily be sharpened by the user, and hence have been ruled out. Instead of sharpening all the angle from one side, one user at least has been very successful using a blade sharpened at the normal angle, and then a grinding taken off the face side of the blade, thus making a cutting angle approximating to the one recommended above.

Chapter 7

Holding the Bench Plane

(i) Take up a position at the bench exactly as if you were about to fight an opponent standing on the other side of the vice. This will bring the left foot forward parallel with the bench, and the right foot pointing towards the bench. (See Fig. 89.) The position of the feet is exactly the same when using either a bench plane or a circular plane. Drop the hands on the plane and proceed to swing. Left hand falls naturally on the knob; forefinger of right hand extended to give more control. The body and feet will be in exact position to get the free swing so essential to good and easy working.

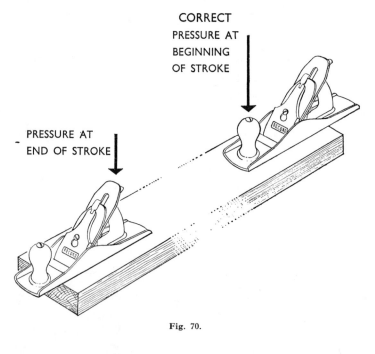

CORRECT
PRESSURE AT
BEGINNING
OF STROKE

PRESSURE AT
END OF STROKE

Fig. 70.

INCORRECT: RESULT OF "DIPPING"
Fig. 71.

(ii) At the beginning of the stroke put slight pressure on the knob.

(iii) At the finish of the stroke put pressure on the handle. (See Fig. 70.)

Fig. 71 shows the usual fault of a beginner, and is due to "dipping" the plane at the commencement and at the finish of the stroke. Rules (ii) and (iii) above, properly carried out, will prevent this. Put another way: in planing, you should endeavour to plane the work **hollow,** not round, as in Fig. 71. It is, of course, almost impossible to plane hollow, but the very attempt will prevent that wearisome and common fault of "dipping".

In planing very long lengths it will be necessary to walk along the board, but when the principles have been mastered on shorter lengths walking along offers no difficulty whatever. Fig. 89 shows a 10 ft. length being planed on edge.

Chapter 8

Squaring up a Piece of Wood

Select first the side of the wood that is best and plane it free from unevenness and blemish.

Carefully test this side with a straight edge in all directions by laying on the straight edge and holding it up to the light. If the side is perfectly true no light will appear between the straight edge and the board in any position of the straight edge. It is essential that there should be no "wind". To test for this apply two similar straight edges as in Fig. 72 and sight along the line of the arrow. If the board is free

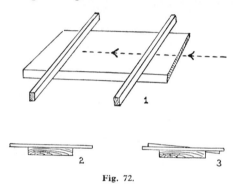

Fig. 72.

from "wind" the edges of the strips will appear as at 2, *i.e.*, they will coincide: if winding is present they will appear as at 3, and will immediately show the least deviation from truth. The longer the straight edges (or winding laths) the more apparent will be the error. As a board in winding is bound to cause serious trouble in fitting up later on, elimination of the wind cannot be too seriously stressed. Winding strips will be made by the worker as a pair and are an interesting exercise in accurate planing. They are best made from a dark-coloured wood such as mahogany. It must of course be bone dry and when finished the strips should be kept in a place free from wide variations of temperature and humidity. The strips are planed true and parallel, and it is an advantage to inlay a boxwood strip on one edge of each, in the case of a pair, made from mahogany, or an ebony strip in the case of a pair made from a lighter-coloured wood. The contrast in colour is a help when sighting across. The inlaid strips may be about $\frac{1}{8} \times \frac{1}{8}$ in. squares, or slightly more if preferred.

Beginners are apt to use a smooth plane for this process, but the short length of the smooth plane makes the operation a very tricky and laborious process. This will be apparent from a consideration of

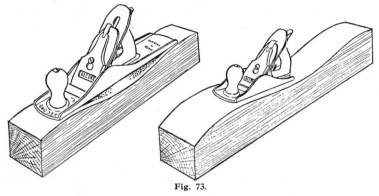

Fig. 73.

Fig. 73, which clearly shows that a smooth plane can not only ride over a convexity but can also work in a concavity, leaving a perfectly smooth, but not a perfectly true, surface.

The Jack Plane and the Jointer, by virtue of their long length, are unable to do this, for whilst they can plane the "hillocks" off, their length prevents any action in the "valleys" until the "hillocks" are removed. (Fig. 73).

Thus, however strong the temptation to use the smaller plane, the longer (not less than 15 in.) plane should be used: and once the iron jack has been used for this purpose, the worker will never revert to its wooden ancestor.

There is sometimes a desire on the part of the worker to increase the amount of "iron", *i.e.*, to lower the blade still farther when he finds the plane is moving over the wood without taking off a shaving the full length of the stroke. A test with a straight edge will frequently reveal a depression and the natural inference is that the high spots must first be taken off, leaving then the depressions level with the rest of the surface. Then the shavings will be continuous. Generally speaking, it is unwise to use too much iron, for the coarser the cut, the harder the work and the more frequently must you sharpen your iron; and unless you are using the mildest of timber with the sweetest of grain, you will tear up long chunks of fibre, leaving blemishes which are heartbreaking to remove later. Take a moderate cut, paper thin. The work is easier, more accurate, and time is saved in cleaning up.

Having planed up the side, now proceed to plane the edge. This must not only be straight in length and breadth, and free from winding, but must also be "square", *i.e.*, at right angles, to the first or "face" side.

67

Although this sounds a difficult proposition, its accomplishment is easy, provided the plane is held correctly. This is clearly shown in Fig. 89, where a long face edge is being planed. The fingers underneath the front of the plane hold it in position, and at the same time, by taking a gentle bearing on the side of the work, hold the plane at right angles to the face. The right hand pushes the plane.

Test with straight edge and try square in all positions, and when correct you have planed the face edge. This should be marked straight away, as in Fig. 74.

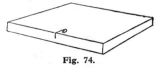

Fig. 74.

Now gauge the desired thickness of the wood, making sure that the stock of the gauge is on the face side, as marked (Fig. 75):—

Fig. 75.

and proceed to plane off the waste just as far as the gauge line. You will find it convenient to stop just before the gauge line, leaving a little margin which is useful for later cleaning up.

The next step is to get an even width. This is done similarly to the last step, only by gauging this time with the stock on the face edge:—

Fig. 76.

and you will proceed then to plane off the waste with the wood in the vice, again just leaving one shaving thickness more than the gauge line.

You have now squared up your wood. It should be perfectly straight and true, of an even width and thickness throughout.

After planing the face side and the face edge, many craftsmen prefer to gauge and plane the width before the thickness. Two advantages are claimed for this method—first that the lines are easier to see on the edge, second that the plane has a better bearing on the wider edge than it has on the narrower one. Both ways get to the same end; and neither rule is hard and fast, much depending on the ultimate purpose of the piece, the character of the wood being worked, and the whim of the worker. Beginners, especially boys, will get on better by planing the width first and then the thickness.

Chapter 9

Difficulties in Planing and their Solution

(i) Sometimes, instead of leaving a smooth surface, a series of corrugations is produced (Fig. 77). This is due to the grinding of the

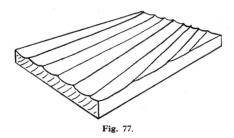

Fig. 77.

iron, which is ground as at D, Fig. 53. In very rough "hogging" this may be done deliberately, with the idea of quickly working down a surface. To remove the corrugations, work all over the board with a sharp, finely set smooth plane, with the iron ground as at E, Fig. 53; or, if the board is at all long, with an iron jack, fore or jointer. Corrugation may be avoided by the use of a properly ground iron (see Grinding, Chapter 5). The ease of working an iron plane removes the necessity for a steeply cambered edge.

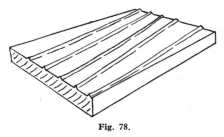

Fig. 78.

(ii) Slight ridges appear in the planing (Fig. 78). These are due to "snicking" the plane iron. If the iron be examined it will be found that a little piece has been chipped off the edge of the cutter (see A, Fig. 53). There is only one cure for this, and that is grinding the cutting edge.

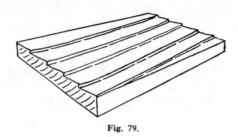

Fig. 79.

(iii) Sharp depressions (Fig. 79) occur in the planing. The cause of this is that the cutting iron is set more deeply on one side than on the other. The Cure—use the lateral adjusting lever to bring the cutting edge in alignment with the sole of the plane. (See Chapter 4 and Fig. 49.) This is one of the cases where an iron plane is immeasurably superior to a wood plane, accurate adjustment being made in a second.

(iv) The wood tears up roughly, leaving an uneven patch of rough fibre. The cause of this is working against the grain. Look at the grain on the edge of the board. To plane the top side of the board (Fig. 80) you must work "uphill" of the grain, *i.e.*, from A to B, as the arrow

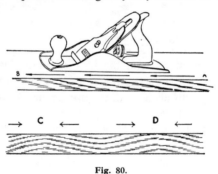

Fig. 80.

shows. If you work from B to A you are against the grain and the wood will tear up. Sometimes the grain will be wavy, as shown C D. Here you have an awkward grain. You must plane "uphill" of the grain and that may mean working in several directions, as shown by the arrows. Frequently, this kind of timber can be cleaned up best by working with a circular motion with a keenly set smoothing plane with a very sharp cutter. It is in this kind of work that the iron plane shows its immense superiority over the wood plane, its accurate and sensitive adjustments allowing it to perform work quite impossible with a wood wedge plane.

(v) Planing the end grain of a board, when it is desired to shoot the end. If the wood be planed right through from A to B (Fig. 81) the end fibres will break through as at C.

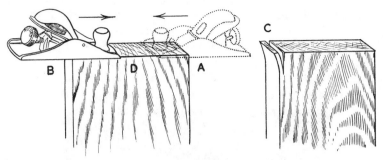

Fig. 81.

The way to plane is from A to D and then from B to D, *i.e.*, from the outer edges to the centre. This can quite well be done in the vice. The low set angle of the Cutter of an iron plane, together with the ease with which it can be adjusted to cut a very fine shaving, makes this process quite easy and accurate. On account of the extra low set angle, the iron block plane (see Chapter 2) is most suitable for this kind of work (Fig. 82).

Fig. 82.—Shooting end grain of a draining board.

(vi) To shoot an edge on the shooting-board. (The stop may be at 90°, or at a mitre of 45°, etc.) The further edge may be chamfered to the line with a chisel before planing. Hold the wood hard up to the stop as shown in Fig. 83. Lay the plane on its side in the rebate, holding it with the right hand as shown. Slide the plane along, taking very fine cuts. The iron must be very sharp and finely set. Three thin cuts are easier and more accurate than one thick one. Rub a candle lightly on the sole and on the rubbing face to give an easier passage for the plane.

Where much shooting is done it is a great saver of time, as well as being easier to cut, if the bottom of the rebate of the shooting-board forms a ramp instead of being made parallel. The effect of this is that much more of the blade is in active service and the time for honing or whetting is postponed. When the blade is run on the ordinary shooting-board to shoot $\frac{1}{2}$ in. boards, only $\frac{1}{2}$ in. of the edge is at work. This is

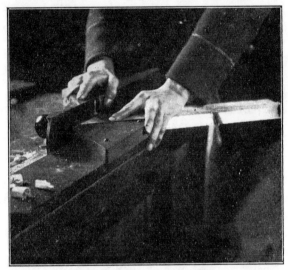

Fig. 83.

dulled while the rest of the blade is still sharp. By using a cant on the board more of the edge is in action; the cut, being oblique, is easier, and the sharpness of the blade lasts longer.

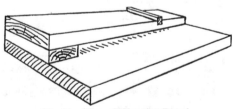

Fig. 84.—"Ramp" Shooting Board.

The sides of Record Planes are ground at right angles to the soles and are therefore eminently suitable for use with a shooting-board. It sometimes happens, however, that although this is so, and the shooting-board is in perfect truth, the cut is unaccountably out of truth. The cause of this, should it happen, is that in setting the blade, it has been set slightly out of alignment with the sole, one corner of the blade projecting farther than the other. The remedy is to correct this by using the lateral adjusting lever. Record T5 Jack Plane is especially suitable for use on the shooting-board, having wider wings which have a greater bearing on the shooting-board, and being provided with an extra side handle which assists considerably in the control of the tool. (See pages 35-40.)

Apart from the use of the shooting-board in the preparation of end grain cuts, there is an enormous advantage in its use in the preparation of pairs of boards entailing long grain cuts. The butt joints of the parts of an occasional table top can be quickly prepared on a shooting-board of moderate length. In using this dodge, it is wise to shoot the first board face side up, and the next one face side down, and so on. (Heart sides should alternate to minimise the effect of any warping.) A typical example is the making of a chess-board where, say, sycamore and black walnut strips are shot on the long grain in the manner indicated, and then glued together alternately. Saw cuts are then made across the face, and the new strips thus separated shot again, this time on the end grain. They will then be finally glued together with a white square opposite a black one. When making the first set of strips, one extra strip should be included so as to make allowance for matching up, the odd pieces not required being discarded after the second glueing. Final support may be given by glueing the whole to a plywood base; a frame may be added; or the board may be embodied in a table top.

(vii) To shoot a mitre for a wide plinth. When only one or two have to be done, they can be done in a vice, similarly to (v) on page 70,

Fig. 85.

using the plane as indicated in Figs. 81 and 82, but at the required bevel. If the job is likely to occur at all frequently, a "donkey's ear" (Fig. 85) should be constructed, and the mitres shot on it as in Section vi.

An alternative way is to screw a pair of squared fillets to both cheeks of the vice at the required angle to the top, in such a manner that they are exactly opposite each other. The board to be shot can then be laid on the two supports, and held in the vice jaws whilst being shot. The two fillets are screwed to the wood facings, and can easily be attached or removed. They should each project about $\frac{1}{4}$ in. or so above the iron jaws of the vice, so that there is no danger of "snicking" the cutter on the iron vice.

The same dodge can be used at times by setting the work in the vice by the use of a carpenter's bevel, dispensing with the use of screwed fillets; but the fillets are well worth the little time they cost in preparation when making 45° mitres.

(viii) To shoot an edge cut at any other angle than 90° to the length.

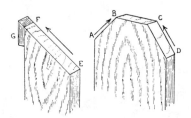

Fig. 86.

A consideration of the way of the grain (Fig. 86) will show that in (1) the plane must travel from E to F. The point at F can be saved from chipping off by cramping a small piece G there until the planing is finished. In example (2) B to C offers no difficulty, and is planed as in Section (v) on page 70. The grain will show that you must plane from A to B and then reverse the job and plane from D to C.

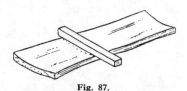

Fig. 87.

(ix) "Warped" and "Cast" Boards, due to faulty seasoning, present difficulties in planing. Warping (i.e., hollowing in width) may be straightened out by damping the hollow side and warming the round side; but the board will probably warp again on drying out if not fixed (after planing, etc.) by the construction, as in a groove or a rabbet.

Casting (*i.e.*, curvature in length due to bad seasoning) is difficult to cure, and cast boards are seldom worth working up.   There is nothing else to do in this case but to plane the high spots away, and that will reduce the ultimate thickness of the board.   Fig. 87 shows a board both warped and cast: not worth the labour of planing up, except, possibly, after cutting up into smaller pieces.

Chapter 10

Fundamentals of Planing

To join boards together to make one wide board.

1. BUTT (or SLAPE) JOINTS

There are two very sound reasons why every woodworker should be able to join two or more narrow boards together.

(a) Wide boards are seldom obtainable in these days. Even when they are, their scarcity makes them command high prices. The price per **square** foot is always higher for the wide boards than it is for narrower ones. Thus, a table top 3 ft. × 18 in., would cost more as a single board than it would for three lengths six inches wide which, joined together would make an equal area to 3 ft. × 18 in.

(The scarcity of wide boards has resulted in the great strides which have been made in the manufacture of plywoods and laminated boards, and the perfection attained in this has been reflected in cabinet design, the making of plywood being so closely allied to the cutting of veneers.)

(b) The shrinkage and warpage of wide boards is very much more apparent than that of the narrower boards, and narrower boards can be "reversed" to minimise the tendency to warp.

In the case of a table top it is essential that boards shall be joined, and that they shall stand up true without showing the joint.

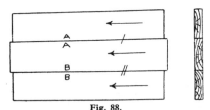

Fig. 88.

Proceed in this manner. Lay out the boards as in Fig. 88, putting the way of the grain as shown by the arrows, and "matching" the grain as nearly as possible for appearance's sake. Arrange the boards with heart sides alternating as in the side view, the effect of this being that any upward pull of one board in subsequent warping will be counteracted by the downward pull of the next. You need not plane the wide sides of the boards, yet; that can come after gluing. Mark the edges to be joined AA, BB, or with a series of strokes (both ways are shown in the figure) so that you can quickly recognise the pairs.

Fig. 89.—Shooting long edges in vice.

Take the first two boards, put them lengthwise in the vice as in Fig. 89, and if necessary on account of their length, cramp the loose ends with a G cramp. The two marked edges AA (Fig. 88) must be outwards. Plane straight and true. If you should be slightly out of square that will not matter very greatly as a slight deviation that way is compensated by the fact that you will reverse one board in fitting (see Fig. 90), but you **must** plane straight in the length.

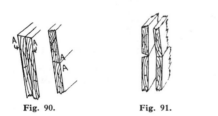 

Fig. 90.   Fig. 91.   Fig. 92.

Jointing boards in this way must be done with a Try or Jointer Plane, the long length of which is specially adapted for truing long lengths. Short planes cannot work straight enough on a long length.

The adoption of the method given above prevents exasperating failures such as are indicated in Fig. 91.

Proceed with the other joints in the same way until all are completed. The boards should now be glued.

Make sure before you start this process that the glue is ready for use and that you have sufficient of it. (Cold glues such as Croid are very satisfactory for this purpose and are easier to use than the ordinary glue which must be heated and applied hot.)

Arrange the boards on the bench in the proper order of fitting. Place the first board with edge A upwards in the vice, and hold the corresponding edge A towards it and along it. Glue both edges where they are to be joined, and then place the glued edges together (the first still remaining in the vice) and rub them together until they "suck". Make sure they are in correct alignment and that the edges are not overlapping. Leave them so whilst you glue in a similar manner the next pair, and so on to the finish.

The ideal is perfectly true edges, with no line of glue showing. If the edges are planed true they will hold for ever, the glued joint being stronger than the fibre itself.

When there are but two or three small pieces they can be left as they are for 24 hours, or moved carefully and supported at the back as in Fig. 92, but where the work is at all large, the joints should be cramped, and left in the cramps for 24 hours.

Another way of temporarily holding a job like this until the glue is set is by the use of carpenter's dogs, which are much like large staples. The 2½ in. size will be found best. They are driven in the end grain at each joint at each end, thus holding the two boards together. They are easily withdrawn after the glue has set.

When arranging the cramps, it is wise to have one at each end and one in the middle; the latter being placed at the opposite side from the former. Thus any tendency the tightening of the cramps may have to spring the boards will be counteracted by the bar of the cramp on the opposite side. The edges of the boards should be protected from bruising by the cramps by having pieces of waste wood inserted between the edge of the board and the cramp. Screw the cramps up firmly, but not too hard. All surplus glue must be squeezed out, as excess of glue weakens, not strengthens the joint. See below, however, on Resin glues.

Fig. 93.—Boards cramped with 3 Record Cramps.

If the cramps are required for another purpose during the 24 hours, you can lightly nail a couple of splines across the boards to hold them, and then remove the cramps. In any case you must allow 24 hours for the joints to set, and whenever possible it is preferable to leave the cramps *in situ* for that period.

It is an advantage when the cramping is done, and before the glue sets, to wipe off the surplus glue with a rag dipped in hot water, or even the glue brush dipped in hot water. Hot water from cast-iron gluepot wells is likely to stain the wood, however. This process may be omitted, in which case the hardened glue must later be removed with a chisel.

The next day you may proceed to square up the board. Select the better face. Cramp it face up to the bench top with G cramps or other suitable means, and proceed (after removing the surplus glue) to clean up the top. If the wood is hard wood (say, a mahogany table top with a troublesome grain) plane with a fairly fine set **across** the grain. Go on in this manner until you have evened it up practically true. Then with a **very sharp** iron set to cut a tissue paper shaving, plane along the grain to leave a nice surface. **Only by this method can a cross-grained hardwood be brought to shape in a reasonable time without undue fatigue.** Sweetly grained soft pines and deals will not require planing across the grain, but for hard woods with irregular grain and wide surface, there is nothing to beat a properly sharpened and set iron plane worked in the manner indicated across the grain for quickly reducing it to dimension and a state of presentability.

Gauge to thickness, and clean up the other face in a similar manner.

The top, or better face will possibly require a final scraping and sanding. Notes for this process will be found under the "Use of the Scraper".

Of late years, improvements in manufacture and length of pot life have made resin glues much more popular both with the trade and with the amateur. Some of these glues require a separate hardener whilst others are of the "one shot" type, but all of them can be applied cold— which is a considerable advantage. The makers' instructions for each individual glue should be closely followed, as there are slight differences in application, but all of them, provided instructions are carefully carried out, will make a sound joint. The gap-filler type will often make a good joint when animal glue would fail. Another advantage these modern glues have is that they are waterproof and so can be used for joints which are exposed to the weather and for boat work. One word of warning should be given: the makers recommend a somewhat light cramping, because if all the glue is squeezed out, the joint will be starved of glue, and the joint will subsequently fail. Cramps, both G cramps and sash cramps, can give heavier pressures than the ones usually recommended, even when screwed up by hand. Hence the amount of pressure given should be carefully watched so that it is not excessive. And finally, the resin glues are deservedly popular for another reason— the cramping process can be considerably shortened. The type of hardener and the temperature of the room both affect cramping times, and here again it will be necessary to refer to makers' instructions.

Excess glue is preferably wiped off before it has set, as when the glue is set, though it can be planed, it is not kind to plane blade edges.

2. TONGUED JOINTS

It may, on occasion, be desired further to strengthen a joint such as is indicated in the last section by adding to the glueing surface. This can be done in a variety of ways, such as by putting in a "loose tongue" (which may have the grain running the same way as the boards or may have its grain running at right angles to the boards—a "cross tongue"); or by having a tongue on one board and a corresponding groove on the other (tongue and groove); or by a number of tongues and grooves.

The Butt Joint as in section (a) Fig. 88 is a perfectly sound joint which will hold up indefinitely so long as it is kept dry, and is eminently suited for cabinet work for tops, etc., and for panels which are set in rebates or ploughed grooves. There are occasions, however, where, if the glue should give, and shrinkage occur at some later date, it is advisable that there should not be a gap through, as for example, a kitchen table top. Then we must have a tongue of some sort.

There is one difference in the preparation of this joint—and all others where the plough is used—as compared with the Butt joint. In the latter case the edges may be planed and joined without any planing of the face. Where grooves are to be put in, it is essential that the face sides of the boards be prepared first and carefully marked.

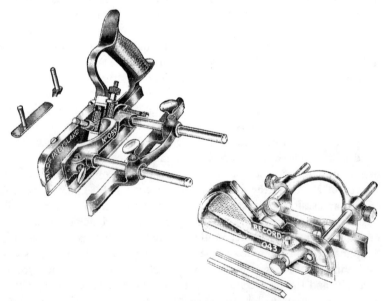

Fig. 94.—Two Record Ploughs (see also Chapter 14).

Plane up the edges exactly as if you were making a Butt joint as in the previous section. Then, if you are going to make a tongued joint, select an iron that will be approximately one-third of the thickness of the wood, e.g., for a table top a $\frac{1}{4}$ in. iron. (Some prefer a thinner tongue than one-third.) Set your plough cutter in your Plough, Combination Plane (050) or Multi-Plane (405) so that it will cut the groove in the centre, and plane **every time from the face side,** *i.e.,* the marked ones. If the fence is not working on the face side every time, you may find  the grooves come unevenly and the result will be so:  Set the plane to cut the groove deeper than its width. For instance, if you are cutting a $\frac{1}{4}$ in. wide groove, your tongues should be from $\frac{3}{4}$ in. to $\frac{7}{8}$ in. deep, so that the depth of the groove should be just full half of the depth of the tongue on each board (Fig. 95). (The method of setting the Combination

Fig. 95.

Fig. 96.

Plane and the Multi-Plane will be found under those headings.) The central position can be accurately determined by fixing the fence either by measurement or by trial on the board itself.

To cut the groove, place the board, edge to be cut upwards, in the vice, face side towards you. Commence at the end further away and take short strokes at first, each stroke commencing a little farther back than the last (Fig. 96) until you have worked back the full length of the board. Then take a stroke the full length of the board and continue this until you can no longer cut a shaving. This will indicate that you have an even, predetermined depth— a perfectly accurate groove in both width and depth.

[In using these planes—the Plough, the Combination Plane and the Multi-Plane, there is no need whatever to bear downwards heavily. It is vitally important, however, that pressure shall be applied **towards** the wood, so that the fence is always in close contact with the side, particularly in the early stages of the cut. Once the groove has been started the iron will keep in the groove and the plane will work very sweetly indeed. Do not use too much iron. Two or three thin shavings are better than one thick one, produce more accurate work, and are less laborious to remove. If you are "forcing" any woodworking tool, you may safely assume that

F

you are not getting the best out of it, out of your material nor out of yourself.]

Work each board the same way on each of the edges to be joined. Then prepare the tongues.   If stuff is available of the right thickness, well and good.   Cut strips off the correct width and they are made. If not, plane up some wood the same as the boards so that it is a keen fit in the groove.   These pieces need not be as long as the boards to be joined if you are going to cross tongue, so that you can use up any odd pieces that are available.   Saw pieces **across** the grain so that their width is that of the two grooves combined and they will fit along the groove end to end as in Fig. 97.   The fact that the grain runs opposite

Fig. 97.

to that of the boards nullifies any reason for their absolute continuity.   When the boards are glued together, all the pieces, as well as the boards become cemented into one strong whole.   Loose tongues should always be crossed like this.   They are strong against any tendency the board may have, when completed, to bending, whilst a long grained tongue is weak in that very respect.   Good plywood may be used for the tongues, the only precaution to be taken being that you must choose an iron that will make a groove the plywood will fit.   For instance, in the case we have just considered, $\frac{3}{16}$ in. or $\frac{1}{4}$ in. plywood could have been used for the tongues, so long as our $\frac{3}{16}$ in. or $\frac{1}{4}$ in. irons cut grooves that the plywood fits.   Millimetre cutters are available as extras, if desired.

The cross-tongued joint is a very strong joint indeed.

Immediately before glueing up, it is good practice to run a thin shaving off the inside corners of the groove with a rebate or shoulder plane finely set (such as the 042 or 077a).   This assists the egress of surplus glue when cramping up.   The shaving taken off must, of course, be very light, but this is not difficult with a rebate plane of the type just mentioned.

A special case.   It may be desirable that a joint should be strengthened with a cross tongue, but that the tongue should be invisible.   In this case the grooves must be "stopped" (Fig. 221, right). A mitred framed top for an occasional table forms a good example. The job **can** be done by ploughing from the centre first and working as far as possible.   The spurs will gauge that part that cannot be reached by the plough, and which must be mortised out with a chisel.   The centre portion being filled with a tongued panel hides any joint on the inside; the stopped portion hides the tongue from observation from the outside ends.

82

The same construction can be used for a lady's work table or similar top where it is desired to give access to a recess by means of a movable panel. In the latter case the movable panel will sit on a rebate, the depth of which will be so arranged that it just misses the tongue, and only a plain mitre then appears inside the rebate.

A very much easier and more satisfactory method of cutting this type of stopped groove is now available, by using the fenced Router Plane, which is able to travel right through to the stopped portion. The method is described under "Routers". (See Chapter 16 and Fig. 215.)

There are times when exceptional strength is called for in a tongued joint. This strength is secured by a variation of the above method, *i.e.*, by using two, three or even more tongues. Anyone who can work single tongues can work multiple tongues. Set the plane for cutting the groove for the first tongue and then work it **from the face side** on one piece (Fig. 98). Then work a similar groove on the second piece **also from the**

face side. Now release the fence: set it for the second groove and work it on the first piece, and then on the second piece, each time making sure that you work with the fence on the face side. Again release the fence; set for the third groove and proceed as before. The tongues are made as before.

Fig. 98. The extra gluing surface that one gets on this type of joint makes it practically unbreakable.

3. TONGUED AND GROOVED JOINTS

A joint which is in common use and much more widely known than the foregoing, is the tongued and grooved joint—the joint which is used on "matching" boards. It has the weakness that any bending strain on the joint is apt to break away the tongue in the direction of the grain, but

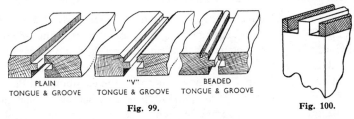

PLAIN	"V"	BEADED
TONGUE & GROOVE	TONGUE & GROOVE	TONGUE & GROOVE

Fig. 99.   Fig. 100.

it is a joint that is eminently suited for matching-boards which are not glued together, as for partitions, hut making and lining, the backs of Welsh dressers, etc. The Combination and the Multi-Planes make this kind of work quite easy. For a plain tongue and groove such as is used for flooring, the edges must first be planed straight and square. The tonguing cutter is then set so that the gap in the cutter which leaves the tongue shall be central. The depth of the tongue is regulated by the little button gauge on the cutter; its position on the edge of the board is regulated by adjusting the fence to suit. If the thickness of the board is more than the cutter that will not matter, as the spare ridge can be taken off afterwards with a plough cutter or a rebate plane (the shaded portions in Fig. 100 show these parts which are later removed).

Keep the fence well up to the work, have a keen edge, and take light cuts. Commence at the farther end of the board and work backwards as advised when starting a groove (see (Fig. 96); only this time you will be leaving a tongue and cutting on each side of it. When you get down to the button gauge on the cutter your tongue will be the height you want it.

The tongues being cut, remove the tonguing cutter and set in the $\frac{1}{4}$ in. plough cutter. With a tongued board in the bench vice **face side towards you,** adjust the fence so that the plough cutter sits **exactly** on the top of the tongue, and screw up the fence. Adjust the depth stop on the plane so that your groove will accommodate the tongue with just a little (about $\frac{1}{16}$ in.) to spare. Check your setting, and then plough the grooves as described above. The object of setting the plough cutter about $\frac{1}{16}$ in. deeper than the tongue is that the tongue may have clearance and so leave no gap on the outside edges.

You must plane your board true and straight first, and you must be sure to work from the face side for cutting both tongues and grooves; or you will find your boards joint up unevenly—some farther back than others.

There is always the possibility of shrinkage to be thought about, and the chance of the joints opening some time after they have been in position. To improve the appearance of a tongued joint, the two front edges are occasionally chamfered, thus giving a V-shaped opening. The chamfering can easily be done with an iron jack. (See Figs. 99 and 113).

A much more effective method of masking the joint is by means of a bead (Fig. 99). The bead is planed on the side that carries the tongue (as obviously, if planed on the grooved side the quirk would so weaken the board that the bead would break away). Cutting a bead on matching-boards is an easy and rapid operation either with the Combination Plane (No. 050) or with the Multi-Plane (No. 405) and instructions for making it will be found in the chapters devoted to those two planes. As in ploughing the cut should be started at the farther end and worked back-wards, and the top of the bead should be slightly below the rest of the surface, so that it does not suffer in subsequent cleaning up.

Use of centre beads on beaded tongued and grooved boards.— Beaded tongued and grooved boards always look best when the boards are narrow, say, three inches or four inches wide. It may be, however, that the boards are six inches wide, or even of varying widths. The work entailed and the wastage of area involved in cutting the wide boards into narrow ones may not be worth while, or the widths available may not be suitable. In this case bead, tongue and groove all the boards on their edges as before described. Then set out even (or approximately even) distances in the widths, and run a centre bead down with the same cutter as used for the edge beads, setting the fence suitably for the distance and the depth stop so that the bead is **just below** the surface. It is always wise to run the beads a little below the surface as, when you come to clean up and sandpaper to a finish, the beauty of the bead is not ruined by the acquisition of a flat which has an annoying habit of catching the light and proclaiming its presence.

The appearance of such boarding on a dresser back is very beautiful.

4. DOWELLED JOINTS

Joining two boards along their length with dowels is done very often, but it has to be admitted that a dowelled joint will often spring when a Butt joint holds. However, the method of doing it is here given. Place the boards, face sides together, face edges upwards in the vice, so that their face edges are in the same plane. Mark off, at intervals, the places where the dowels are to come, in such a manner that the mark appears at the intersection of face side and edge on both boards. Then release the boards and square each board on each mark from the face side, marking on the face edge. Set a cutting gauge accurately to half the thickness of the board, and from the face side gauge across the squared marks. The crossings of the two markings will give the positions of the centres of the dowel holes. These should be approximately one-third of the thickness of the boards, and care must be taken to bore at right angles to the face edge. The dowels should be slightly rounded at each end, and many workers like a slight groove along the length of the dowel; the object in each case being a provision for the escape of excess glue. Fit the boards dry to make sure all goes up well. Then take apart, glue the dowels into one board, which is best held in the vice for this purpose; then glue both edges and the projecting dowels, making sure the free holes get their share. Bring all together and cramp up, leaving the cramps on for 24 hours. The operation must be done quickly, or the glue will chill; consequently, everything required must be ready at hand before any glue is applied. Most failures can be traced to chilling of the glue through some delay in the assembly.

It is a good plan when jointing long lengths to plane the edges very slightly hollow; the ends of the joint then tend to pull together more.

A dowelled joint that embodies a rebate is a particularly strong joint. The boards are prepared as described for ordinary dowelling first and the dowels are fitted dry. A shallow rebate is then taken out of each edge, on opposite sides. The extra glueing surfaces presented, and the interlocking angles, make the joint very strong indeed. Care must be taken, of course, that the width taken out of the one side for the rebate is equal to the amount left on the other, so that when the boards are put together the faces of the two are flush; any air space left in a joint makes a weakness.

5. TO PLANE A ROUND OR AN OVAL ROD

There is always a tendency by a beginner to solve this problem by using a spokeshave. The usual result is a keen disappointment. First, accurately square up your piece as already described. Then join the diagonals as at A or B (Fig. 101) and strike out accurately the circle or ellipse required. Make a pair of cradles as at C to rest the work in against the bench stop. Now plane the corners off straight as at D and E, leaving the piece truly octagonal. Plane off the corners now to make it 16 sided; then again to make it 32 sided; again to make it 64 sided, and the use of a scraper or file and sandpaper will finish off your job accurately.

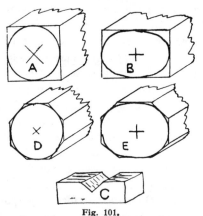

Fig. 101.

6. TO CLEAN UP THE EDGES OF A FRAME TOO BIG TO HOLD IN THE VICE

When the job cannot be secured in the vice, it can often be held between the knees, or one can sit on it, or it may be cramped to the bench top or end. Sometimes an awkward size of frame may rest on the trestle whilst part is secured in the vice. This usually works if the planing is done **towards** the vice. Other dodges will occur to the ingenious worker.

7. TO MAKE A RAISED PANEL

Square up the panel to its finished length and breadth. Make sure the sides are square with each other and the sides parallel. Set your Plough, Combination Plane or Multi-Plane with a $\frac{1}{4}$ in. iron to the width and depth required and plough grooves as at A (Fig. 102). Now set the panel in the vice and plane the slope away, at first with your iron jack,

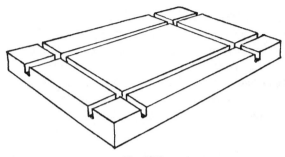

Fig. 102A.

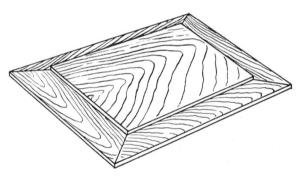

Fig. 102B.

and finish off with Rabbet Plane No. 010 or 010$\frac{1}{2}$. In working the ends, plane in the direction of the arrows, as shown in Fig. 81. You will find it best to work the long way of the grain first. Make a nice, clean straight mitre where the slopes join at the corners.

An alternative method, which is very pleasing when finished, is, instead of ploughing with a $\frac{1}{4}$ in. iron for the grooves, plough them with a narrow fluter cutter (using No. 405 Multi-Plane), which must be very sharp and finely set. In this manner, the groove is concave, so that the edge of the fielding is left finally quarter round instead of straight as in the first case. The play of the light on this quarter round has a very fine effect if the work is cleanly carried out.

8. TO CUT A GROOVE OR RABBET WIDER THAN YOUR WIDEST CUTTER

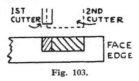

Fig. 103.

The widest cutter on the Combination Plane 050 is $\frac{7}{8}$ in. and you wish to sink a groove, say, 1 in. wide. Work a groove of any width on the side **farthest away** from the face edge at the place where the edge of the required groove is to come. Now take a cutter slightly wider than the remainder and take this off at a second cut, letting the cutter make the near edge at the required distance from the face edge. Keep the depth gauge the same for both cuts. (Fig. 103).

A similar method is used for cutting a wide rabbet.

In this case the spare wood, after the plough cut has been made, can be taken off with a Jack Plane.

9. TO START THE MORTISES FOR HAUNCHED TENONS

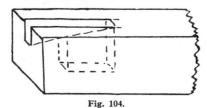

Fig. 104.

The joints of, say, a kitchen table are stronger if the tenons are haunched. The work of mortising is very much lighter if the Combination Plane or the Multi-Plane is used in the preliminary cuts, working as if you were going to groove them. There is no need to mark out the width of the mortises, as the spur cutters do this for you, and at the same time the part for the haunch to fit in is brought to depth by the cutter of the plane. Any slight cut made beyond the limit of the mortise is hidden by the lower part of the rail when glued up. This is a great time saver (Fig. 104).

The haunches, and the mortises to the depth of the haunch can also be quickly and accurately cut with the Router 071, using the straight side of the fence as in making a stopped groove (see page 180).

10. MAKING DOUBLE OR TRIPLE, etc., REEDING
with the Combination Plane or the Multi-Plane when only a single bead cutter is available. (Fig. 105).

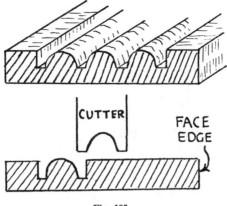

Fig. 105.

Start on the side farthest away from the face edge and run on the first bead. Slacken the fence and so adjust it that the next bead will come as shown, *i.e.*, so that the farther flat of the second cut will coincide with the near flat of the first cut. Continue this for as many beads as are required. This is a popular form of decoration for relieving any flat surface, *e.g.*, the front face of a pilaster, or a drawer front. If the beads are cut slightly below the surface they do not suffer in the final clean up.

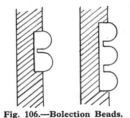

Fig. 106.—Bolection Beads.

Horizontally placed Bolection beads as a decoration to the lower parts of furniture carcases can be made separately and planted in a shallow groove as shown in Fig. 106. When neatly proportioned to the rest of the work these can be very effective, and on modern work have a tendency to become more popular.

11. TO MAKE A RETURN BEAD

Whilst this presents a difficulty with wooden bead planes, the process is simple with either the Combination Plane or the Multi-Plane. Work a bead first on the face edge, leaving just a small quirk only on the face side, by setting the fence under the quirk cutter as at A (Fig. 107). Then work on the face side, setting the plane in such a manner that the little quirk is just taken off as at B (*i.e.*, by setting the fence just level with the round of the edge).

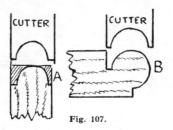

Fig. 107.

12. TO MAKE A TORUS BEAD

This is easily done with the 050 or the 405.   Mark first from the edge of the board with a plough cutter distance as shown under cutter. Now set the plane so that the bead cutter will have the quirk as shown in the lower diagram (Fig. 108).   Cut the bead first, and then plough away the shaded part with the plough cutter.

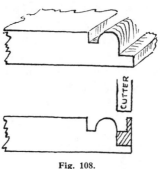

Fig. 108.

13. TO MAKE AN ASTRAGAL MOULDING

Work a bead on the edge of a board and then cut off as shown by the dotted line (Fig. 109).   It can be grooved on the reverse side by ploughing a groove in the edge of a board and using this as a rest, as at A.

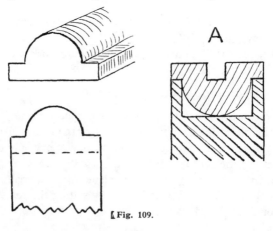

Fig. 109.

90

Another way is to use wood of the same *thickness* as the required astragal. Plough the groove first; reverse the wood and cut the bead. Then sever with a fine saw or the slitter cutter (No. 405), and trim the last edge with a block plane.

Further types of rectangular astragals and the method of sticking them will be found in Fig. 166B, page 137.

14. TO MAKE ROUND RODS

Though of limited application this dodge is useful at times. A bead is planed on both sides of a board, which should be of the right thickness (Fig. 110). If care be taken and the board is the right thickness, good rods can be made requiring very little cleaning up.

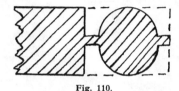

Fig. 110.

15. TO PLANE VERY SMALL PIECES

Set the Iron Jack sole upwards in the vice and draw the piece along. Keep the fingers clear of the blade. When small dimensioned fillets or keys for joints are to be planed, it is often of advantage to cut out a shallow housing in a spare piece of wood similar to that shown in Fig. 111, minus the guide. The thin piece can then be placed in the housing and planed. Using this method it will not buckle as it might if placed in the ordinary way against the bench stop.

16. TO CUT A STOPPED HOUSING FOR A SHELF

Fig. 111. Square the lines and gauge for depth and mark the set back of the stopped part. Bore a hole the width of the housing as at A.

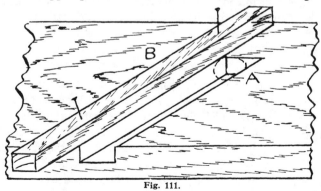

Fig. 111.

Tack on a squared fillet at B and with a tenon saw cut to the depth required. Remove the fillet and repeat the cutting, using the fillet as before on the other side of the housing. Take out the rough with a chisel and router down to correct depth with an 071 router (Chapter 16). Clean up round the hole with the chisel.

The same effect can be achieved by making a mortise at A instead of boring, taking care of course that the chisel cuts are made across the grain.

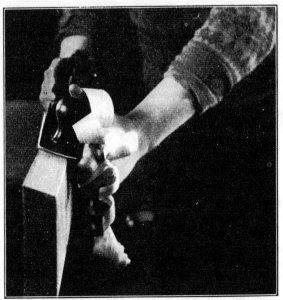

Fig. 112.—Planing a Bevel.   Note fingers of left hand taking a bearing.

17. TO CHAMFER

When chamfering always set out the chamfer with a pencil.   If set out with a gauge the ugly gauge marks are left, or you have to proceed farther than you intended so as to remove them.   When chamfering along the grain, proceed as for bevelling (Fig. 112), except that less is taken away.   When working chamfers or bevels across the grain, it is an advantage to use a block plane, tilting the plane slightly across the chamfer so that the cutter works obliquely, as before described.

Both through and stopped chamfers are easily and quickly made with Record Chamfer Spokeshave A65, an unbreakable tool fitted with two adjustable fences which eliminate tedious marking out, as once the fences are set, all the chamfers will finish uniformly and without waviness.   Through chamfers need no marking out at all, and for stopped chamfers only the two ends need be marked.   Very effective curved entrances and exits will come after a little practice (see page 196).

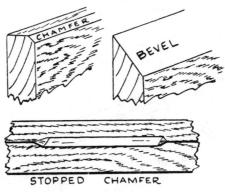

Fig. 113.

18. WORKING A MOULDING ON A TABLE TOP

First plough a groove $\frac{1}{4}$ in. wide, as shown at A (Fig. 114). Remove the shaded portion with an Iron Jack, rebate, or shoulder plane, as most convenient. The ovolo at B can be done by working two grooves and by using a No. 073 Shoulder Plane. Ovolo cutters are available with the Multi-Plane (see page 166). For moulding end grain see fig. 193.

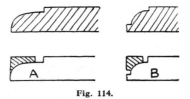

Fig. 114.

19. TO MAKE DRAWER SLIP

Drawer Slip (Fig. 115) can easily be made from waste pieces or short ends by ploughing a groove $\frac{3}{16}$ in. or $\frac{1}{4}$ in. wide, and $\frac{3}{16}$ in. deep, on the edge of a board which should be about $\frac{3}{16}$ in. thick. After the groove is cut, the thickness of the slip is gauged; the corner is rounded off as previously described, and then the slip is sawn off (Fig. 116).

The width of the groove chosen should be in accordance with the thickness of the drawer bottoms. Centre slip for drawer bottoms is made by ploughing a groove the same thickness as the drawer bottom on both sides of the slip, and then rounding off the two upper corners, *i.e.*, those which will appear inside the drawer.

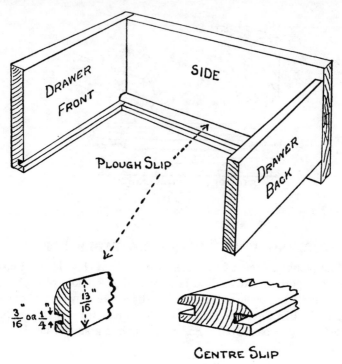

DRAWER FRONT

SIDE

DRAWER BACK

PLOUGH SLIP

$\frac{3}{16}$" OR $\frac{1}{4}$"

$\frac{13}{16}$"

CENTRE SLIP

Fig. 115.

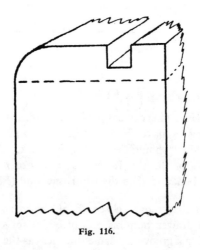

Fig. 116.

20. A RABBETED CORNER JOINT

A very neat corner can be quickly made by rebating one piece as at A (Fig. 117) and nailing the second piece as indicated. If the little end grain which is slightly rounded as at B the joint is much improved.

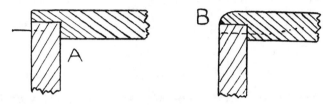

Fig. 117.

This joint may be used when making small cabinets of plywood, the rabbet taken out being equal to all the plies but one. In this case the plane spur should be used (078 and 778 Rabbet, 050 Combination, 405 Multi-Plane). If desirable, the joint may be further strengthened by glued blocks on the inside. If rounded as at B a veneer can be laid around the complete corner.

21. A VERY STRONG CORNER JOINT

This joint which may be seen in much of the work of the Chippendale period, is an ingenious combination of straight-forward planing and glue jointing, and is shown in detail in Fig. 118. A is the end of a bookcase or the like, and B the door. The fluted quarter column is glued into a rebate formed in the piece D, which in turn is rebated for the door, and is tongued into piece A as shown; A, C and D, when glued up, making one very solid, yet charmingly effective corner, having a rich appearance. The small sketch E will clearly show the parts which are to be rebated to form part D, the sizes, of course, depending upon the material being used. The quarter column C may be made in several ways, but if only two are required they may be planed up as described for circular work and the flutings may be cut with a scratch stock, or with a gouge, or the round may be left quite plain. Four parts may be turned up in the lathe if previously glued together with paper between, the paper facilitating the division after turning.

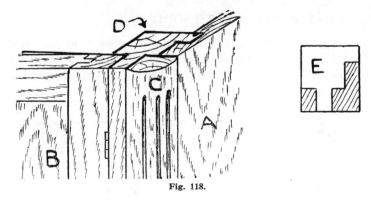

Fig. 118.

22. SIMPLE METHODS OF MAKING CORNER JOINTS

Simple methods are shown in Fig. 119. A offers no difficulty, being merely rebated and rounded. B is a simple variation, where a groove is first planed as at dotted line at D, and after the rebate is cut, the corner

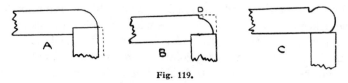

Fig. 119.

is rounded, the rebate being cut a trifle less than the thickness of the material to butt into it, so that the ovolo is thus formed on the edge. C shows the familiar staff bead, rounded off at the back, the bead appearing on the front edge (as in a cupboard). These joints may be glued, or glued and nailed, or nailed only on commoner work.

23. OTHER CORNER JOINTS

These can be made by the plane by introducing a little more work, and the result, particularly if the job is one for the home, well repays the extra trouble taken (Fig. 120). The dotted line at D shows the shape

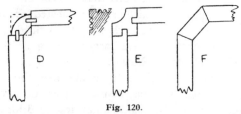

Fig. 120.

before ploughing the grooves for the loose tongues. The sides to be joined are ploughed with the same iron, but the groove set back about $\frac{1}{8}$ in. Loose tongues (as before described) are inserted. The quadrant may be rounded off with the Jack Plane (or with the Multi-Plane), and the inner corner taken off similarly, finishing straight or hollow. This is a very effective corner for a wardrobe. Extra strength may be given to joints such as D, E and F by glue blocking on the inside of the corners. E offers no difficulty. The quarter hollow is cut with the Multi-Plane, using the special bottom and cutter (Chapter 14). If the concavity is troublesome because no hollow plane is available, the section may be planed straight, convex, or may be stop chamfered (see Fig. 113). Alternatively, two, or three narrow beads may be used. F is a nice-looking corner calling for accurate bevelled planing which has been described.

24. STRENGTHENING MITRED CORNERS

G (Fig. 121) shows a two-tongued mitre. Piece K has its edge at right angles. The groove is first ploughed out the full depth, and then

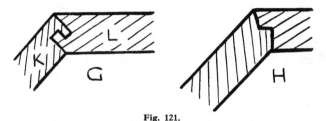

Fig. 121.

the side removed with the rebate plane. Piece L is planed off to the required bevel, the groove ploughed, and the spare rebated off. H is not so strong as G. It can be worked with the Jack Plane first and the rebates cleared with the Rebate Plane. Extreme accuracy is called for in such corner joints as have been described in the last four paragraphs; but the advent of the Metal Plane has made this accuracy easily attainable by anyone who will take reasonable care; and the results are well worth while, giving an effect truly reflecting the finest traditions of craftsmanship.

25. MITRED BOXES

A box structure having mitred corners may be strengthened with parallel keys. The mitres can be shot on the Donkey's ear (Fig. 85). The two sides and the two ends should be checked for equal length, and the mitred corners should be square with the face edge. To plough the grooves, the pieces should be carefully set in the vice back to back as at B (Fig. 122) when it will be found that the fence of the plough will rest on one mitre whilst the other is ploughed. The second groove is ploughed by resting the fence on the mitre already ploughed. When all the grooves are completed, slips or "keys" can be fitted as at A. The keys

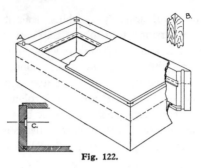

Fig. 122.

not only strengthen the joint, but they are also of considerable assistance in preventing the tendency of the mitres to slip during assembly and glueing.

Small boxes such as cigarette boxes and jewel cases may be made in the manner indicated. Before the mitres are glued up, sides and ends are ploughed as at C. This is for the insertion later of a slip on to which the lid falls. The position of this groove should be gauged on the outside of the box as shown by the dotted line (Fig. 122). Any groove for the fitting of the bottom or top should also be ploughed at this stage. The box is now assembled and glued, top and bottom being fitted. After the glue has set, a saw cut is made through the gauged line, thus separating the lid from the box. The sawn surfaces are then trued up with a Record Smooth or Jack Plane with cutter finely set. A thin slip is now fitted flush with the inside of the box into what will now be the lower part of the groove C, letting it project about $\frac{1}{8}$ in. or $\frac{3}{16}$ in. to suit the other part of groove C, which is left in the lid.

Whilst for a quick job the bottom may be nailed or screwed on, a better method is indicated in Fig. 122, where the sides and ends are ploughed with an iron approximately half the thickness of the bottom, and the bottom rabbeted to suit. In assembling, the mitres only (with their keys) should be glued, and the bottom left dry, thus leaving allowance for any subsequent shrinkage of the bottom. Similar allowance could be made for the top; in this case the sides and ends would be ploughed suitably and the top treated as a bolection panel (see Fig. 123).

This method of box construction is much more speedy than might appear from the description, and very effective boxes can be so made, as, for example, when the box (with slips) is made of satinwood and the outside veneered with burr elm. Ebony or boxwood squares or strips may be inlaid and a handle of ebony or walnut may be fitted.

Further variation is possible in the treatment of top and bottom. Recessing the bottom slightly can give a pleasing shadow. The top may be fielded in one of many ways; or the edges may be chamfered or rounded over; or may carry a simple ovolo or ogee moulding.

Serviceable boxes for the storage of special tools, *e.g.*, bull nose, shoulder plane, etc., can be made by this method; and with a slight variation of the design which will suggest itself, the lid may be made to slide. A thumb notch can be made with gouge and chisel.

26. DOORS AND PANELLING

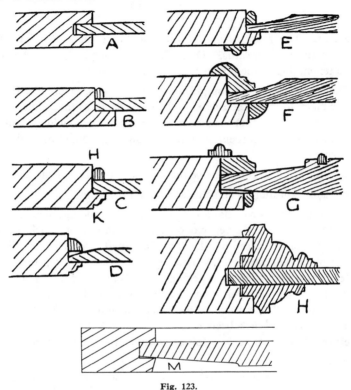

Fig. 123.

A to M (Fig. 123) show various methods of framing the panels of doors. A shows a plain ploughed groove. The tenons for the door frame are often made the same thickness as the width of the grooves so that their entry is through the groove into the mortise. Make the mortise and tenon joints first, and plough last. Don't forget to leave a haunch on the tenon that will fill that part of the groove which comes on the end of the stile (A A Fig. 124) or the result will be a nasty gap.

For better convenience when cutting the mortise, it is best to leave a horn about an inch long on the ends of the stiles. These horns will be cleaned off after the frame is glued up.

B shows a plain door which has the advantage that the panel can be left out until after polishing is finished, and then the loose bead can be

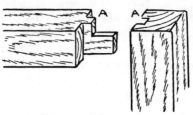

Fig. 124.

tacked in. The mortises and tenons should be made first, and the rebate taken out afterwards. Don't forget the long and short shoulder of the tenon, due to the rebate being taken out later.

C offers a little more complication, though in principle like B. If care be taken to make the rebate H the same depth as the moulding K, the shoulders of the tenons can be made equal and the mouldings mitred at the corners. For carpentry work the mouldings should be scribed at the corners.

D is the same as C but shows the panelling bevelled at the back.

E has the addition of an astragal fixed on the front.

F, for a heavier door, has a bolection (*i.e.*, protruding) moulding on the front, whilst G, for a heavy door, has the addition of a cocked bead on the front of the raised panel. This is a fine finish to a heavy door. The groove should be carefully ploughed out with an 071 Router, using the fence provided, after accurately marking its limits on both sides with a cutting gauge. It requires careful workmanship, but is a joy to see when finished. When using the Router, plane into each corner. Set in the groove for the cock bead first and later take the bevel off. The panels in a large door such as this are frequently bevelled on both back and front.

H shows a method of inserting a panel by means of which the use of nails, with their consequent disfigurement, is obviated. The patterns of the mould may be varied a good deal. it being the tonguing that is important. Another variant of this method is by using one mould only having multiple tongues to fit into corresponding grooves in the frame, and one other groove into which the panel fits. In the latter case, of course, the panel does not run **through** the moulding as it does at H, but sits, as it were, on top of it, in a groove. These last two methods are only used on very high class work where labour charges are not a primary consideration.

The slight bevel shown on the frame at M gives a very interesting play of high lights on the door when completed, and has a more chaste appearance than has a stop chamfered frame, besides being easier to dust. When setting out, notice that the rail has a long and short shoulder, the front shoulder being undercut to fit in with the chamfer of the stile. The hollowed part of the fielding of the panel here shown may be done with a narrow fluting cutter of 405 Multi-Plane before the bevel is planed off. The refined appearance of a pair of four-panel doors made in this manner has to be seen to be appreciated.

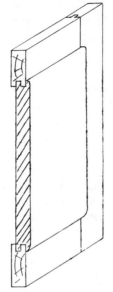

Fig. 125.—Door with raised Panel.

The door shown in Fig. 125 indicates a modern method of panelling, and may be used singly or in multi-panelled doors. It is very strong, as a thick panel can be used; it does not collect dust; and it has a fine appearance. Whilst needing accurate workmanship it is not really difficult if a Record Plough is used. In arranging the construction of the frame, make the grooves (say $\frac{1}{4}$ in.) the same distance from the edge of the frame. Then when ploughing the panel the same distance can be used. Before the panel is grooved, it should be shot square and accurately to the size of the rectangle at the bottom of the groove in the frame (e.g., if the frame is 18 in. × 15 in. and the frame grooves $\frac{3}{8}$ in. deep, the panel must be accurately squared to $18\frac{3}{4}$ in. × $15\frac{3}{4}$ in.). The Record Ploughs will plough the groove across the grain of the panel as easily as they will plough with the grain. Before fitting the panel it is as well to slightly chamfer the "tongue" that enters the frame groove. If a slight easement has to be made in fitting the panel the No. 2506S Side Rabbet Plane will be found most useful. The bolection edge of the panel may be treated as indicated, or it may be fielded, or finished with two small rebates stepped, etc.

101

Fig. 126.—Record Side Rabbet Plane No. 2506S, with Depth Stop.

The variety of door constructions shown is indicative of many, and by no means exhaustive. There is sometimes a doubt in the mind of the worker of limited experience as to whether he should groove the panel in, or fit it with a rabbet and bead. The grooved door is undoubtedly stronger, but the method of finish will frequently be a deciding factor. If a grooved door is to be French polished, the panel must be polished or nearly so before the door is glued up; for it is impossible to get a good finish in the corners of the panels after the door is up. If the door is to be painted and varnished there is no difficulty. When the door is to be French polished, it is usually best to rabbet the frames. The panel can then be polished apart from the glued-up door, and the bead can be tacked in after finishing. The inner edges of the frame are better to polish also when the panel is out.

27. SIMPLE FLUSH DOORS

The variety of ways in which flush doors can be constructed is manifold, and three simple ways only are shown. The quickest way, of course, is to use ready-made laminated board when that is available, merely cutting to size. A quick method for ordinary work is shown at A (Fig. 127) where two pieces of plywood are glued to the front and back of a mortised frame. If need be, lock rail and muntins may be set in to strengthen this. On account of the enclosed air space a small hole is often bored from the edge for ventilation. At B a better method is shown. The splines are planed true on their edges (planing in pairs as in Fig. 88) so that when butt glued up the surfaces are flat. When dry, the whole is toothed, and the inside face of the plywood toothed (see Toothing, page 207) and then glued together under pressure. Fig. 128 shows how Record G Cramps are used in cases like this. The edges of the battens are rounded slightly in planing so that when the two cramps are applied the batten is made to press in close contact along its whole length. At C (Fig. 127) a variation of this is shown, which reduces the

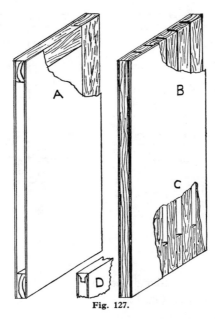

Fig. 127.

amount of core wood required and reduces the weight of the door.   The
shorter pieces are trued up in longer lengths and then cut off.

When veneering the edges of flush doors a piece of solid long grain
should be let in as at D on the end grain.   A groove is first ploughed, and
the bevels shaped with a shoulder plane; the shaped fillet being similarly
worked to a fit and then glued in.   This fillet may be wood of the same
kind as the veneer used, or it may be of a cheaper wood and afterwards
veneered.

Fig. 128.—Showing method of Cramping Flush Door with G. Cramps.

28. MEETING EDGES OF DOORS

The problem of breaking the joint between two doors is overcome
by the carpenter by making each door wider to allow for the overlap.

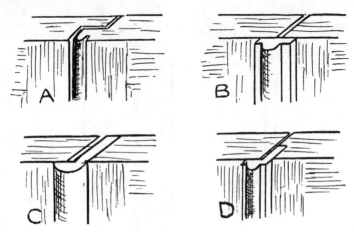

Fig. 129.

A rebate is cut on the left-hand door, a bead on the right, and a rebate behind the bead as at A (Fig. 129).

The cabinet-maker in cheap work plants an astragal with glue and pins as at B.

In better work C and D are used. At C a rebated slip is prepared with the edge rounded at the front. This slip is then glued on to the right-hand door as shown, a gap being left for the purpose.

In the best class work the slip has an astragal on the front, and besides being rebated itself, it is glued into a rebate in the right-hand door. The slip is easily made on the edge of a board by making the rebate first, and then the bead, and lastly cutting the whole slip from the board with the saw, or it may be severed easily from the board by using a $\frac{1}{8}$ in. plough cutter in the No. 050, or the slitting cutter in the 405.

A modern rectangular method of breaking the joint of two meeting doors is shown in Fig. 166B, page 137.

The advantage of making these mouldings oneself are:—(a) they are well made, (b) they are made of the same material as the work itself, (c) they are made to the individual size required, and do not have to be "adapted" to meet standard machine-made sizes, (d) the cost of the material is negligible—you make just as much as you require and do not have to buy considerably more than you need. In good class work hand-made mouldings of this description are always worth while, giving that human touch which is so often absent from machine work together with the real satisfaction that comes from work well done.

29. PANELLED BACKS

The back of a Welsh Dresser may be done with matching by any of the methods shown on page 83.   Alternatively, the muntins may be thicker than the panels, as at A, Fig. 130, which enables wide, thin

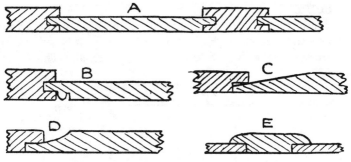

Fig. 130.

boards to be used whilst keeping a rigid construction.   The panel may be relieved with a bead, as at B (see Beading), or in the case of a wardrobe, may be chamfered as at C and D.   The panelling on the back of a wardrobe door may be arranged in a simple rebate, the framing being screwed to the door, in the manner shown at E.

30. FACING

Where expensive woods are being used, it is permissible to face up, *i.e.*, glue a thin piece of the expensive wood ($\frac{1}{4}$ in. or $\frac{3}{16}$ in. thick) to a cheaper wood.

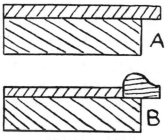

Fig. 131.

A (Fig. 131) shows a thin piece of, say, mahogany or walnut glued to a thicker piece of pine or good red deal or baywood.   B shows a similar combination with the addition of a moulding, which may be of any desired section.   All that is necessary is that the pieces shall be planed accurately on their abutting sides (for this purpose use No. 06, 07 or 08). The abutting sides are then glued and the pieces rubbed until they "suck".   They must then be left for 24 hours.   If there is any tendency for the thin piece to rise, two or three Record G Cramps should be placed along the length; or they may be weighted down and left under the weights. Frames may be constructed in any of the orthodox manners, and the facings may be glued on with the frames complete.

31. LIPPING

A considerable economy of material may be effected in shelving for bookcases and the like by glueing up a strip of the hardwood as used on the carcase to a width of less expensive ·material. This is called "lipping".

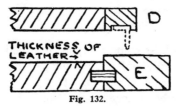

Fig. 132.

C (Fig. 132) shows a plain lipping, and D shows the lip having a shallow, ploughed groove underneath where a narrow length of scalloped leather or such material may be tacked. This saves a great deal of dust from accumulating on the tops of the books which stand on the shelf below. When lipping a writing table top, the lipping should be cross tongued and should stand higher than the centre by the thickness of the leather covering (E, Fig. 132).

The outer edge may be suitably moulded or rounded, and the corners mitred. Cross tongues may be fitted in the mitred corners, as already indicated.

Some saving in expensive material may be effected also by facing up the members of a wardrobe cornice, etc., etc. The "backings", whilst of cheaper wood, must be quite dry and of even grain; otherwise, in time, the frames will pull and twist.

32. DECORATIVE APPLICATIONS OF THE PLANE ON DRAWER FRONTS

The appearance of a plain drawer front may be considerably enhanced by a simple, yet intelligent, use of the plane.

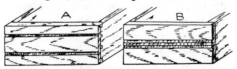

Fig.. 133 A. & B.

A and B (Fig. 133) suggest an infinite variety of treatments that is possible with the use of the centre bead in the Combination Plane 050 or the Multi-Plane 405.

Fig. 133. C.

C shows a refined effect that may be obtained by various rebates, easily and quickly worked with the same planes.   In cutting across the grain, use the spur cutter keenly sharpened, or there is a danger of tearing the fibre afterwards, giving endless work cleaning up.   If the grain is very intractable, run a cutting gauge down first, and set the plane to the cut so made.   The fielding may be done with a finely set Rabbet Plane No. 010 or $010\frac{1}{2}$; and as an alternative to the square edged part of the fielding a fluting (additional fluting cutter $\frac{3}{16}$ in. or $\frac{1}{4}$ in. for multi-plane) may be used.   This will call for care in taking very light cuts with a very sharp cutter, and in running the fielding into the line of the fluting.   It may have to be touched up lightly with a scraper.   Whilst calling for a somewhat high degree of skill, it has a very pleasant appearance, and it has the virtue from the housewife's point of view that it is easy to dust.

One of the richest effects of all is that given by a cock bead, as at D, which can be quite thin—$\frac{1}{8}$ in. and looks very well.   The drawer should

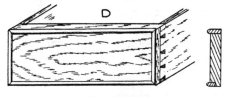

Fig. 133. D.

be completed plain and fitted.   The top should be planed away the full thickness to the depth of the bead.   The sides and bottom should be

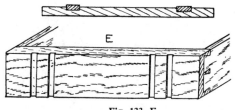

Fig. 133. E.

rebated to the ends of the dovetails for width, and the thickness of the bead for depth. The bead should be mitred at the corners, keeping in mind that for the two top corners the top bead will be mitred part way only. The planing should be true, and the beads are glued in position, cramping securely until dry.

A modern treatment (which may be varied a great deal in detail) is indicated at E where vertical grooves or inlays are run in the drawers

and sometimes the rails also, so that a continuous vertical line of ornament is shown throughout. This is a case where a plane of the type 050 or 405 is indispensable—the cross-grained work being done as shown under "Dado work" (Chapters 13 and 14). The grooving can also be carried out expeditiously with the No. 071 Router.

Drawer fronts may also be decorated by a small moulding planed on the edge, or by having a moulding glued on, as in Jacobean work. They may be relieved by inlaid bandings or lines, or may be veneered. The fenced Router has made the laying of bandings a very easy process. F is

Fig. 133. F. & G.

typical of a quartered veneered drawer front, having cross bandings around the edge, and an inlaid band which may be plain or fancy, or may be a very narrow line of box or other wood. The fitting of the edges of the veneers is simplified when they are shot with a thicker piece of wood, either in the vice or on the shooting board. Before being laid, the abutting surfaces should be toothed, an operation neatly done with the toothed cutter of the scraper (No. 080). See Fig. 256.

G shows a narrow moulding worked on the edge. Such mouldings can be worked up with the hollows and rounds of the Multi-Plane in great variety, or when very small, with scratch tools.

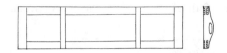

Fig. 134.—Panelled Drawer Front, Muntin Handles.

The drawer front shown in Fig. 134 is made up of a frame and three panels. The muntins are set at right angles to the drawer front, and are shaped to form handles as indicated in the side elevation. The shape of the handles may be varied; and the panels may be left plain as shown or they may be fielded or otherwise decorated. It will be obvious that a panelled-front drawer such as this cannot be satisfactorily dovetailed, the grain of the stiles running the wrong way, so the sides of the drawer are tenoned into the front, and pegged. This method is at its best in large drawers such as in wardrobes, etc. The shrinkage of the front is negligible, owing to the method of construction, and the handles, being tenoned into the frame, get a sound grip on the drawer when pulled out; whilst they can never come adrift, being an integral part of the construction.

33. DRAWER FITTING

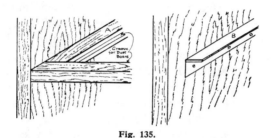

Fig. 135.

Drawer Rails and Runners are traditionally worked as at A, Fig. 135. The rail is tenoned into the carcase end, and the runner is housed in a stopped groove (see Fig. 111) and stub tenoned into the rail. Rail and runner are ploughed on their inner edges as shown for the insertion of the dust board from the back.

A much less laborious method is shown at B, where a length of angle metal (about $\frac{5}{8}$ in. $\times$ $\frac{5}{8}$ in. $\times$ 14 or 16 gauge) is let into a stopped groove in the carcase end and screwed home. The drawer fronts will need to be deeper than the openings by the thickness of the metal. No rails are needed, and no dust boards are fitted. The drawers glide exceptionally easily on the runners, and the time and material saved is considerable, and drawer space is greater. The corner joints of the carcase must be sound, as there is no bracing by rails on the front.

Chapter 11

Rabbets and Rabbeting

The word Rabbet, in use from late Middle English times, would appear to have an Old French derivation, authorities being at some variance with each other, some working from *raboter, rabouter*—to plane, to thrust against; others preferring *rabat, rabbat* from *rabattre*, to beat back or down. The form *Rebate* appears to have crept in later, probably in the 17th Century; though when thus spelt it was pronounced rabbet, the pronunciation "rebate" being a fairly modern interpolation. The antiquity of the name is an indication that a rabbet,—a channel or slot cut along the edge or face of a piece (or surface) of wood and intended to receive the edge or end of another piece or pieces of wood,—has been known for several centuries. Indeed, the word, used in the sense of cutting a rabbet occurs before the end of the 16th Century. In its simplest form a rabbet may be seen in the open channel of a door frame, possibly its earliest appearance; and as such is one of many indications of the manner in which the early craftsman surmounted the difficulties presented by the material in which he worked. No matter how carefully and accurately he made his door fit the frame, natural shrinkage was bound to occur, giving rise to draughts. A rabbet was the natural solution of the problem; and whilst a fillet nailed on would have served the same purpose, the craftsman preferred a planed rabbet as being, with the means at his disposal in those days, not only more workmanlike and lasting, but actually quicker and easier—for it must be remembered that the days of machine saws had not yet arrived, and the cutting of comparatively thin stock at a time when boards were cut with a pit saw, was a laborious process.

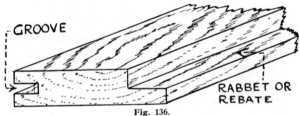

GROOVE

RABBET OR REBATE

Fig. 136.

The rabbet is used in many other ways than around a door. Rabbeted boards are often used to cover a wide surface, as on the walls of outdoor timber structures, etc., where the boards are free to move with atmospheric variations whilst still remaining weather-proof; and certain constructions in cabinet and other work depend upon it, *e.g.*, meeting stiles of doors, joints, sliding lids, etc.

There are various ways of forming a rabbet, depending a good deal upon the type most frequently met with in any particular shop. In cabinet work and in much joinery, quite a lot can be done very conveniently with the Combination Plane, No. 050, and the Multi-Plane, No. 405; and instructions for cutting rabbets with these tools will be found under those headings (Chapters 13 and 14). Modern mouldings depending for their character upon the rabbet may also be stuck with these planes (see Fig. 166); the spur of these tools will be found of great assistance in making the top and bottom rabbets of a flush panel, where the rabbet cuts across, and not with the grain. It would indeed be difficult to find a rabbet that the Multi-Plane could not negotiate successfully.

In most shops, however, the rabbet is so frequently employed that a single purpose plane has advantages; and by and large, it must be admitted that a tool designed for a single purpose is likely to perform its function with some superiority over a tool mainly designed for some other purpose, and having rabbeting as a secondary adjunct.

The Record range of Rabbet Planes is now quite a wide one, and a short examination of the various patterns will prove a profitable study. The larger rabbets, No. 010 and No. 010½, are designed for the larger work which falls to the lot of the joiner, and to that of the carriage builder. No. 010 is a Jack Rabbet, having the proportions of a Jack Plane, *i.e.*, a length of 13 in. and a cutter 2⅛ in. wide; whilst the No. 010½ has the proportions of a smoothing plane, *i.e.*, a length of 9 in. with a 2⅛ in. cutter. Neither of these planes is fitted with a fence or depth stop, and it will be necessary to gauge the limits of the rabbets when using either of these tools; and to use some form of guide when working, as will be explained later. The cutter is made the full width of the sole, so there is no difficulty in working from either side, or even, if necessary, working left handed. Both planes are made of malleable iron which is practically unbreakable.

Fig. 137.—Record Rabbet Plane No. 010.

To make a rabbet using either No. 010 or No. 010½ (the performance is very similar; the shorter plane is lighter and in some fingers a little "handier"—the longer plane is more likely to give a straighter cut on long lengths owing to its extra length)—one of two ways is generally employed. A very good way indeed is to gauge the limits of the rabbet, and then make a plough cut on the inner gauge line, just inside the waste, this plough cut being set for depth with the depth stop of the plough. The remainder of the waste can then be taken away with the Rabbet plane, working just up to, but not past, the gauge line. It will be appreciated that this allows a rabbet to be made either on the face edge, or on the edge opposite the face, as the plough may be set to cut from the face whilst the rabbet plane takes away the rest, whichever way the rabbet lies. It will also be noted that there is practically no limit to the depth to which the rabbet may be cut; and the width of the cutter, $2\frac{1}{8}$ in., is wide enough for all practical cases likely to come within the scope. The plane handles like a smooth or a jack, so there is nothing new to be learned in the way of handling; and the vertical and lateral adjustments are similar to those of the bench planes, so there is no need to wonder why these two planes are so popular with the skilled tradesman.

In the second way of using the smooth and the jack rabbet, No. $010\frac{1}{2}$ and No. 010, it is still preferable to gauge on both side and edge of the work, and then, on the side of the work, a spline is fastened temporarily to act as both fence and guide. This spline is usually nailed on, leaving the nails projecting so as to ensure their easy removal when the spline has accomplished its purpose; or, when as in work which has to be polished in finish, and where nail holes would be an unpardonable blemish, the spline may be temporarily secured to the work by means of Record G cramps. The nature of the work will suggest the size of cramp required—usually 4 or 6 in. will be used. Some little thought may have to be used in positioning the cramps so that they do not foul either the tool or the fingers, but a little experience goes a long way in these matters, and learning by making a few mistakes is usually lasting learning. The spline having been attached, it will be apparent at once how the rabbet is to be cut; and whilst it is easier as in Fig. 138, if the

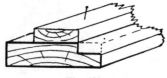

Fig. 138.

grain proves *very* contrary, it will not be found very difficult to turn the work about and work the other way. Often it will be found advantageous to work as with a plough, *i.e.*, making short strokes at the end farther away, gradually working backwards and deeper, but with a sweet grained

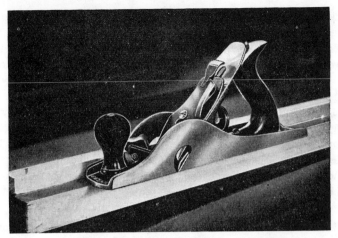

Fig. 139.—Method of cutting a rabbet with No. 010 Rabbet Plane.

wood as used in normal joinery the plane may take a long cut such as is done with an ordinary jack plane.

Sometimes, as is done to fit a heavy back to a wardrobe or cupboard, an obtuse angled rabbet is called for. It is easiest to work this square first and then work to the angle—having of course gauged the limits before the rabbet is started. An acute angled rabbet, used occasionally but not so frequently, should first be cut square, and then the undercut made with a Side Rabbet, Record No. 2506.

Record No. 010 and No. 010½ are sometimes erroneously referred to as "Badger" planes. A Badger was a wood rabbet, about the size of a jack plane, evolved to do the fielding of door panels. Its blade projected as far as the edge on one side only, and it was sometimes provided with some sort of fence. But the essential difference was that it had a skew blade, which was very advantageous in the top and bottom fielding which were of course cross grained cuts.

Whilst it is generally preferable to gauge a rabbet and work to a gauge line, it is very convenient to have a rabbet plane that is fitted with a fence and a depth stop. The Record Rabbet and Fillister No. 078 is so fitted, and for many years has been a very popular tool both with the

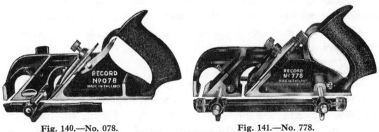

Fig. 140.—No. 078.　　　　　Fig. 141.—No. 778.
Record Rabbet and Fillister Planes

113

H

craftsman and the amateur. It is a simple tool, and has done, and will do, its work very well. There is now available a very much improved pattern of Rabbet and Fillister in Record No. 778, and it will be interesting to examine the two a moment or so to see where the difference lies. Both planes have the same capacity—they will both cut a rabbet up to 1½ in. wide; this of course is less than the larger rabbets we have been discussing; but these two planes are not designed for the heavier work, being more suitable to the cabinet maker than the carpenter and joiner, or shall we say more suitable to the smaller work than the larger. Both planes are 8½ in. long. Both are fitted with fence and depth stop, the former controlling the width of the rabbet, the latter the depth of it. And both are fitted with a spur, which can be used on cross grain, so that one may make a rabbet across the grain, as for a flush panel.

But whilst the thickness of the shaving is controlled in the case of the 078 with a lever, it is controlled in a much more positive way in the 778 by means of a screw. In the case of 078, to increase the cut the lever is pushed upwards; to decrease the cut the lever is depressed. The lever happens to be close to where the thumb lies when the plane is in use. There is a tendency to rest the thumb on the flat of the lever, and as one works, an unconscious, slight, but continuous, pressure is put on the lever, resulting in the plane making thinner and thinner cuts, and then, none at all. The answer of course is to put the thumb *under* the lever when working. With No. 778 the screw adjustment is very positive, and once set it will remain so until a deliberate change is made.

From Fig. 140 and Fig. 141 it will be seen that whilst No. 078 has only one arm rod for the fence, No. 778 has two arms, these passing right through the body. This results in a much more accurate setting, and allows a little more lateral adjustment. Both planes, of course, may be used to start a fillister—this being cut on the opposite side from the face, in the case of 078 the arm rod may be screwed in from either side; with No. 778 the rods are pushed right through. When the planes are used in this manner, it will be noticed that the arm rods touch the wood fairly soon after the rabbet (or fillister) is started. The fence must then be removed and the rabbet finished to the gauge line. No. 778 cuts this initial cut deeper than 078 does. (To clarify the confusion of the uninitiated arising from "rabbet" and "fillister"—a fillister may be considered as the rabbet which holds the glass and the putty; and it is thus a rabbet which is cut on the side *opposite* the face, but it must be cut *parallel* with the face.)

In Record No. 078, when assembling the arm rod and fence, the arm rod will normally be screwed into the left hand side of the body, and it will be noticed that a small hole has been drilled in the arm rod so that a tommy (a nail will do) may be used to screw the rod up tightly. Thumb screws for adjusting the fence and depth stop should be finger tight. The use of pliers, etc. on these screws is very apt to damage the thread, which will eventually cause slipping.

The arm rods of No. 778 pass right through the body and are secured by set screws. In normal use they will project from the left hand side of the tool only, as if they are made to project on the right hand side the projecting ends will be in the way. Only when the fence is required on the right hand side will they project through on that side.

The depth stop requires no explanation, being simply set to the depth required. There is a point to watch, however, in this simple setting. The distance should be measured from the sole of the depth stop to the edge of the cutter—and not to the sole of the plane if very accurate work is attempted; hence it is wise to try a cut first before finally setting the depth stop. Similarly, in setting the fence, measure from the face of the fence to the edge of the cutter rather than to the side of the plane.

In setting the cutter in the body, the side of the cutter may project very slightly outside the side of the body, or it may be set flush with the side; but it should never be set inside.

When grinding and sharpening the cutter, care must be taken to keep the edge square with the sides, or one side of the rabbet will be deeper than the other; and in adjusting the cutter, the projection of the cutter must be even all the way. Beginners always favour thicker shavings, believing this to be a saver of time; but experienced craftsmen have learned that two thin shavings are better than one thick one. And probably this is even more true in rabbeting than in other types of planing.

Seldom will the spur be required when one is rabbeting *along* the grain. Only when the wood has a very difficult grain will this be required, and it must be noted that there will be left the score mark in the corner when this is done. Should this be objectionable, the last few strokes should be done with the spur in the "off" position. Usually when rabbeting with the grain the spur can be forgotten.

But when rabbeting *across* the grain, as in the end of a shelf where the thickness of the shelf is reduced to form a shoulder, or in the fitting of a flush panel, one cannot do without the spur very well, as it dispenses with a preliminary saw cut—often not too easy to do across a wide board. It is essential that the spur be sharp, as it must make a clean cut vertically in front of the cutter proper. And here let us remember that both spur and its screw are very small, and easy to lose if dropped on the floor, so it is very wise when manipulating the spur to do all the operations *over* the bench. The best way of sharpening the spur is to hold it in a pair of flat nosed pliers, resting the spur on the end of a spline (say,

1 in. × 2 in.) held at a convenient height (usually the height of the elbow when one is standing up) in the vice. A few strokes with a smooth file are taken on the bevelled side, swinging the file to the curve but keeping the bevel quite straight. The slight wire edge on the flat side can then be taken off with one stroke of the file, taking care to make no bevel on this—the face side. Still holding the spur in the pliers, take a few strokes on the oil stone, making no new bevels, but working up to a keen edge. Insert the spur flat side outwards and screw up tightly, checking up that no dirt, etc. is resting on the seating which would cause the spur to project beyond the side of the body.

Some little practice with either No. 078 or No. 778 will soon enable the worker to make a clean rabbet. Having assembled fence and depth stop and adjusted these as required, and fastened the board to the bench, either in the vice or by means of G cramps, or buttons, or otherwise, the action is very similar to that of using a plough.

Both Record No. 078 and No. 778 have two positions for the cutter. For all normal work the cutter is inserted in the rear position. The forward position converts the tool to a bull-nosed rabbet, used when the tool is required to work close up to an obstruction. For both tools adjustment of the cutter when the tool is used bull-nosed, will be by sighting along the sole, as the mechanical adjustments are for the normal position only.

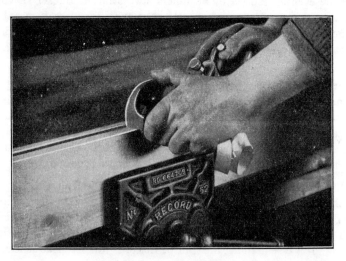

Fig. 142.—Method of cutting a rabbet with a No. 078 Rabbet and Fillister Plane.

Hold the plane level, pressing the fence against the wood. Take each and every stroke evenly and carefully. Start (as in ploughing) at the further end, making at first short strokes, gradually increasing the length and depth, until a stroke can be taken the full length of the work, and continue so until the depth stop rides on the face of the work, preventing any further cutting, and the rabbet is then complete.

A slight variation of this procedure is required when working across the grain. As explained above, the spur is required for this, and the first few strokes will be taken at the end of the cut which is away from the worker, slowly and carefully allowing the spur to cut downwards before anything is taken off with the cutter, and then proceed as above described. These few preliminary spur cuts are important, as upon the skill with which they are made depends the cleanliness of that end of the rabbet. If they are carelessly done, the wood will almost certainly break away at that point. To make assurance doubly sure, some workers will score a line with a sharp knife; but properly used the spur should do this without the knife cut. Don't be discouraged at initial failures; skill can only be acquired with constant practise; but once having attained that skill there remains a very permanent sense of personal satisfaction.

If there is any pitfall for the beginner, it is in the keeping of the fence fair and square to the work: the thing to bear in mind is that what pressure is applied, should be to the fence rather than to the cut. If the cutter is properly sharpened and set, very little downward pressure is required. Another aid towards keeping the plane under control is the extension of the index finger of the right hand forward rather than wrapped around the handle. At first, the beginner can profitably set the cutter back (so that the plane does not cut at all) and practise "working" with the tool until the "feel" of it comes along, later making short and then longer cuts as above described.

It will be noticed that when either Record No. 078 or Record No. 778 is divested of fence and spur, a very efficient square plane appears. This has quite a number of uses in cleaning up certain work; and it can be used in the making of many mouldings, and in the making of oblique walls to a rabbet, etc., much in the same way as the larger rabbets; but its length and width make a much handier tool for a lot of smaller work. Although with care and a very fine cut it *can* be made to trim a shoulder (on the ends of the fibres of the wood), it is not very strongly recommended for this purpose, as the pitch of the cutter is too high. This work is better done with a low pitched shoulder plane as described later.

When the worker has become accustomed to using the rabbet planes, many adaptations will suggest themselves to him. Fig. 143 shows a very strong carcase joint the work on which can be considerably curtailed with the intelligent use of the rabbet plane. The joint should be set out after the ends of the sides have been shot true, square and

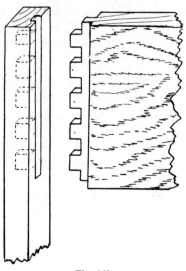

Fig. 143.

accurately to length, and the tenons and mortises should be the width of the mortise chisel. The tenon length can be cut with the rabbet plane, using the spur after the tenon saw cuts have been made. The recesses can be quickly removed with the bow saw. (For the leg, make the mortises first, then plough the groove, (which is a stopped groove) using Record Router No. 071 and the fence, as described on page 184.)

As with all iron planes, a little lubrication of the sole and fence is very desirable from time to time, and a rub—little and often—with a paraffin wax candle is probably the best method.

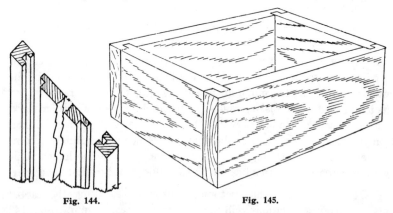

Fig. 144. Fig. 145.

Figs. 144 and 145 show two useful adaptations of rabbeted work. For the cutting of the grooves see Chapters 12, 13, 14—they are quite speedily cut across the grain as dado cuts, using two spurs with either the Combination Plane (No. 050) or the Multi-Plane (No. 405). For the box construction, it is as well if a trifle extra is left for final cleaning up on the outside of the dado cut—the end of the box is thus left at its full thickness. In the cabinet end (Fig. 144), if the grooves only occupy part of the length of the leg, they are best cut with the Router (071), using the fence, as in Fig. 215. Very handy boxes can be made as above for the safe storage of such tools as the Multi-Plane, the Plough, the Router, etc. If a slide lid is preferred, the two sides and one end may be grooved before gluing up, and the other end made narrower to suit. The bottoms may be grooved in, or may be glued, or simply screwed or nailed on. This construction is often used for veneered boxes, but it is not free from objections for this purpose, the joints and the end grain being weak spots for veneering upon. If it is used as a base for veneer, the end grain should be well treated first with a mixture of thin hot glue and litharge. This will prevent the end grain showing through the veneer, but there still remains the possibility of the line of the joint showing through at some future time, owing to unequal contraction.

Another operation which calls for the use of the Rabbet Plane is the shooting of mitred rebates as in Fig. 146. This corner joint is used on

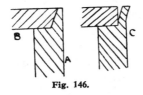

Fig. 146.

small cabinet and other work, but has a special application in the fitting of rebated frames to the backs of carcases (*e.g.*, a wardrobe). When a fairly heavy back frame has to be fitted into a rebate, if it is fitted as at C, it will frequently result in the narrow slip which is left curling outwards as shown at C. To prevent this the rebate should be mitred as at A, and the framing shot to a corresponding mitre as shown at B. The Rebate Plane is used with the fence to cut the square part, and then canted without the fence for the mitre part. The mitred part of B offers no difficulty, being simply shot with the Jack Plane.

SHOULDER PLANES

The method employed in Fig. 143, and the use of a sharp spur should ensure dead accuracy of fit of the shoulders to the post, as they can be worked parallel to the edge, which has been previously shot with a jointer. There are cases in which this method cannot be employed, as for instance in the sloping shoulders of a gun stock stile, and other shoulders, particularly when these are wide, as in the lock rail of a door, when these come from the saw. However skilled the workman may be, there are times when some adjustment must be made. It is for such work as this, and for the very close fitting of shoulders to the stiles, that the Record Shoulder Planes have been designed (Nos. 041, 042, 073).

Fig. 147.—Record Shoulder Rabbet Plane.

No. 041 is a short and narrow tool, 5 in. long, ⅝ in. wide; No. 042 is slightly larger, 8 in. long and ¾ in. wide, and these two are both of great service on smaller shoulder work and in general accurate fitting. They are used by many as small rabbet planes. Such a small plane as this will be found very useful in many such operations as the cleaning up of the edges of shaped small brackets, *e.g.*, the two brackets of a towel roller. Often the terminal members of the curves are awkward to clean up, but if the two pieces are placed together in the vice, and the square and curved portions planed crosswise with No. 041 or 042, the process is much simplified; the brackets will be exactly similar in shape and the finish of the smaller parts that the spokeshave cannot reach quite clean. Along mouldings they are equally useful, and for small work generally they will be found a great asset.

Shoulder work proper (Figs. 148, 149) calls for extreme accuracy of cut on short grain, and as the plane must "run through", leaving a

Fig. 148.—Method of shooting a shoulder.

dead true surface, it needs a very sharp iron, and a mouth which can be adjusted to varying conditions of timber, grain, etc. A break of grain at the end of the cut would be fatal, so, in addition to the adjustable mouth, the blade must be set at as low an angle as possible, and the adjustment of the cutter must be of micrometer fineness. And all these exacting conditions must be combined with the utmost rigidity in the plane itself, so that the tool may work with smoothness and regularity throughout. Finally, the tool must have a correct "balance" and a comfortable "feel".

However fastidious the craftsman, however meticulous he may be in his work, he will find that the shoulder plane, No. 073, will answer to his every demand. No iron will take a sharper edge, and retain it longer

Fig.149.—Method of trimming a secret dovetail with Record No. 073.

than will the Tungsten Steel of the Record Cutters fitted to these planes. The adjustment of the mouth, from O (completely closed) to $\frac{3}{16}$ in., securely locked in any intermediate position is not only ingenious, but it is an engineer's job, with all the accuracy that that implies. The adjustment of the cutter is quick and positive, yet of extreme fineness; and the ease of handling may be judged from the two examples in the accompanying illustrations.

Adjustment of the Blade is by means of the milled nut at the upper end. When removing the blade, slacken the tightening screw under the lever. This allows the lever to be removed. Give the blade a slight cant and then it can be withdrawn. Reverse the operation for replacing the blade, watching the edge that it is not dulled by a sharp contact with the front of the escapement. Note that the bevel side goes upwards, and see that the slot at the top of the blade engages with the collar of the feed screw, and that the blade "beds down" nicely. *When* *making any adjustment of the blade, up or down, with the feed screw, slightly slacken the tightening screw of the lever, and tighten this when adjustment is complete.*

To adjust the Mouth (073 only) first slacken locking-screw which will be found on the top of the plane, over the nose. (This screw has a ½ in. head and generous slot. It is sunk below the level of the plane, and has a particularly strong grip.) The locking-screw being slack, to open the mouth, turn the screw on the front of the plane, to the right; to close the mouth, turn the same screw to the left, pushing up the whole of the slide bottom towards the cutter.

Having obtained the width of mouth required, tighten locking-screw on the top of the plane.

The argument crops up in workshops as a hardy annual as to whether shoulders should be shot or not, but space forbids that the constantly recurring arguments should be repeated here. Suffice it to say that some of the best craftsmen of recent years, whose work is already considered typical of the best examples of modern work, make a regular practice of shooting their shoulders. It is suggested to those who do not do so, that they should compare the final appearance of work—in which the shoulders have been shot with that left from the saw—with or without deep knife cuts. Correctly shot shoulders contribute something to that feeling of joy that a true craftsman experiences in a job well done.

BULL-NOSE PLANES

The value of these planes is immediately apparent both to the cabinet-maker and to the carpenter and joiner; in fact, to both, they are indispensable, in fine fitting and in the construction of diminished (gunstock) stile work, etc., and in the trimming of such mouldings as ovolos, when slight adjustment must be made, and so on. No. 076, whilst possessing the advantage of a receding nose, is not adjustable by a screw for depth of cutter. The blade is removed by slackening the tightening screw under the lever. A slight cant sideways allows the blade to be easily withdrawn for sharpening, etc. As for all low pitched

Fig. 150.—Record Bull-nose Rabbet Plane, No. 076.

planes, the blade is used with the bevelled side upwards. The blade is quite rigidly held when set by tightening screw under the lever, which latter provides a convenient hold, fitting nicely to the hollow of the hand.

No. 077A has the great advantage that the blade is adjustable by means of the milled nut at the upper end of the cutter. When removing the blade for sharpening, etc., slacken the tightening screw under the lever, and remove the lever. A slight cant of the cutter will enable you to withdraw the cutter.

When replacing, return the cutter, bevelled side up, in the same way, *i.e.*, by canting the projections through the aperture (alternatively you may "feed" the cutter from the bottom). See that the slot in the cutter engages with the washer on the feed nut, and that the cutter beds down nicely. Replace the lever. Feed the cutter by means of the milled nut in the rear, either back or forward, as required, and tighten all by means of the tightening screw under the lever. *Always slacken the tightening screw before altering the adjustment, and tighten it when adjustment is complete.* This plane is capable of very fine and accurate work.

Fig. 151.—Record Improved Bull-nose Rabbet Plane No. 077A.

No. 077A has the very desirable feature of an adjustable mouth, in addition to the cutter adjustment. It can further be used, when the front is completely removed, as a chisel plane.

To adjust the width of the Mouth

The front of the plane is removable by undoing the centre screw in front. When this is removed you will find two "shims" or spacing pieces, one $\frac{1}{64}$ in. thick and the other $\frac{1}{32}$ in. thick. It will be seen that these give four distinct effective widths of mouth.

(a) When front or nose is screwed down without any spacing pieces, a very close mouth is formed. This will give, with a fine set iron, a shaving less than 1/1000 in. thick.

(b) A slightly wider mouth is obtained by inserting the $\frac{1}{64}$ in. spacing piece alone.

(c) A still wider mouth is obtained by inserting the $\frac{1}{32}$ in. spacing piece alone.

(d) The widest mouth is obtained when both the $\frac{1}{64}$ in. and the $\frac{1}{32}$ in. spacing pieces are inserted.

No. 075 is a cheap bull-nose, 4 in. long and an inch wide. Its mouth is adjustable by means of the screw at the top; but there is no fine screw adjustment of the cutter. Properly sharpened and set it is capable of quite good work in spite of its low price, but somewhat tedious to set.

Fig. 152.—Record Bull-nose Rabbet Plane No. 075.

As the blade is not low set as in the other bull-nose planes, the bevel side of the blade is fitted downwards in this case.

Fig. 153.—Record "3-in-1" Plane.

No. 311 Bull-Nose, Shoulder Rabbet Plane is a three-in-one plane that will appeal to many amateurs, as it may be used as a shoulder plane, a bull-nose plane, and a chisel plane by an ingenious interchange of the fore end, effected by a single screw, which is apparent from Fig. 153. The cutter is adjustable for depth of cut in the same way as 077A (page 123), and the plane is quite efficient in working in any of its forms. No shims are provided for varying the width of the mouth.

It cannot be too strongly emphasised that care in sharpening the cutters of all rabbet, bull-nose and shoulder planes amply repays the worker. The edge must be kept true and square, as it is when it leaves the factory. It will be appreciated that a hollow stone will affect this squareness and truth; when extra fine work is attempted, grindstone and oilstone must be quite true. When adjusting the blade, care must be taken that the cutter does not lie "foul", *i.e.*, it must lie evenly to the sides of the plane. With these simple (and obvious) precautions, there will be no difficulty in doing the finest and most exacting work with any of the planes in this section.

SIDE RABBETS

It so happens sometimes that the wall of a rabbet, or a groove, requires some adjustment and it is not always possible to do this with a rabbet plane. For instance, a panel may be slightly too thick to enter the groove of a frame. If the panel is of wood and unpolished, it may of course be thinned down; if it is polished or veneered this may not be advisable or possible; if it is a glass or mirror, it is obviously quite

Fig. 154.—Record Side Rabbet Plane No. 2506.

impossible—one must widen the groove. For this purpose No. 2506 Side Rabbet will be used. It has two cutters so that it may be used either left or right hand, or may accommodate itself as in a groove to the

Fig. 155.—Easing a groove with Side Rabbet Plane.

lie of the grain; and should the work demand working right up into a corner, this may be done by removing the front, which is held by a single screw.

The plane will also be found of great value in the adjustment of mouldings, as for instance where there is a slight discrepancy at a mitre, for trimming a damaged moulding, etc. The illustration (Fig. 156) shows how the side rabbet may be used in easing the rabbet of a door frame without the necessity of removing the door.

No. 2506S Side Rabbet is the same as the above plane, with a further refinement added in the form of a depth stop, adjustable and reversible, which is fitted to the base.

Regarding the working of these planes, little explanation is called for. The plane falls naturally to the worker's hand, and with very little practice indeed, it is quite easy to take off a continuous shaving from the wall of a groove or to make a slight local adjustment, as required. The

Fig. 156.—Easing a Rabbet with the door *in situ.*

blades should be kept quite sharp, and naturally the set should be fine and not coarse. Work can be accurately done in a few moments with a side rabbet that would be a puzzle with any other tool—and then be indifferently done after expending a long time on it. No kit can be considered complete without a side rabbet.

Ploughs and Ploughing

The modern joiner and cabinet-maker accept the plough as an essential tool in the kit, for without a tool that will make a groove of some sort all work would be very limited; yet there was a time when woodworkers had no such tool. Constructions prior to the 15th century are without grooves. How is it then that the plough has become so necessary a tool since that time?

Probably in no better way is this question answered than in the evolution of the chest—that simple box-like structure from which practically all our modern furniture can trace its ancestry. Chests may be traced back to the 13th century, many of the earlier ones being laboriously "dug out" from a solid baulk of timber, and strongly bound (for conditions were rugged, rough, and precarious in those days) with iron bands. A natural progression from this was a chest nailed up from boards; and a few such chests are still preserved in some of our churches and museums. If an examination of these is made, it will be found that, as a rule, the front and back and the bottom are single boards with the grain running horizontally; the two ends are single boards with the grain running vertically; and it will be found in most cases that the front and back boards are split. This of course is natural, and to be expected, for wood naturally shrinks across the grain, but very little along the grain, and as the boards of the front are nailed across the vertical long grain of the ends, when shrinkage occurs, something has to give way. Hence the carpenter sought a way of preventing this damage.

The practical outcome was the invention of a panelled construction, a construction which is standard practise to this day. If the wood could be free to shrink (and for that matter to expand also—as in a moist atmosphere) the problem was solved; and a frame, grooved for a panel offered the solution. So in the 16th century we find chests the back and front of which are panelled, whilst the ends remained solid. Both frames and panels were often elaborately carved, as indeed had been many of the "planked" chests, and much hard thinking had to be done to solve the difficulties of mitring the mouldings of the frames; but that is another story, not relevant to the present one, however interesting its study may be. Reverting to the main theme, the solution having been found, how was the groove to be made? Perhaps the first grooves were made with a scratch tool, for the ancestry of this tool goes far back— it was used for mouldings long before moulding planes were common.

Yet a scratch tool has its limitations, and it is never a happy tool to use in any case, and so a plough plane made its appearance. It is not easy to say just when it came, or what the early ploughs were like, as none are now in existence, but at all events they were known well enough in 1678 for their name to appear in current literature. In principle they were probably not unlike the wood wedged ploughs,* later improved by screws and nuts of hardwood, that still linger amongst us; drastic improvement did not come until the introduction of iron ploughs much later.

The establishment of such a tool soon led to its extended use in other directions than panelling; and it is common practice to start a wide rabbet with a plough groove, thus reducing the effort required and tending to more accurate results.

The iron ploughs have many advantages over the wooden ones. The material of which they are made does not warp and shrink like wood does; neither is the wear on any part comparable with that of wood. No periodical truing up, with its consequent reduction of material is necessary. The adjustments are much more rapid, and at the same time more accurate. The handling is far more easily mastered, for they are less cumbersome.

It is regularly found that a boy who cannot handle a cumbersome wood plough at all can make accurate grooves with a suitably-chosen iron plough such as the Record No. 044 or 050, or 043. They pack into

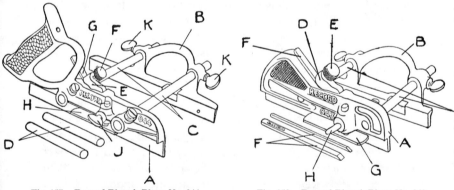

Fig. 157.—Record Plough Plane No. 044.   Fig. 158.—Record Plough Plane No. 043.

A. Main Stock	A. Main Stock
B. Fence with Thumb Screws	B. Fence with Thumb Screws
C. Fence Arms, long-pair	C Fence Arms-pair
D. Fence Arms, short-pair	D. Lever Cap
E. Lever Cap	E. Lever Cap Knurled Screw
F. Lever Cap Knurled Screw	F. Cutters—set of 3
G. Cutters—set of 8	G. Depth Gauge
H. Depth Gauge	H. Depth Gauge Locking Screw
J. Depth Gauge Locking Screw	
K. Fence Thumb Screws	

---

* Plough of 16th century lies on bench, Fig. 8.

less space and so are easier to carry about and store. The Tungsten steel cutters of the Record Ploughs are much more efficient than those of the wood ploughs. And with all these very real advantages, the price of the iron plough will be found more economical than that of a wooden plough.

In order to understand the function of a plough plane we must first consider what is required from it. We expect a plough plane:—

(a) to plough a groove which shall be constant in width, though this width may not be identical for all projects.

(b) to plough that groove at a constant and predetermined distance from the face side; and this distance must be variable and under the control of the worker.

(c) to plough the groove so that its depth shall be constant, but as in (b) that depth shall be variable and yet under control.

(a) The width of the groove is determined by the width of the cutter; and that cutter is held in the mainstock, in such a way that it is rigid, but the thickness of the shaving is controllable. In both Record No. 043 and Record No. 044 ploughs, the cutter is held in the mainstock by means of a lever cap; and whilst in No. 043 the thickness of the shaving is regulated manually by setting the cutter to project more or less below the runner of the mainstock, in No. 044 a screw adjustment is provided which gives quick, easy and critical setting. No. 044 has a further refinement in that a side screw is provided for the temporary holding of the cutter whilst the adjustment is correctly made.

(b) The distance of the groove from the face side is determined by the setting of the fence, and the mainstock is provided with two arm-rods on which the fence may slide, easily, parallel and square. The arm-rods are themselves adjustable, in that they pass through holes carefully drilled in the mainstock, and are secured thereto by set screws. It will usually be found that a position for the arm-rods approximately half-way through the mainstock will be handiest. For those odd occasions when the groove is to be further away the arm-rods can be moved suitably, but when approximately half-way through the tool is easier to handle and usually the balance will be found better. The fence can now be passed towards or away from the mainstock, and can be secured by means of the two thumb screws in any predetermined position. In measuring for this, the cutter must be in working position, and the distance is measured between the edge of the cutter and the fence, (*not* the mainstock and the fence).

It will be noticed that the fence has two drilled holes. These are provided for the worker who prefers a deeper fence; a fillet of hard wood can be screwed to the fence with No. 8 round head screws. The size of the fillet will be as the worker wishes; but it must be planed parallel and square and a recess will have to be taken out of it (continuing the recess on the plane) in order to allow the egress of shavings.

The deeper fence, taking a bigger bearing on the face side of the work, tends to make the operation easier, but it seriously limits the amount of work which can be done in the vice (the vice jaw is in the way of the deeper fence) and so usually it will be found better to plough with the narrow fence without any extension.

It cannot be too strongly emphasised that there is no need whatever to use any tool to screw up the thumb screws of any of these adjustments. Fence, depth stop and lever cap as well as side cutter screw will all do their work when secured finger tight, and any further forcing of them will tend strongly to damage the thread either of the screw or the female portion in the castings.

To ease the working of the plough, a wax candle may be drawn from time to time along the fence and the runner. This will provide a lubrication superior to that provided by oil.

(c) The depth of the cut is controlled by the depth stop. In setting, measure from the depth stop to the cutting edge of the cutter; and here again finger tight with the securing screw will be enough.

Having thus considered the essential features of the plough, we may now see in what respects Record No. 043 plough differs from Record No. 044 plough. No. 043 is a smaller plough, and is provided with three cutters only, viz. $\frac{1}{8}$ in., $\frac{3}{16}$ in. and $\frac{1}{4}$ in. Thus, with a simple, single cut, only grooves of those sizes may be cut; but it will be noticed that these sizes are the ones most usually required by the skilled amateur. It does not follow that a wider groove cannot be cut, for if the limits of the groove be first marked on the wood (*e.g.* $\frac{3}{8}$ in.) the plough may be set using a $\frac{1}{4}$ in. cutter to cut that part of the groove nearer to the face side; and then the fence released and re-set to cut the part away from the face side and thus a $\frac{3}{8}$ in. groove will have been made using only a $\frac{1}{4}$ in. cutter. But it takes time, two cuts had to be made where a $\frac{3}{8}$ in. cutter would have taken only one cut.

Thus then, the joiner or the cabinet maker, who has no time for double cuts when single ones will suffice, requires a plough with enough cutters to do anything in the way of ploughing that ever arises, and Record No. 044 with its eight cutters ($\frac{1}{8}$ in. to $\frac{9}{16}$ in. by $\frac{1}{16}$ in.) is the tool such craftsmen prefer. Indeed this plough is nowadays regarded as the standard plough of the craft. Where millimetre grooves are required (as for some types of plywood) 4, 6, 9 and 12 mm. cutters are available as extras.

Where it is desired to make a groove to fit plywood or other wood or hardboard which was of standard size and was then, say, veneered on one or both sides, the best method of enlarging the groove is to use the Record Side Rabbet No. 2506 to take a shaving from one or both walls of the groove as desired. (See Chapter 11, page 125.)

Record No. 043, thus, may be considered as a very suitable tool for the skilled amateur who wishes to plough accurately the smaller grooves $\frac{1}{8}$ in., $\frac{3}{16}$ in., and $\frac{1}{4}$ in. and occasionally a groove somewhat wider. On account of its smaller size it is also eminently suitable for beginners in schools, and it has the virtue that when its manipulation has been mastered, there is nothing to unlearn when passing onto the larger modern ploughs 044, 050 or 405, the handling of which is practically the same as the smaller one. For the craftsman who demands a plough as good as he can get it with a range of cutters that will see him through any work that may crop up right throughout his lifetime, there is the Record No. 044 which will never let him down.

Fig. 159.—Record Plough Plane No. 043.

Fig. 160.—Ploughing a groove with Record Plough Plane No. 043.

From the moment of its introduction, Record Plough Plane No. 044 has been immensely popular with all sections of woodworkers in all parts of the world; and by reason of its handiness, accuracy, and ease of operation it has been almost universally adopted in woodworking classes and Technical Colleges, and the improvements which were incorporated some years ago have thoroughly justified their existence. Its range of eight cutters as we have seen, enables it to plough grooves from $\frac{1}{8}$ in. to $\frac{9}{16}$ in.; with wider grooves making two cuts; it will plough $\frac{5}{8}$ in. deep at any distance from the edge up to 5 in.; and narrow rabbets can be made by moving the fence up to the cutter. Wider rabbets are best made by first ploughing a groove, and then removing the rest with a rabbet plane. The 044 is of very solid construction, and weighs $2\frac{3}{4}$ lbs. It packs into quite a small space.

Fig. 161.—Record Plough Plane No. 044.

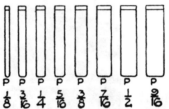

Fig. 162.—Standard Cutters for Record No. 044 Plough Plane.
(4, 6, 9 and 12 m/m Cutters are also available as extras)

Fig. 163.—Record Plough Plane 044 in use.

Two pairs of arms are provided, and whilst some ploughing may be done with the shorter arms, these are primarily packing arms, to enable the plane to be packed into a smaller space for boxing, transit and storage. So normally the longer arms will be most used. In the extremely rare event of the standard arms not being long enough, longer ones may easily be fitted, and in case of difficulty they may be specially ordered. This is, however, an extremely unlikely request, as the pair of longer arms are likely to meet all the demands of the worker.

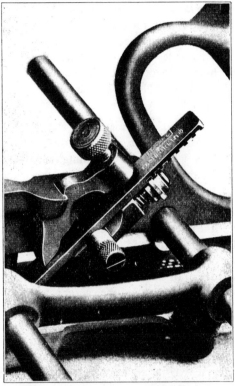

Fig. 164.—Improved Housing of Lever cap; screw adjustment to cutter; and knurled locking screw of Record Plough Plane No. 044.

Each of the two ploughs we have been considering will make accurate and clean grooves, and the handling of them is simple and may be seen from the illustrations. The handles are both designed for comfortable working. The main thing is to keep the fence well up to the face of the wood, in close contact everywhere so that the groove is the same distance all the time from the face side; and to keep the plane upright so that the groove is parallel to the face side. What pressure there is should be applied with the left hand to keep the fence up to its work. Very little pressure is required from the right hand beyond the necessity to propel the plane—if the cutter is properly sharpened and set, hardly any downward pressure is required. Grooves should be started at the end of the wood that is farthest away, gradually deepened backwards as the work proceeds (see Fig. 96). The work is much easier if the fence and the runner are occasionally lubricated during the ploughing—either with a spot of oil or with a wax candle. The wax candle, used little and often, is strongly recommended.

The worker should not find much difficulty in sharpening the cutters, this being in keeping with the sharpening of other plane cutters, but it should be noted that in the case of a plough plane, the angle of 35° is desirable; and it is better to keep to the one bevel rather than make two bevels. The flat side should be kept flat—no bevel on this side. Beginners who have not enough confidence in sharpening may use Record Edge Tool Honer No. 161 with advantage—it is described earlier under "Honing".

In ploughing rails and stiles for doors, etc., the mortises and the cheeks of the tenons should be cut first, the ploughing next. The shoulder cuts are best left until the ploughing is completed, this leaving a better bearing for the fence all the way than when the shoulder cuts have taken away the bearing at the two ends.

It is frequently found that constant pressure of the vice has hollowed out the facing of the back jaw (the one on the bench) particularly when this is of deal or other soft wood. This may result in the stile or rail being ploughed being bent to a slight curve when set in the vice for ploughing the edge. In such a case the worker finds difficulty in ploughing, and, not being aware of the cause, is apt to lay the blame on the plough. The straight fence of course cannot accommodate itself to the curvature the wood assumes, and it would not be desirable that it should do so. A temporary remedy is to pack up from the back with a piece of wood which will keep the stile being ploughed straight; but the real and lasting remedy is to cut away the worn and bruised jaw facing and replace it with another piece of hardwood. Indeed, when bench tops are made of softwood, as many are from the need to economise, it is a good practice to face up the whole of the front edge with a 2 in. piece of beech or similar hardwood. It is mentioned here because it is a common trouble with a much used bench, and often enough it has escaped observation.

Nowadays the use of the narrow fence is almost universal; and only those workers who have been used to an old fashioned plough will feel the need to deepen the fence, but as we have already noticed, should this be required it is an easy adaptation well within the capacity of anyone who is likely to be using a plough.

Whilst naturally the plough will most often be called upon to make the grooves for panelling, this does not by any means represent the full measure of the work the plough may be called upon to do. As will be seen from Figs. 165 and 166 the plough may be used also for work both constructional and decorative—the decorative detail being modern in spirit, and sound in taste, as springing directly from the use of the tool used in a natural manner. The sketches shown here are suggestions only, much being left to the imagination and ingenuity as well as the experience of the craftsman, who should bear in mind that in the majority of this work it will be the disposition of the proportions of the members of his decoration, and the proportion of this decoration to the whole that will be the deciding factor in the success or otherwise of his efforts. An extra rabbet on the fielding of a panel may make or mar the whole appearance by being a sixteenth of an inch too big or too little. This will not always be apparent from a drawing, which has a two dimension limitation; the flat drawing cannot show the subtleties of the light and shade of the finished work in the solid. It is best to experiment a bit with spare pieces. And in any case, unless the workmanship is of the first class, any attempt at this kind of decoration will certainly be a dead failure.

The cross sections illustrated in Fig. 165 are examples of what may be done with Record Plough Plane No. 043. It will be noticed that if the

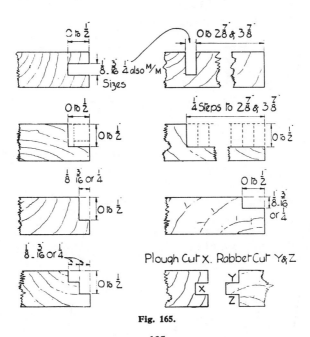

Fig. 165.

135

occasion arises, the fence may be used left- as well as right-handed, and with a little care a groove may be planed on the end of a board as well as along the grain of it; but neither of these ploughs is recommended for cutting housings or dados (*i.e.*, grooves across the board as for receiving a shelf—sometimes also called a raggle) as they are not fitted, as are Record Planes No. 050 and No. 405, with spurs for this purpose.

The cross sections shown in Figs. 166A and 166B illustrate some examples of work which may be done with Record Plough Plane No. 044 which has, as we have seen, a greater capacity. And any cut which may be made with Record No. 043 can also be cut with Record No. 044.

In concluding this chapter, we would draw attention to subsequent chapters which describe Record Combination Plane No. 050 and Record Multi-Plane No. 405, both of which, in addition to their more extended repertoire, are very efficient plough planes.

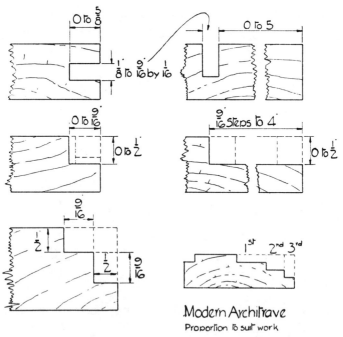

Modern Architrave
Proportion to suit work

Fig. 166A.

136

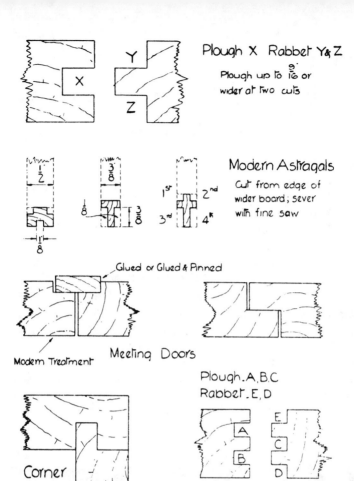

Plough X Rabbet Y & Z

Plough up to $\frac{9}{16}$ or wider at two cuts

Modern Astragals

Cut from edge of wider board; sever with fine saw

Glued or Glued & Pinned

Modern Treatment   Meeting Doors

Plough. A, B, C
Rabbet. E, D

Corner

Fig. 166B.

Chapter 13

The Combination Plane, No. 050

Range of Operations:—
Ploughing.
Rabbet and Fillister.
Dado (Housing).
Edge Beading.
Centre Beading.
Matching (Tongues and Grooves, with or without beads).

All the above operations are common to Carpenters, Joiners and Cabinet-makers, and of frequent occurrence both in hardwoods and softwoods. At first sight, it would appear that a claim to do all of them well with a single tool would be hard to sustain; to do them with a single tool with precision and good finish almost impossible, for in a general way it is admitted that a single purpose tool is the best. A closer acquaintance with the Combination Plane, and a consideration of its design will, however, soon dispel any doubts; and a practical demonstration will show that the operations, at first sight dissimilar, are actually very closely related.

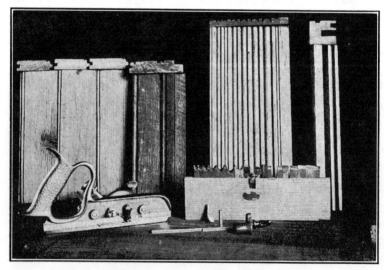

Fig. 167.—Combination Plane (No. 050) and some of its work.

A comparison with the plough planes will show that whilst the ploughs have a mainstock and a sliding fence, the Combination Plane has both these and also a Sliding Section (Fig. 171B), the sole of which bears on the wood in the same plane as the mainstock. This allows the cutter to rest in parallel machined grooves, providing with the cutter bolt and nut a rigid seating for the cutter; and although it does not in any way interfere with the function of the plane as a plough, it does allow the use of a bead-shaped cutter, seven sizes of which are provided, ranging from $\frac{1}{8}$ in. to $\frac{1}{2}$ in. With any of these cutters, used in the same manner as a plough, therefore, a centre bead may be stuck. As the Sliding Section is provided with a Beading Stop (Fig. 171E), so arranged that it cuts out one quirk of the bead, any of the Beading Cutters may be used for edge beading. This arrangement provides, therefore, the equivalent of seven Centre Bead Planes, and seven ordinary Bead Planes, which with the Plough represents so far fifteen planes.

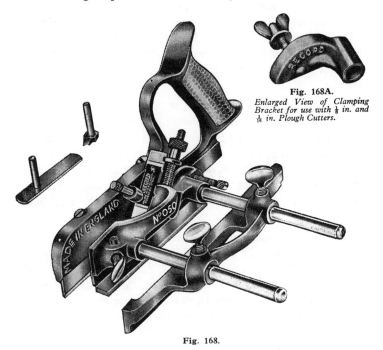

Fig. 168A.
Enlarged View of Clamping Bracket for use with $\frac{1}{8}$ in. and $\frac{3}{16}$ in. Plough Cutters.

Fig. 168.

The Fence is so designed that it can slide under the sliding section, and thus Rabbet and Fillister work may be undertaken at one cut up to a width of $\frac{7}{8}$ in. (or wider, of course, taking two cuts). Adding a Rabbet and Fillister to our list we have now an equivalent of sixteen planes.

Both the sliding section and the mainstock are fitted with spurs which, by cutting through the fibres before the blade takes its shaving,

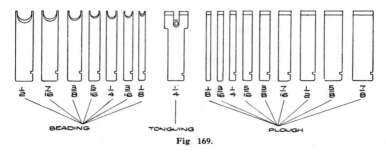

Fig. 169.

allow the tool to make a groove *across* the grain. As this operation may be done with any of the seven plough and rabbet cutters, the equivalent of seven dado planes is added, bringing the total now to twenty-three.

Any plough of course will make a groove on the edge of a board, and by careful manipulation may be coaxed into making the tongues; but the Combination Plane carries a special tonguing cutter, which will make a $\frac{1}{4}$ in. tongue of predetermined height at one setting—(an adjustable depth stop is provided on the cutter); and thus a pair of Matching Planes is added to the list, bringing the total plane equivalent now to twenty-five.

As planted ovolo and astragal may be made with any of the seven beading cutters, a further plane equivalent to fourteen planes may thus be added, a grand total, excluding extra cutters, of thirty-nine planes in one. Yet this Combination Plane, a precision tool in every sense of the word, is packed in a compact box taking less space than that taken up by an old-fashioned wood plough and its cutters—and is sold at a price which is below that which would have to be paid for the bead planes alone.

It should be noted that millimetre cutters are available as extras for the Combination Plane in the usual millimetre plywood sizes where these are at variance with inch sizes, *i.e.*, 4, 6, 9, and 12 millimetres. Also additional tonguing cutters for $\frac{1}{8}$ in. and $\frac{3}{16}$ in. tongues are obtainable. These millimetre and extra tonguing cutters are not supplied with the tool, but may be ordered separately through the tool dealer.

HANDLING THE PLANE

Hold the plane as in Fig. 170. The main thing to remember is to apply the slight pressure required in the right place, *i.e.*, on the fence, with the left hand. The fence must be kept well up to the edge of the work, and care must then be taken not to cant the plane over. This can be avoided by "feeling" all the fence in contact. A canted plane will give a groove that is not square with the face of the work.

If a lubricant should be desired on the fence, a rub with the side of a wax candle will do the trick; or a spot of oil may be applied.

A great deal can be done with the work held in the vice, as the fence is not too deep on the face. Where work cannot be held in the vice it may be cramped on the bench, "tacked" to the bench, or wood holding stops or buttons may be used. When similar operations are often called for, as in some repetition work, the worker will find that a suitably-ploughed board or strip will be useful—a "sticking" board. Thus, strips could be held in a ploughed groove whilst they were planed into astragals, etc. The advantage of the narrow fence is that so much work can be done in the vice. There are some workers who prefer a deeper fence, maintaining that this is an extra assistance in keeping the fence vertical and close to the work. Should a deeper fence be desired, screw a parallel fillet of wood as deep as desired to the face of the fence. Screw

Fig. 170.—Using the Combination Plane.
Keep the fence well up to the work with the left hand. Very little pressure is required with the right hand.

holes for this purpose will be found in a suitable position. Any well-seasoned hardwood will do for this; rosewood or beech will be found excellent. At first it will require slight lubrication before it works freely, but it will soon settle down with use to free and easy working.

SIZES OF CUTS
Ploughing

Any ploughing can be done from $\frac{1}{8}$ in. to $\frac{1}{2}$ in., ranging by sixteenths of an inch; also $\frac{5}{8}$ in. and $\frac{7}{8}$ in. at one cut with standard cutters. Extra

Cutters will plough 4, 6, 9, or 12 millimetres at one operation. By a simple expedient (see Fig. 103) any wider groove may be cut.

Dado Cuts (*i.e.*, Grooves across the grain).

Any dado or through housing may be cut the same sizes as for ploughing.

Beads and Centre Beads

Any bead or centre bead can be cut from $\frac{1}{8}$ in. to $\frac{1}{2}$ in., ranging by sixteenths of an inch. The bead may be on the edge of a board (plain or tongued) or in any position on the board up to $7\frac{1}{2}$ in. from, and parallel to, the edge. (With the fence in the ordinary position, centre beads may be made up to 5 in. from the edge; by reversing the fence a further $2\frac{1}{2}$ in. may be spanned. This is beyond the usual limit for such beading, but if a case should occur where the bead must be more than this, the makers can supply extra long arms to increase the distance.)

Rabbet and Fillister

Using the fence, rabbets may be accurately cut $\frac{1}{8}$ in. to $\frac{7}{8}$ in. wide at one cut. Wider rabbets are made by two cuts, a plough cut coming first. In this way practically any width rabbet may be cut without fatigue.

Matching

Tongues may be cut $\frac{1}{4}$ in. wide; grooves are made with the $\frac{1}{4}$ in. plough cutter.

ASSEMBLY OF THE COMBINATION PLANE

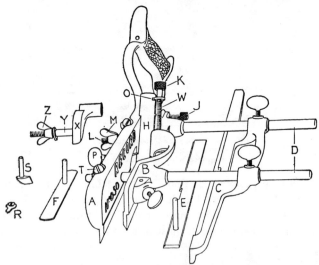

Fig. 171.—Parts of Combination Plane.

A—Main Stock.   B.—Sliding Section.   C—Fence.   D—Arm Rods.   E—Beading Stop.
F—Depth Gauge.   H—Cutter.   J—Sliding Section Fixing Screw.   K—Cutter
Adjusting Nut.   L—Cutter Bolt.   M—Cutter Bolt Wing Nut.   R—Spurs with Screws.
S—Shaving Deflector.   W—Cutter Adjusting Screw.   X—Narrow Cutter Clamping Bracket.
Y—Cutter Clamping Bracket Bolt.   Z—Cutter Clamping Bracket Washer and Wing Nut.

There will be no difficulty in assembling the plane. Slacken the screws in the Mainstock which secure the short arms, and replace the latter with the long arms, locating them normally approximately half-way through, and tighten up the screws. (When working a long distance from the edge the arms can be located farther to the right.) Slide the section B on the arms as shown until the Cutter-bolt L projects through the hole in the Mainstock. Slip on the washer and the wing nut M loosely.

Insert the cutter from below. See that the notch in the upper part of the cutter engages with the Collar O of the Adjusting Nut K.

Draw L up nearly tight by means of the Wing Nut M, seeing that the cutter is properly bedded in the slots in A and B.

The projection of the cutter below the edges of A and B controls the thickness of the shavings, and can be accurately adjusted to very fine limits by means of the Adjusting Nut K.

When adjusting the cutter, always slacken the Wing Nut M, tightening again after adjustment is made.

The adjustment of the depth of the cutter is worth more than passing notice, for, whilst it is possible to obtain any desired setting with a moment's manipulation, that adjustment is positive. When any adjustment is made to the depth of the cutter by means of the screw feed, it is impossible for any sideways displacement of the cutting edge to take place, as may occur when the cutter is held, as in some places, by a taper bolt. In the Combination Plane the cutter sits inside the two accurately-machined grooves which, when the cutter is screwed up tightly, always maintain a permanent lateral position of the cutter.

For Ploughing

Insert cutter of desired size and tighten up. Use Depth Stop F at P (forward of the Wing Nut on Mainstock A) and adjust to depth of required groove.

Slide Fence C to required distance from edge and tighten up thumbscrews which hold the fence to the arms.

For Rabbeting

Proceed as for ploughing. When possible, it is advantageous to use a wider cutter than the width of the rabbet, and slide the Fence C under the near edge of the cutter. Otherwise use a cutter the width of the rabbet, and slide C to edge of cutter.

(For cutting a rabbet or a ploughed groove wider than the widest cutter, see Fig. 103.)

143

For Beading

(a) On edge of board.

Insert Beading Cutter and tighten up after adjusting. Use Beading Stop E and Depth Gauge F. In this manner also tongued boards can be beaded.

(b) Centre Beading.

Select beading cutter and proceed as for ploughing. It is not necessary to use the spurs for Beading.

For Cutting a Dado (Housing)

Nail a $\frac{3}{16}$ in. thick batten (plywood is excellent for the purpose) on the edge of the dado to be cut. Use the spurs but not the Fence C. The batten acts as a guide. When the shoulder of the main body casting reaches the batten, if it is desired that the dado should go deeper, remove the batten. The depth of cut already made will keep the remainder of the cut straight and square. The Depth Stop F will limit the depth to be cut. Dados of all the usual depths can be easily cut in this way with great speed. (Fig. 172.)

To cut a groove or a rabbet deeper than $\frac{3}{8}$ in. Remove the Depth Stop. When the cutter reaches its natural limit and can proceed no further on account of the shoulder on the Mainstock A, slack the Wing Nut half a turn, screw the Cutter a little forward by turning the Adjusting Nut K, and tighten the Wing Nut. Then take off a shaving. Repeat this forward feeding of the Cutter in the same manner until the required depth is cut. A groove or rabbet may thus be cut to a depth of $\frac{15}{16}$ in., and will be even in depth.

Fig. 172.—Cutting Dados. The plywood strip used for guidance in starting the dado cut has been removed so that the dado may be deepened.

Fig. 172 shows clearly the method of cutting dados. The problem here was to cut a number of cross housings in a number of parallel strips, the housings to be evenly spaced. The strips were arranged in order, and cramped together with a sash cramp. The whole was held on the bench with a G Cramp. The required cutter being inserted and the spurs being set down, a plywood strip was tacked at the position of the first groove. This being completed, the strip was moved into position for the second groove, and so on. At the moment of taking the photograph, the third groove was being finished off. The plywood strip has been taken away so that the depth could be increased. In the manner indicated here, housings for shop shelving, etc., can be very speedily done across the grain as quickly as ploughing can be done with the grain; and all the housings will be at even and accurate distances on each and every piece. All shelves will fit fair and square provided that the precaution is taken to use a cutter the same width as the thickness of the shelves, partitions, etc., which are to be inserted.

It should be carefully noted that there is need for very little marking out. All that is necessary is that the position of one side of each dado shall be indicated. The strip of plywood gives the straight line, the cutter gives the width. There is no need to do either sawing or chiselling. The method can be used in the making of shop blinds, where continuous hinges are to be inserted in large numbers of strips. The number of strips which can be worked at a time is limited only by the length of cramp available. When a large number of strips are worked, there may be a tendency for the middle ones to work up when the cramp is tightened, but this can be overcome by tacking on temporarily a spline, as shown at the back of the cramp in the photograph. If any tendency shows itself of the initial cut of the spurs "ragging", the plane should be drawn backwards a time or two, using a fair downward pressure whilst doing this. The effect of this is that the spur makes a clean cut before the cutter takes its shaving. When this is done, no matter how rough the grain of the wood, the dado will have clean edges on both sides.

The Spurs can be put in or out of action by means of the Retaining Screws. Spurs are used in dado work, and sometimes in ploughing or rabbeting, especially when the grain is at all crossed. When adjusting the Spurs, take care to work well over the bench, as both Spurs and Screws are very tiny, and once lost among the shavings are apt to try the tempers of the mildest among us.

When sharpening the spurs (and they must be sharp if good, clean work is to be done) hold them in a pair of flat-nosed pliers on a piece of odd wood held in the vice. File the bevelled edge with a fine saw file, but do not file the flat side—merely wipe off the wire edge with one light wipe of the file.

Using the $\frac{1}{8}$ in. and $\frac{3}{16}$ in. Plough Cutters

A valuable improvement to the Record Combination Plane No. 050 has been introduced, enabling the Plane to be used with $\frac{1}{8}$ in. and $\frac{3}{16}$ in. cutters for ploughing, rabbet and dado work. The No. 050 Plane has this improvement fitted as standard, the parts being X, Y, Z, *i.e.*, the narrow cutter clamping bracket complete with one plough cutter $\frac{1}{8}$ in. and $\frac{3}{16}$ in. When using these cutters, the sliding section C is not required. For these two cutters, the Cutter Clamping Bracket is used in place of the sliding section as indicated in Fig. 173. Otherwise, the operations are as previously described. The $\frac{1}{8}$ in. and $\frac{3}{16}$ in. cutters will be found extremely advantageous when framing up plywood of these thicknesses, and in cutting the grooves for tongued clamps on thin tops as for wireless cabinets and the like.

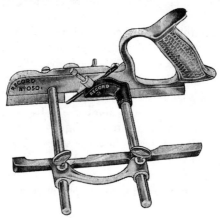

Fig. 173.—Clamping Bracket of Combination Plane in position.

Another useful application of the $\frac{1}{8}$ in. cutter to the Cabinet Maker is in the fitting of inlaid black or box lines on corners. The fence is run up to the edge of the cutter, and the depth stop set to the thickness of the line to be inlaid. When working across the grain, the spur should be used, or a cutting gauge run down first, to get a clean edge. The rabbet being cut, and the line fitted to length, a little thin, hot glue is applied. To cramp up, half-inch or so wide cotton tape is bound round as one would do bandaging, stretching the tape as tightly as it is possible to do. This should be left on a few hours (overnight, if possible) to give the glue ample time to set. It is a wise precaution to take to cover the line with a strip of newspaper before the tape is bound round, as this facilitates the removal afterwards of the tape. If the newspaper is stuck it can be easily scraped or damped off in cleaning up.

146

For Tonguing and Grooving

For grooving, as already indicated, the $\frac{1}{4}$ in. plough cutter is used, and there is no essential difference from the operation of ploughing. The tongues should be cut first, and the grooving cutter (*i.e.*, $\frac{1}{4}$ in. plough) should then be set for the grooves at the appropriate distance from the edge, using Fence C, and regulating the depth with the Depth Stop F.

For Tonguing, use the tonguing cutter. The height of the tongue is regulated by the screw stop on the tonguing cutter itself. There is no need for either Depth Stop F or Beading Stop E. The distance of the tongue from the edge of the board is regulated by the Fence C. The cutter will cut a $\frac{1}{4}$ in. tongue in the centre of boards $\frac{5}{8}$ in. to $1\frac{1}{8}$ in. wide. Double tongues may be cut on boards from $1\frac{1}{4}$ in. thick and upwards by taking two cuts, and by a similar method triple tongues can be cut on wider boards.

The Shaving Deflector

When tonguing, under certain conditions it may be found that whilst the shavings clear themselves from the right-hand prong, there may be a tendency for them to fail to clear themselves from the other prong. Should this be experienced, the Shaving Deflector provided can be attached. The Shaving Deflector S is inserted loosely in the hole P before the Cutter is inserted from underneath. When both Deflector and Cutter are in position, the Deflector is set so that its squared recess fits the side of the Cutter closely before it is secured by the Thumbscrew. The Cutter is then adjusted for cut in the usual way and secured by its wing nut. When the cutter is properly ground and sharpened, and correctly set for depth, it will be found under most conditions that the operation of tonguing can be performed quite satisfactorily without the aid of the deflector.

The edges of matching-boards can be "Veed" or beaded. The bead should be on the face of the tongued board, and is cut as previously indicated. (See also Fig. 99.)

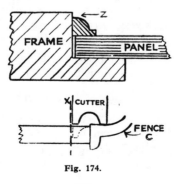

Fig. 174.

Mouldings

An ovolo for planting can be made by sliding the fence under a beading cutter of suitable size so that half the cutter only is in action. The depth gauge should be set to correct depth as required. Choose wood of suitable thickness, and after planing the half bead, saw off on the line XX (Fig. 174), later trimming off the sawn edge with the jack or smooth plane. The moulding can then be planted the depth of the quirk as at Z for panelled work in doors, framings, etc., being glued and pinned. The panel should neither be glued nor pinned, being left free to shrink. Thus only one of the flats should be glued, *i.e.*, the one that fits to the frame, and the pins should be through the moulding to the frame only. If the panel be pinned, it may at some later time crack.

A suggestion of further mouldings is shown by Fig. 175, the manner of cutting them being indicated with the drawings. Many rectilinear mouldings can also be made with the Combination Plane, suggestions for which will be seen in the Fig. 166 accompanying the description of No. 044 Plough. Any work which can be done with this plough can, of course, be done equally well with the Combination Plane.

SHARPENING THE CUTTERS

Plough and Matching Cutters are sharpened as ordinary plough plane cutters, and offer no difficulty.

The Beading Cutters are best sharpened with a carver's slip. It is best not to make a second bevel, as the grinding cannot be done on an ordinary grindstone. When honing the beading cutters, hone the full width of the bevel, thus retaining the shape and obviating grinding.

A Carborundum slip will quickly hone the Cutters at the grinding bevel, but does not leave a keen enough edge, and must be followed up with a Washita, or preferably an Arkansas slip. When rubbing off the wire edge from the face of the cutters, hone perfectly flat. A bevel on the back of the cutter is very detrimental to the working. A round rod wrapped in flour grade emery cloth, touched with a spot of oil, will sharpen the cutters, or a round hardwood rod can be used with flour emery and oil, but a carver's slip is best of all.

Chapter 10 has many operations which will provide further suggestions for the use of this very versatile plane, all the parts of which are standardised. In the rare event of any part requiring replacement, spare parts are always available through the tool merchants and the manufacturers.

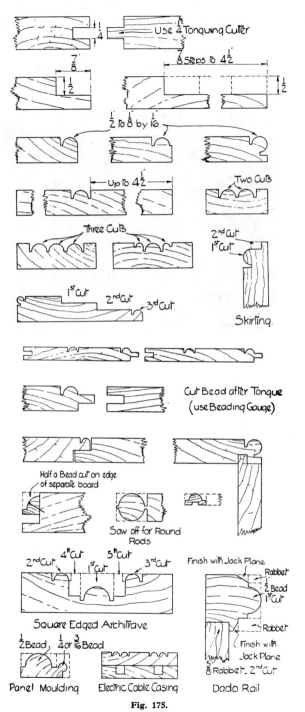

Use ¼ Tonguing Cutter

¼

⅞

½

8 Steps to 4½

1½

½

½ to ⅝ by 16

Up to 4½

Two Cuts

Three Cuts

2nd Cut

1st Cut

1st Cut 2nd Cut 3rd Cut

Skirting.

Cut Bead after Tongue
(use Beading Gouge)

Half a Bead cut on edge
of separate board

Saw off for Round
Rods

2nd Cut 4th Cut 5th Cut 1st Cut 3rd Cut

Square Edged Architrave

Finish with Jack Plane

Rabbet

½ Bead
1st Cut

Rabbet

Finish with
Jack Plane

⅝ Rabbet 2nd Cut

Dado Rail

½ Bead ¼ or 3/16 Bead

Panel Moulding   Electric Cable Casing

Fig. 175.

149

The cross sections, Fig. 175, illustrate various cuts which can be made with the No. 050 plane, and also indicate the methods. In addition, all cuts shown for No. 044, Figs. 165 and 166, and smaller Plough Planes can be made with these Combination Planes.

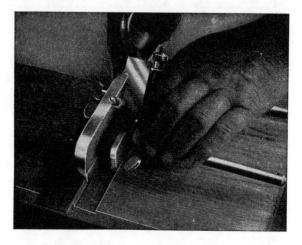

Fig. 176.—Cutting a plain dado or housing.
Note use of Plywood strip.

Chapter 14

The Multi-Plane, No. 405

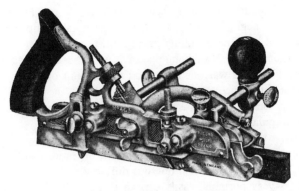

Fig. 177.—Record Multi-Plane No. 405.

The craftsman in wood may ask himself "Why should I possess a Multi-Plane?" The answer to this may be considered under various headings:—

(i) The Multi-Plane is capable of a wide range of operations—

(a) It replaces numerous **Beading** Tools. It can bead on the edge in seven sizes from $\frac{1}{8}$ in. to $\frac{1}{2}$ in., and can centre bead equally well in the same sizes in the width of a board up to 8 in. from the edge, or further when fitted with longer arms. Extra beading cutters and **Reeding** cutters (with 2 to 5 beads) may be obtained.

(b) It is a most efficient plough. Eleven plough cutters ($\frac{1}{8}$ in. to $\frac{13}{16}$ in.) are provided in the standard equipment.

(c) It can be equally well used for cutting a dado (or housing) across the grain, using the cutters as for ploughing.

(d) It replaces two pairs of matching planes, cutters being provided for $\frac{1}{4}$ in. and $\frac{3}{16}$ in. matching (tongues and grooves).

(e) It is a first class rabbet and fillister plane.

(f) It is a sash plane, capable of producing easily and accurately sash mouldings of various sections.

(g) Used as a slitting plane, it will cut off, accurately, strips of wood more quickly than ripping with a saw.

(h) Used with the special bases and cutters, it will work hollows and rounds, and nosings as for stair treads, etc.

(ii) Using special cutters it will stick ovolos without the use of an extra base.

(iii) The initial outlay on the Multi-Plane is considerably less than the amount expended on an assortment of planes covering the same range of work.

(iv) The amount of storage space taken up by the Multi-Plane is almost negligible. Compare the space taken up by plough, several beaders, matching planes, fillisters, etc.

(v) In common with all metal planes, it possesses a freedom from any possibility of warp or twist, and the amount of wear, even after years of service, is almost imperceptible.

(vi) It possesses fine adjustments for cutters, stops, fence, of easy manipulation and positive action.

(vii) It has the great advantage that once having got the "feel" of the tool, you can perform any or all of the operations without having to learn the "feel" of numerous differing tools.

(viii) It is very portable, easily carried to any job where a variety of operations may be needed.

(ix) Apart from the Standard Cutters, which are illustrated on page 169, and the Special Cutters, others may be made from blanks by the user.

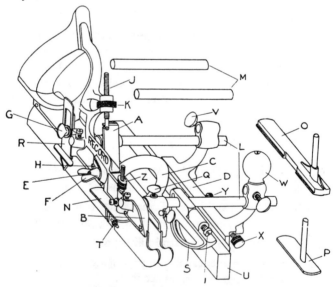

Fig. 178.—Record Multi-Plane, No. 405, showing parts.

There are three main parts to this Plane:—

    B. The Main Stock
    C. The Sliding Section
    D. The Fence

The function of the **Mainstock B** is to carry the Cutter A (with its adjustment K), the Slitter and the Depth Gauge N. It carries the Handle and provides a bearing for one edge of the Cutter.

The bearing for the opposite edge of the Cutter is provided by the **Sliding Section C.** This slides on the Arms L, allowing cutters of various widths to be used, and is secured by two Thumbscrews Q (only one of these shows in the Fig. 178; the back one being hidden by the Cutter).

The **Fence D** regulates the distance of the various cutters from the edge of the work. It is used for ploughing, beading and fillister work. It is secured on the arms by the two Thumbscrews, and may be set in two positions for height. When it is desired to use the Plane left-handed the arms should be pushed through the Main Stock (by releasing Set Screws) when the Fence can be attached on the opposite side.

The bearing of the Fence U is of rosewood and carries on its outer side an extra adjustment for fine work. This adjustment is locked by Screw X.

Two sets of arms are supplied with the Plane (4¼ in. and 8¼ in.), and longer ones can be supplied by the makers, or made from round steel rod by the user.

Spurs are provided in mainstock and sliding section. These are only used in cutting cross-grained wood, and when not required can be reversed out of action.

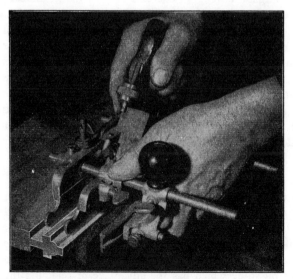

Fig. 179.—Method of handling the Multi-Plane. Keep fence well up with the left hand.

The Cam Steady S is used when centre beading, etc., at a long distance from the edge, and its purpose is to provide an interim bearing which prevents the fence from sagging, thus making for easier handling.

The rosewood Knob W provides a handle for the left hand, with which the fence is kept up to the work.

Though the description of the parts may at first perusal seem a little complicated, it will be found in actual practice that the Plane is very simple indeed to use in every one of its many applications and, after an hour or so of actually using the Plane, no craftsman will ever be happy without it.

We will now show the method of using the Plane. Fig. 179 shows clearly the way to hold the Plane. The important thing is that what pressure is applied should be with the left hand, which keeps the fence well up to its work. There is no need for heavy downward pressure anywhere. The fence should be lightly rubbed with the flat of a candle which is better than oil, as the latter has a tendency to pull the fence out of truth.

The cutters provide no difficulty in sharpening. The straight cutters are sharpened precisely as any other plane irons (Chapters 5 and 6). The shaped cutters are sharpened with a slip. A carver's Arkansas slip is ideal for the purpose. It will be found a great advantage to hone the full bevel of these cutters rather than make a second bevel as with a straight cutter, as by this method the original curve is always retained as well as the original bevel. If a second bevel is made, difficulty will be encountered later in grinding. This can be done fairly quickly with a carborundum slip of coarse grade. Another method of sharpening these cutters is by using a boxwood stick and flour emery with a little oil; and still another by using a round rod wrapped in fine emery cloth just touched with oil. A carver's slip of Arkansas, however, will usually be found best. It takes a little longer to hone the full bevel, it is true, but the edge given by the Arkansas slip is particularly keen and free from wire edge, and pays for the little extra time it takes. The honing in any case should be on the bevel, only a couple of wipes over the stone being taken on the flat or face side.

When sharpening the beading cutters care must be taken to retain the shape of the quirks. If these are inadvertently made narrower, they may be narrower than the bevelled runners, which will prevent them from cutting at that part. Another fault to avoid is taking more off the flats of the quirk than off the curved portion. Some workers avoid sharpening the bevelled part by working the face side of the cutter only flat on the oil stone which has the advantage of retaining the original shape easily and in practice this works quite well, and there is no practical disadvantage other than that the cutter may be worn down somewhat quicker, but the cutters have a very long life.

The Cutter is inserted by slacking the Wing Nut F on the cutter bolt, setting as in Fig. 180, the slot engaging with the Pin on screw J. The knurled Nut K is then turned so that the cutter edge just projects very slightly below the Mainstock B. Tightening Wing Nut F now holds the cutter firmly in position.

When adjusting cutter for a thinner or thicker shaving, always slacken Wing Nut F before turning Nut K; and tighten up after adjustment.

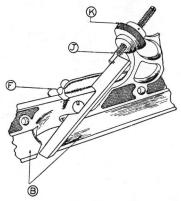

Fig. 180.

TO CUT A DADO (housing, *i.e.*, groove across the grain)

Set the spurs, which must be sharp, edge downwards on Sliding Section C and Mainstock B. Insert the cutter of desired width. Set the sliding section so that its spur is in line with the edge of the cutter. Nail a straight edged batten on the edge of the groove to be cut. Use the extra Gauge P to gauge the depth of the groove. The batten acts as a guide; the spurs cut the edge clean. Housings for shelves, stair treads, etc., are thus accurately and cleanly cut. (Fig. 181).

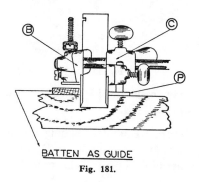

BATTEN AS GUIDE

Fig. 181.

TO CUT A RABBET

The Multi-Plane is set up as a rabbet and fillister by using a cutter a little wider than the desired width of the rabbet. The sliding section

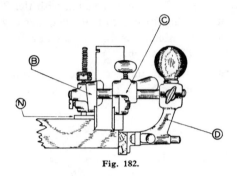

Fig. 182.

C, with its spur out of action is slid up about half-way across the cutter to form a bearing. The spur is in action on the Mainstock B. The Fence D is set to regulate the width of the rabbet, and the Gauge N regulates the depth.

FOR BEADING

The spurs are not required when cutting **any** Beads.

(a) **Ordinary Beading.** Set the cutter of the desired size so that the outside edge of Sliding Section C is in line with outer edge of cutter. The Fence D regulates the distance from the edge of the board, and the Gauge N regulates the depth. The top of the bead should finish just below the surface, so that it suffers no damage in subsequent cleaning up (sandpapering, etc.) of the work.

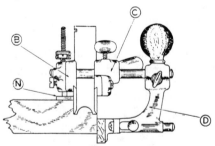

Fig. 183.

If outer quirk is not required, slide fence D further under cutter, or use beading stop as in Fig. 184.

(b) **Beading Matched Boards.** Sliding Section C is used as for ordinary beading, but instead of using Fence D, use the Beading Stop O as a bearing on the edge of the board. This prevents the left hand quirk from being cut and has ample bearing above the tongue. Depth of cut is regulated by Gauge N as before. Fence D is not used. No spurs. (See Fig. 184.)

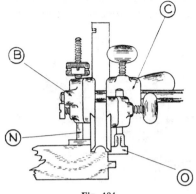

Fig. 184.

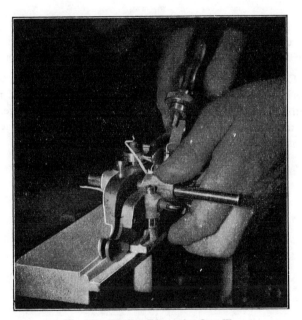

Fig. 185.—Beading Edge, using Stop W.

(c) **Centre Beading.** Set the Plane as for ordinary beading (Fig. 183) and regulate distance from edge by means of Fence D. The Cam Rest S can be attached to either arm to steady the Plane. In this way a bead can be cut 5 in. from edge. No spurs. Special cutters are obtainable to cut 2, 3, 4 or 5 beads for reeding.

FOR MATCHING BOARDS (Tongued and Grooved)

(a) **Cutting the Tongues.** Use the Tonguing Cutter, regulating the height of the tongue by means of the adjustable Stop which is attached to the cutter. The Depth Gauge N is not required, nor the spurs. The distance from the edge is regulated by the Fence D. With

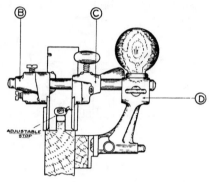

Fig. 186.

the two cutters ($\frac{1}{4}$ in. and $\frac{3}{16}$ in.) any board from $\frac{3}{8}$ in. to 1 in. can be tongued in the centre. (See Fig. 100 for tonguing thicker boards.)

(b) **Cutting the Grooves.** Use the plough cutter of the same width as the thickness of the tongues. The Depth Gauge N regulates the depth of the groove, and Fence D its distance from the edge. Spurs are not required. When using $\frac{3}{16}$ in. cutter Sliding Section C should not be used.

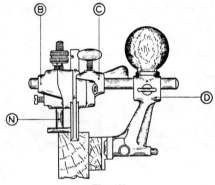

Fig. 187.

FOR PLOUGHING

The procedure is exactly as in Fig. 187. Section C should be used for $\frac{1}{4}$ in. and wider cutters, but for narrower cutters it should be removed. The spurs are not used.

FOR SASH WORK

There is little difference between this and cutting tongues, except in the shape of the tool. The adjustable Stop on the cutter regulates the depth of the cut. The fence D is used as in tonguing. Spurs are not used. Cut one side of the moulding first, and then reverse the board and cut the other side as indicated by the dotted line. It is easiest to cut the mouldings on the side of a wider board, ripping off with a saw when both sides are cut. The board can be nailed to the bench. See Fig. 179, which shows this method. When it is desired to mark and joint the sash bars first from the squared-up stuff and mould afterwards, all the bars can be moulded on one side with the flat lying on the bench top. To mould the other sides, the pieces should be reversed, and laid in a sticking board. (This is merely a ploughed board with the near edge of the groove bevelled off with a rabbet plane to accommodate the ovolo. It is not essential that the exact replica of the moulding be made; so long as the moulding lies firmly in the channel it will be all right. The board should be about three feet long, which will be long enough for all such work.) The sticking board should have the groove so made that the face edge of the sash bar projects slightly over the edge of the bench, so that Fence D is able to get a bearing on it. Then all the bars can be moulded on the second side. By this method, the Multi-Plane does the work of the sash fillister and the sash ovolo at the one cut.

Make sure that the sliding section C gets a bearing on the wood when using the sash cutter. (Fig. 188.)

It will be noticed that a certain amount of variation in the shape of the moulding can be obtained by sliding the fence farther in or out, and the diagram (Fig. 188) shows the maximum, which is not usually required. Generally speaking a $1\frac{3}{4}$ in. sash cutter will cut a $1\frac{1}{2}$ in. moulding; a $1\frac{1}{2}$ in. cutter a $1\frac{1}{4}$ in. moulding.

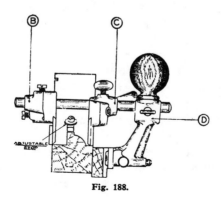

Fig. 188.

FOR SLITTING

Strips can rapidly be cut from thin boards by means of the Slitting Cutter, which is attached on the right hand side, just in front of the handle. It should be placed in the slot, with its Depth Gauge R over it, both being screwed together and to the main stock with the one screw. The Fence D gauges the distance of the cut from the edge of the board. When the boards are thick, slit them from both sides (see dotted lines).

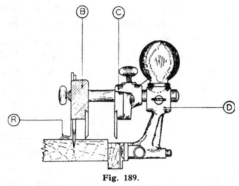

Fig. 189.

Ovolo cutters $\frac{1}{4}$ in., $\frac{5}{16}$ in. and $\frac{3}{8}$ in. are available as extra cutters. To stick an ovolo, the cutter is inserted in the usual way and the sliding section, which is not required, is removed. The fence is then put in position so that it may slide underneath the cutter, thus adjusting the size of the quirk. The depth stop is then arranged in position to adjust the depth of the top quirk. The cut may be made from either face side or face edge as most convenient, but as the face side gives a wider bearing, it is usually to be preferred. The spurs are not required, and with a sharp cutter and a fine feed, mouldings may be cut with confidence on either long or end grain. The plane is held exactly as for other operations, and there is no canting over as with the old-fashioned wooden ovolos—a great advantage. As in cutting any mouldings it is essential that the cutter be quite sharp. No extra base is required for ovolo cutters.

TO CUT HOLLOWS AND ROUNDS

The Multi-Plane may be used to cut hollows and rounds by attaching special bases and using the corresponding cutters. The Sliding Section C is not used, and the hollow or round bottom is slid up into its place. The cutter is then inserted. According to the nature of the work in hand, the Sliding Fence D may, or may not be, required. The special hollow and round bases are made in four sizes. The extreme widths and diameters of the circles they will cut are:—

Hollow and Round, $\frac{1}{2}$ in. wide cutter, $\frac{3}{4}$ in. circle

,,	,,	$\frac{5}{8}$ in.	,,	1 in.	,,
,,	,,	$\frac{3}{4}$ in.	,,	$1\frac{1}{4}$ in.	,,
,,	,,	1 in.	,,	$1\frac{1}{2}$ in.	,,

Fig. 190.—Hollows and Rounds and Nosing Cutters.

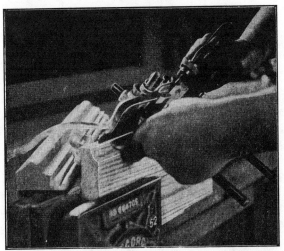

Fig. 191.—Note fingers of left hand in guiding hollow. On the left is a section of Architrave worked with the Multi-Plane by the methods described.

The cutters will cut more than their extreme width, of course, by varying the angle at which the Plane is applied (see Fig. 194), and they can be used in combination with the other cutters to produce mouldings of almost any conceivable shape, using methods similar to those indicated in Fig. 192.

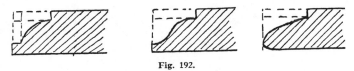

Fig. 192.

With the fluting and the ovolo cutters, it will be realised that the sliding section will not be required, as this would prevent the cutter from working. Thickness of shaving (and this should be as thin as practicable and the cutter sharp) is adjusted from the sole of the mainstock.

L

The beginner is often puzzled by moulding on end grain, as on the ends of a cabinet or similar top. It is really quite simple. Suppose the piece in Fig. 193 has to be moulded on all four sides. Work the

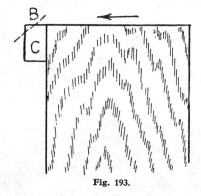

Fig. 193.

end grain first from A to B. Before starting the cut, attach a small piece of similar wood as shown by C to the panel at B. This can be glued on, but that will necessitate waiting until next day for the glue to dry. It will usually be found that it can be held on by a long sash cramp. This piece will allow the Plane to run through without breaking the corner at B, as the broken fibres will only occur on C, and even then only to a limited extent if a chamfer be taken off as shown by the dotted line. The other end grain is then worked in the same way, and the two long grain sides will then offer no difficulty, the plane running straight through.

In the case of a simple round or hollow, of course, the Plane may be worked from each end, as on page 71; but with a fancy moulding such as an ovolo or ogee, that is obviously an impossibility, but the job is quite simply and easily done when a block is attached as indicated.

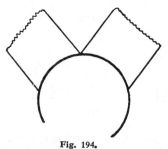

Fig. 194.

It will be clear from Fig. 194 that a 1 in. hollow or round is not confined to the $\frac{3}{8}$ in. of its width, as it will follow any part of the curve which is 1 in. diameter.

An example is given in Fig. 195 of a common moulding with several members indicative of the wide scope of application of the Multi-Plane. Set out first the section of the required moulding on the end of the wood. It will be noticed that much work can often be saved by running off two narrow plough grooves which meet. In Fig. 195 piece A could

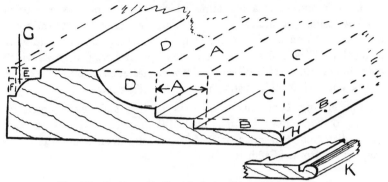

Fig. 195.—Architrave and method of striking with Multi-Plane.

be cut first with a suitable ploughing cutter. Piece B could be ploughed away with a $\frac{1}{8}$ in. plough cutter; piece C then falling away. D is then cut away with the 1 in. round. Working on the opposite edge, E and F are taken away with the Plane set as a fillister (see page 156), and the remaining piece G worked off with the 1 in. hollow. Alternatively G

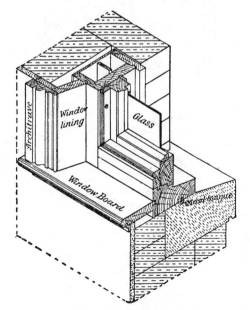

Fig. 196.—Sash Windows. From "A Manual of Carpentry", Riley, MacMillan & Co. (also Fig. 197).

163

could be worked away with a rabbet plane (q.v.). It now remains to work off the edge H, which can be a simple rounding worked with a Jack (Fig. 30), or more interestingly, it can be run off as a bead with the 405, as at K. The ovolo at G can be made with one cut by using the special ovolo cutter of suitable size.

Fig. 195 represents a moulding which would appear as a door or window casing, and indicates the method by which an infinite variety of mouldings can be struck, either for new work or for matching old work in repairs. Figs. 196 and 197 give the detail of a sash window, which aptly indicate the value of the 405 Plane, inasmuch as all the sections can be cut with its aid, as shown in the foregoing sections.

The Nosing Tool consists of a special base and cutter which are similar to the hollows, but it is made $1\frac{11}{16}$ in. wide, and cuts an exact $1\frac{1}{4}$ in. diameter semi-circle or half-round. Its main application is in shaping the fronts of stair treads.

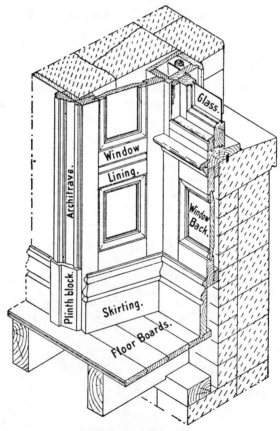

Fig. 197.

The "feel" of the Multi-Plane 405 is quickly acquired, and its operation very easy. When commencing cuts with it, as with the Combination Plane 050, it is preferable to start at the end farthest away, and work backwards along the board. Take nice, steady, even, firm cuts, always keeping the Fence D well up to the work. Don't forget a rub with a candle on the bearing face of the fence, and on the soles of the hollows, rounds and nosing tool is well worth while; the Plane works all the easier for it. Remember that fine work is only got with sharp tools, and that two or three thin shavings will leave a better surface and are more easily cut than one thick one. The Plane will, on occasion, stand a lot of "iron" for ploughing, but beads, sash mouldings, hollows and rounds must have a sharp cutter finely set for a thin shaving if you want first class work. With the screw feed to the cutter this is quite easily and rapidly secured.

When planing a hollow, the first part is often cut out with a gouge. With the Multi-Plane this may be done, if desired, but it is not necessary as the Plane will cut all the hollow from the start quite quickly, and the knack of taking a steadying bearing with the fingers of the left hand is one that is very quickly learnt. (See Fig. 191.)

Among the "special" cutters for the Multi-Plane which are available are a $1\frac{1}{2}$ in. Sash Cutter—the counterpart of the one supplied; a range of fluters from $\frac{3}{16}$ in. to $\frac{3}{4}$ in., which are very useful for relieving pilasters, etc., and a wide range of reeding cutters which cut at the one operation, 2, 3, 4 or 5 beads. Ovolo Cutters are made in $\frac{1}{4}$ in., $\frac{5}{16}$ in., and $\frac{3}{8}$ in. sizes.

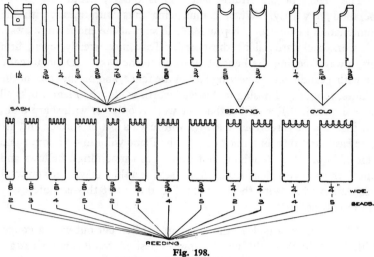

Fig. 198.
Additional Cutters for Multi-Plane.

LIST OF ADDITIONAL CUTTERS

Size Inches	Type	Size Inches	Type
$1\frac{1}{2}$	Sash Cutter	$\frac{5}{8}$	Beading Cutter
$\frac{3}{16}$	Fluting Cutter	$\frac{3}{4}$	,,
$\frac{1}{4}$	,,	$\frac{1}{8}$	Reeding Cutter, 2 Beads
$\frac{5}{16}$	,,	$\frac{1}{8}$	,, 3 ,,
$\frac{3}{8}$	,,	$\frac{1}{8}$	,, 4 ,,
$\frac{7}{16}$	,,	$\frac{1}{8}$	,, 5 ,,
$\frac{1}{2}$	,,	$\frac{3}{16}$	,, 2 ,,
$\frac{5}{8}$	,,	$\frac{3}{16}$	,, 3 ,,
$\frac{3}{4}$	,,	$\frac{3}{16}$	,, 4 ,,
$\frac{1}{4}$	Ovolo Cutter	$\frac{3}{16}$	,, 5 ,,
$\frac{5}{16}$	,,	$\frac{1}{4}$	,, 2 ,,
$\frac{3}{8}$	,,	$\frac{1}{4}$	,, 3 ,,
		$\frac{1}{4}$	,, 4 ,,
		$\frac{1}{4}$	,, 5 ,,

The beauty of a bead or moulding lies in a great measure on the play of the light on it, and as that varies with the time of the day, and the time of the year, nay it varies from moment to moment, it is that factor which gives mouldings their interest, and explains why they are so permanent and not swamped by the caprice of fashion.

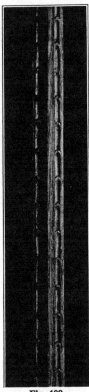

Fig. 199.

There was a recent period during which mouldings tended to disappear, together with all ornaments, owing to the influence of the "get back to fundamentals" school; but sane ornament, and sane mouldings are slowly re-appearing, as it was seen they must, and at the present time much experiment may be observed in the work of the modern artists in woodwork, the true craftsmen who are consciously or unconsciously making the modern style that will rank in days to come with that of the classical masters. In many cases the mouldings which are most effective are such as have for their basis traditional motifs, and Figs. 199 and 200 may be taken as typical of this type. Fig. 199 shows a moulding designed for the edge of a board such as might show on the edges of a wardrobe, linen press, chest of drawers, etc. If the illustration is turned horizontally it will be noted that the effect is altogether different from that obtained when the moulding is placed vertically; and in the solid, with a live play of light and shade, the difference is much more pronounced —its whole character is changed. Variation of effect is not so apparent when Fig. 200 is turned (in spite of the optical illusion), but it is equally variable in the solid, with the light striking the ornament from another

Fig. 199A.

Fig. 200A.

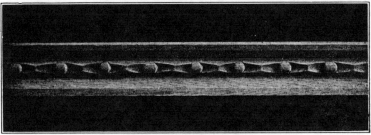

Fig. 200.

angle. Fig. 199 is intended of course for vertical work, and Fig. 200 for horizontal work. Although both appear to be very complex, they are not nearly so laborious to produce as it would seem. It will be seen from the sections that a centre bead is the predominant feature. In Fig. 199 this bead is quite small, $\frac{1}{8}$ in.; and the two outer portions are then rabbeted away at a slight bevel. In Fig. 200 the centre bead is larger, $\frac{3}{8}$ in., and the sloping members are rabbeted away, but not this time so far, a flat being left which catches the light on another plane from that of the slopes. The gouge cuts are made on the mouldings after the beads and bevels are cut, using a carver's gouge (sharpened on *both* sides), and the essentials to remember are that if the two gouge cuts meet, the chip will come away clean; and that it is quite useless to attempt any work of this kind with blunt plane cutters or gouges. These two mouldings are but simple examples of many such which can be similarly treated, and probably look best on oak which is left clean from the tool in its natural colour, unpolished or waxed. It calls naturally for clean and accurate workmanship, but it is well worth the effort; and when such mouldings are used in a restrained manner, keeping the proportion of decoration quite low as compared with the total surface area, the whole effect is one of lasting joy.

In many cases, as in sash work, mouldings are of utility as well as beauty, and their form is the ultimate result of generations of tradition, and by this time well nigh perfection. Thus, if you would have your mouldings ever things of beauty and ornaments to your work, study what has gone before (you can see it any time all around you); endeavour to discover **why** it was so done rather than in some other way; remember the play of light; and then work out your own salvation. Was it Aristotle who said: "It's not the man who makes the box, it's the box that makes the man!" Receding mouldings have lately become popular; there is room for much thought and experiment in this direction. The play of light on a moulding above the eye level is vastly different from that on one below it. (Compare a picture rail and a skirting-board: both have a definite purpose to serve: tradition has evolved the best treatment for that purpose and at the same time discovered the most decorative effect without undue expenditure of labour.)

FINISHING MOULDINGS

Mouldings and beads are at their best when cleanly worked and left from the sharp tool, and they should not require the use of glass paper; a burnishing with a handful of shavings, or a piece of coarse hessian will improve the appearance of clean work in most hardwoods and some softwoods. If glasspaper *must* be used, care should be taken

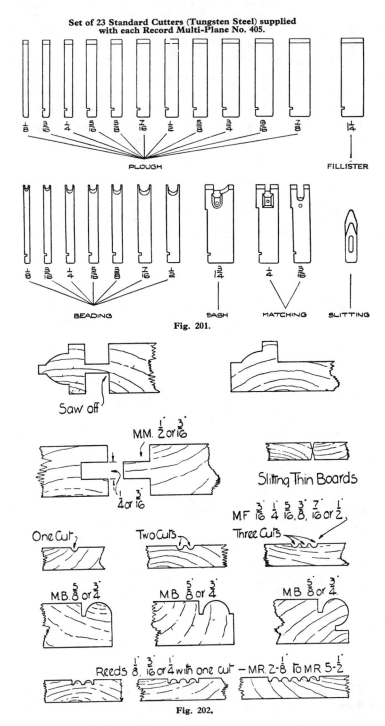

Set of 23 Standard Cutters (Tungsten Steel) supplied with each Record Multi-Plane No. 405.

PLOUGH

FILLISTER

BEADING SASH MATCHING SLITTING

Fig. 201.

Saw off

MM. ½ or 3/16

¼ or 3/16

Slitting Thin Boards

MF 3/16 ¼ 5/16, 3/8, 7/16 or ½

One Cut Two Cuts Three Cuts

M.B. 5/8 or ¾ M.B. 5/8 or ¾ M.B. 5/8 or ¾

Reeds ⅛, 3/16 or ¼ with one cut — MR. 2-8 to MR 5-½

Fig. 202.

not to spoil the edges by rubbing them down or rounding them. This can be avoided by working the glasspaper round a rod for a hollow, and fitted over a hollow (in wood or cork) for a round; the rounds and hollows being made to follow the mouldings. Straights, of course, call for the glasspaper to be folded over a straight surface—a narrow fillet of wood serves quite well, and a steel rule will help in a very narrow quirk. A useful rubber may be made by gluing a piece of cork composition (such as is used for table mats) on a block of wood about $\frac{3}{4}$ in. or $\frac{7}{8}$ in. thick.

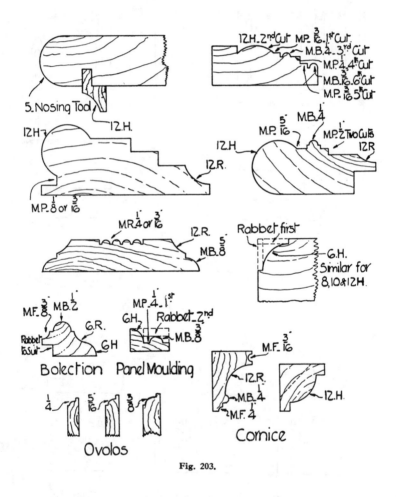

Fig. 203.

Figs. 202 and 203 indicate a number of mouldings, etc., which may be done with the Multi-Plane, and others will be seen in Figs. 204 and

205, all of which are within the capacity of this tool. The number of the cutter required for each is indicated on the sketches, and where one sequence of cuts is better than another the best sequence is indicated also. The table construction shown may be varied by having the top receding (omitting the overhang) and by sticking an ovolo round the table edge, fitting this edge about $\frac{1}{8}$ in. inside the outer edges of the frame top. The mitre of the rails may be secret dovetailed. The appearance of this table is very distinguished, and the construction much sturdier than might be thought from a cursory examination of the drawing. These illustrations while not being exhaustive, will serve to indicate the wide range that the plane will cover. A selection of examples performed with this Multi-Plane are shown in Fig. 206.

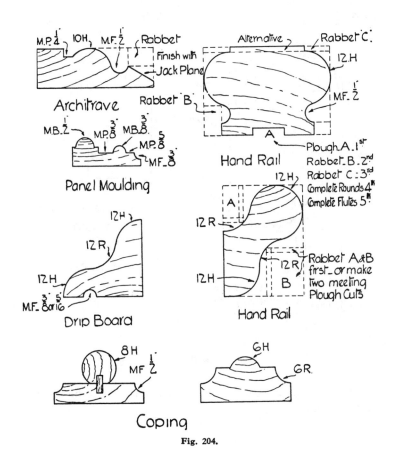

Fig. 204.

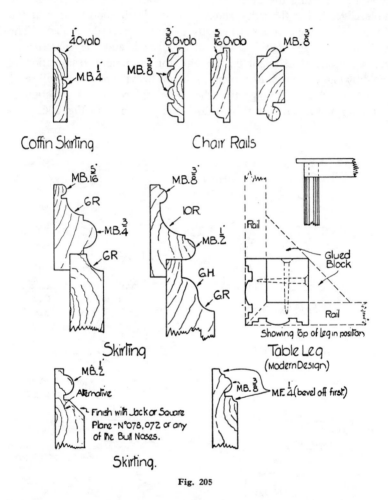

Fig. 205

DADO CUTS, *i.e.*, grooves across the grain, can also be performed with these Planes.

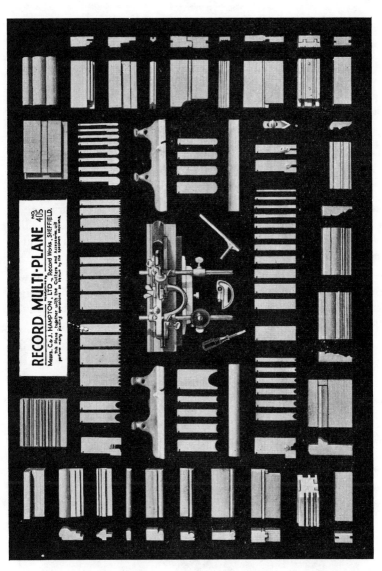

RECORD MULTI-PLANE NO. 405

Messrs. C. & J. HAMPTON, LTD., Record Works, SHEFFIELD.

This Plane, together with the Cutters and Accessories, will perform many planing operations as shown by the specimen sections.

Fig. 206.

173

Chapter 15

The Circular Plane, No. 020

Fig. 207.

The wooden Compass Plane has been known to wheelwrights for many generations, and is limited in its scope to the fixed curvature of its sole. It has been long superseded by the metal Circular Plane, which covers a much wider range of work, and has all the advantages of adjustment that are possessed by the metal Bench Planes.

With the old type of wooden plane, the curvature of the sole was fixed, and convex and concave work necessitated the use of two distinct planes. The metal variety has a flexible steel sole, which can be adjusted both to a convexity and to a concavity. (See Fig. 207.)

The adjustment of the cutter, grinding and honing, are precisely the same as for the Bench Planes. (See Chapters 5 and 6.)

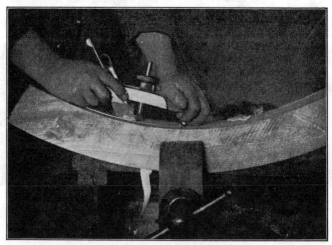

Fig. 208.—Record 020, working concave.

The adjustment of the sole to the work in hand is quickly made, the steel face being anchored at each end to the body. See that the locking screw is not tight, and with the Plane resting on the surface which is to be planed, turn the large adjusting screw at the top until the face of the Plane tallies with the desired curvature. Tighten the locking screw and the Plane is ready for use. The cutter can be taken out for sharpening,

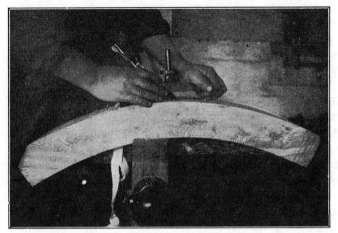

Fig. 209.—Record 020, working convex.

and replaced without interfering with the setting. The frame or body of the Plane is conveniently shaped at each end for a comfortable grip. The method of using the Plane is shown in Figs. 208 and 209, which show the felloe of a wagon wheel being planed.

There is a tendency when first using a Circular Plane to work the Plane at an angle, as is frequently done with a Jack Plane. This, of course, cannot be done when working with a Circular Plane; the Plane must go forward and not cross ways. The direction of the grain must be carefully studied, this, in principle, is explained on page 197 in connection with spokeshaving. The same principles apply when using the Circular Plane.

To the cabinet-maker, the Circular Plane is of great service in the making of circular frames and serpentine work; and to the carpenter in making circular frames for windows and doors. To the wheelwright, of course, it is indispensable.

The construction of serpentine fronts (*e.g.*, kidney-shaped table frames, bow-fronted chests, etc.) is something of a puzzle to the uninitiated. To cut them out of the solid is laborious, wasteful of material, and frequently introduces short grain which not only weakens the construction, but also impoverishes the finished appearance. They are quite simply built up of short shaped pieces much in the same way as a brick wall is built. The parts may be simply glued and cramped, or may be glued and screwed, or glued and pegged. When the glue is dry they are cleaned up and planed accurately to shape with the Circular Plane,

Fig. 210.

toothed, and veneered. To cut the blocks, a template should be prepared from a full-size drawing, and the parts marked off from the template on a trued-up board. If only a few are required, they may be cut by hand with the bow saw, but if any quantity have to be cut, it is better to have them cut out on the nearest band saw. As the top and bottom are true previous to sawing, the assembly is fairly quickly done, and the Circular Plane will look after the faces when the glue is dry.

Patterns may be built up in a similar manner, as well as moulds for concrete castings, etc.

Fig. 211.—17th Century Wheelwright's Plane.

Chapter 16

Router Planes

In the cutting of housings, it is usually essential that the floor of the housing shall be at an even depth from the face of the wood being worked. The carpenter found that this was more easily accomplished if there was some kind of stop to his chisel; and the earliest routers appear to have been blocks of hardwood into which the chisel was wedged tightly. A rounding off of the corners made the block easier to handle; and as the tool—the router or the Old Woman's Tooth—found its way into the toolmakers' catalogues it had become largely standardised in shape.

It served its purpose, but it was clumsy in operation and equally so in adjustment; and it usually called for quite a lot of preliminary work in setting out, sawing skilfully at the right place inside the lines, and a preliminary chopping out with the chisel before it was applied for the purpose of leaving a final level, and its efficiency was very largely due to the skill and experience of the worker, particularly in the preparatory operations.

Today we have little use for such a tool, and it has almost completely been superseded by the metal type of router, which in its modern form has a cast iron body. This body has an open mouth (which, as we shall see, can be converted into a closed mouth readily as required) and it is fitted with three cutters, two for straightforward routering, and one for finishing smoothly, these cutters being controlled by screw adjustment. It is further provided with a fence which may, as occasion warrants, be used either on straight or curved work.

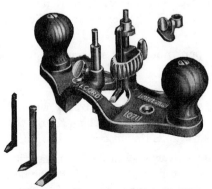

Fig. 212.—Record Router Plane No. 071

177

The shape of the router is the result of much investigation, and has reached a point practically of perfection. Two polished wooden knobs are provided, these applying the power in just the right place for the maximum effect on the cutter with the minimum of effort by the user. The angle of the cutters is such that a clean, easy cut is made; and the casting is made large enough to cover all normal requirements, but as will be seen later, provision is made so that in effect the size of the hollow it will work on has no practical limits.

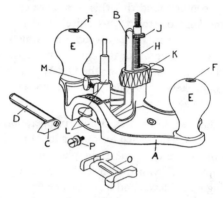

Fig. 213.—Showing parts of Record No. 071 Router.

A.	Body	J.	Cutter Adjusting Nut
B.	Cutter	K.	Cutter Clamping Collar and
C.D.	Finishing Cutter		Thumb Screw
E.	Knobs	L.	Depth Gauge and Shoe
F.	Knob Bolt and Nut	M.	Depth Gauge Thumbscrew
H.	Cutter Adjusting Screw	O.	Fence, with Screw and Washer P

Record No. 071 Router may be used either as an Open-mouth or a Closed-mouth router.

When used **closed mouth,** the shoe (L) is secured as in the illustration. Correct setting is easily obtained by resting the router on a level surface with the thumbscrew M slack, this then being tightened up when the shoe is level with the sole of the router. Experienced craftsmen may prefer to set the shoe one shaving thickness (about .001 in.) below the sole.

When used **open mouth,** the shoe and depth gauge are removed from the router.

The cutters may be used for normal work in the position shown in Fig. 212, or they may be used for **bull-nose work,** in which case they will be set in the rear slot (Fig. 213, behind K), the clamping collar being then reversed, *i.e.,* with its thumbscrew to the front.

To insert the cutter, slacken the clamping collar thumbscrew K, raise the collar, and push up the cutter from the bottom. Engage the slot of the cutter in the cutter adjusting nut J. Lower the collar, adjust nut J to raise or lower the cutter so that its cutting edge is slightly below the sole. Tighten clamping screw K.

Insertion for bull-nose work is similar, except that the cutter goes in the back groove instead of the front one.

Clamping collar K should be set as low down as it will go, this giving a better cutting action than when it is set higher as in the illustration, Fig. 213.

Fig. 214.—Normal work on a through housing.

In **recessing housings,** (Fig. 214) preliminary sawcuts (on the waste side of the line) should be made across the grain. The cutter being set as above, cuts are then made from the end of the housing; in the case of a through housing, from each end—the object of this being to avoid a breakaway at the finishing end. When the cutter has taken this portion out, thumbscrew K is slackened half a turn, nut J is advanced a turn, and K is tightened up. This puts the cutter ready for the next deeper cut, which is made as before. The knack of adjusting the two screws quickly is easily acquired, and can usually be done on the return stroke. This method is quicker than first setting the cutter the full depth of the housing and then "hacking out" the chips; it is easier in operation; and the cutter remains sharp longer. Gauge marks may be made on the work to indicate correct depth; or use may be made of the $\frac{1}{16}$ in. divisions which are scribed on the cutter, by noting their position in relation to the top of the pillar; or use may be made of the depth gauge as described on page 182.

The fence is not required in normal routering.

179

Fig. 215.—Using the straight fence for making a stopped groove.

The **square ended cutters** ($\frac{1}{2}$ in. and $\frac{1}{4}$ in.) are for normal work. The pointed cutter (Fig. 213, C) is for those occasions when the surface of the recess must be left smooth. When using this smoothing cutter, if the dimensions of the work allow it, it will be found advantageous to work with a sideways, shearing cut. The smoothing cutter should never be used for "hacking out".

When the recess to be cut is wider than the router is long, a board about $\frac{1}{2}$ in. $\times$ 4 in. (these dimensions can be varied a lot), and long enough to stretch across the proposed recess, should be attached to the sole with No. 8 C/S screws through C/S holes which will be found drilled through the sole. Before the board is screwed on, it should be marked for the opening (from the sole of the router) and the clearance cut away with the bow saw. The operation is then as described above.

The threaded holes in the sole are for the attachment of the **Fence** (Fig. 213, O) which is fitted under the sole, and may be used on either side of the cutter. The grooves which are milled on the sole will keep the fence square, and the appropriate hole is chosen which will set the fence at the desired distance from the cutter. With the aid of this fence, stopped grooves $\frac{1}{2}$ in. or $\frac{1}{4}$ in. wide, according to which cutter is used, can be made.

For this operation the shoe must be secured in the "close-mouth" position. The fence must then be set with its straight face at the desired distance from the face side of the work. Usually in this type of work mortises are already made at the stopped ends of the proposed grooves. If not, a mortise should be cut at that end as deep as it is proposed the groove should go.

The cutter being set a trifle below the surface of the sole, a cut should now be made from the end of the work towards the mortise, keeping the fence well up to the work (as in ploughing). On the return stroke slacken thumbscrew K, advance nut J, tighten thumbscrew K and make another cut. Repeat until the desired depth is cut. (Fig. 215.)

The operation is not as complicated as the description suggests, and after a little practice it becomes almost automatic.

That face of the fence which is opposite the straight face is so designed that it will follow a curve either outside or inside. It is used in a similar way to the straight face, except that it follows a curved edge instead of a straight one, and that the grain of the wood must be more carefully studied. It will be found that in making a groove in a circular or oval base that two quarters can be done with the fence on one side of the router and the other two quarters can be done with the fence on the opposite side of the router.

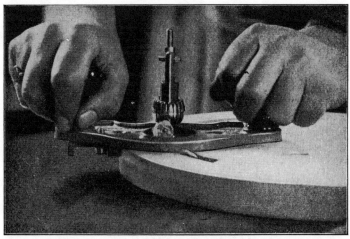

Fig. 216.—Using the round fence for making a curved groove.

The **depth gauge and shoe** (Fig. 213, L) can be used in two ways.

When detached from the router, it forms a handy depth gauge for testing, say, a series of blind mortises which it is desired shall be the same depth. In this case the shoe (which forms the stop) will be so attached that the thinner end of the gauge can be inserted into the mortises (or similar holes or recesses).

When used in conjunction with the router, the router is set up as an open-mouth router. The thin end of the gauge pointing downwards is then inserted into its hole and pushed through until its end projects the desired depth below the sole. The shoe is then attached above the pillar, securing the shoe thumbscrew, but leaving thumbscrew M slack so that the gauge is free to move upwards. Whilst routering is being done the shoe will not fall on to the pillar until the desired depth is reached. As soon as it touches the pillar the worker will know that he has gone deep enough.

The cutters should be kept sharp, and can be sharpened on an oilstone or with an oilstone slip. They should be sharpened on the bevelled side only, merely wiping off the wire edge on the flat side. The edges of the normal cutters should be kept square and the finishing cutter shaped to a 90° point. The cutters may be ground on a grindstone as indicated in Fig. 217. The grinding angle is 35°. It is preferable to sharpen the cutters with the slip to one bevel only; this obviates the need to grind.

Fig. 217.—Sharpening a Router Cutter.

Spare parts are obtainable. In ordering quote Record Router No. 071 and the name of the part required.

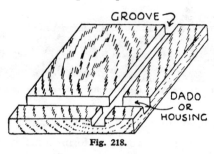

Fig. 218.

Fig. 218 shows clearly the difference between what is usually termed a "groove" and what is known as a "dado" or more commonly a "housing". The groove, which runs the same way as the grain, will normally be cut with a plough; but the "housing", (sometimes also called a "raggle") being across the grain, (as for a shelf), will be cut as above described with the router.

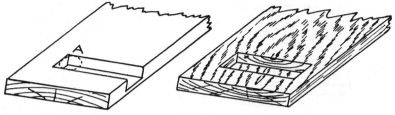

Fig. 219.

Fig. 219 shows two examples of stopped housings, which give a better appearance than a through housing, as the inserted part (as in a shelf) does not show through at the front, and it is stronger as the shoulder on the shelf tends to prevent side play in the joint. To cut a stopped housing, mark out with square and knife; the groove may stop $\frac{1}{2}$ in. or $\frac{3}{4}$ in. from the front; and then bore at A with a bit which is the width of the groove. The front corners may now be cleaned up with the chisel, and then saw cuts are made just on the waste side of the line to the depth of the gauge line, evenly all along. The boring will provide somewhere for the sawdust to go; it would otherwise clog in the kerf. The router may now be used as above described to take out the waste.

The same purpose can be served, if, instead of boring, a mortise is made with a $\frac{3}{4}$ in. or 1 in. chisel, cutting, of course, *across* the grain so as not to split the wood. This may, perhaps, take a little longer than the boring, but if it is carefully done it usually results in a more accurate job at the finish. In all work of this kind it is preferable to set out with a sharp marking knife rather than a pencil. The limits are more positively defined.

When the housing must be stopped at both front and back as shown on the right-hand side of Fig. 221, after marking out, the limits of the housing can be defined with a sharp chisel, tapping with a mallet. A light cut can then be taken with the router towards each end of the housing in turn; the cutter then advanced for another cut, and so on until the required depth is attained. Alternatively it may be mortised out with the chisel for the bulk of the cut and the last $\frac{1}{8}$ in. or so cleaned up with the router.

Recesses for locks, hinges, etc., ("gains") can often be cut better using the router, the limits of the cut being first defined with a sharp chisel, and the fence being used if necessary. The pointed (finishing) cutter will leave a very smooth face where this is required, especially if it

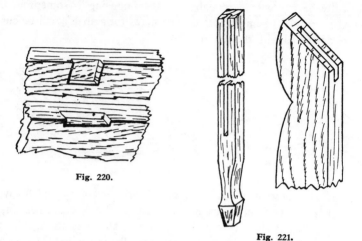

Fig. 220.

Fig. 221.

is used "on the skew", and the point is useful for getting the corners clean. This cutter will cut the thinnest shaving with ease, and it can be of great service when cutting the shallow recesses for irregularly shaped inlays.

Fig. 221 shows two examples of stopped grooves using the fence as in Fig. 215 and as described above. Usually in work of this type it will not be necessary to define the length of the groove with the chisel: but it is advantageous, where there is no mortise, to cut one at the closed end of the cut. The length of the runner on the plough plane prevents that tool from making a stopped groove satisfactorily but the operation is relatively simple with the router when the fence is used. It must be noted that housings, described earlier, are not done by the method at present under consideration.

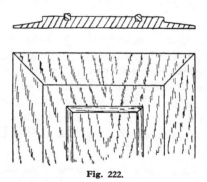

Fig. 222.

The fence may also be used to make the groove for a cock bead on a panel as shown in Fig. 222. It is best to cut the groove before the fielding (*i.e.*, the rabbeting) is done. On the straight grain there may be no difficulty in getting a clean cut, but on the cross grain the fibres should be cut first fairly deeply with a sharp cutting gauge, or with the slitter of the multi-Plane No. 405, Fig. 189, and it will not do a lot of harm if the long grain is similarly prepared. Once the groove has got well started the cutter will then do the rest of the cut both horizontally and vertically.

Precisely the same method can be applied to cut the shallow grooves for inlaid bandings, which are later glued into the grooves. In both this case and that of cock beads it is as well for cutter and bead or banding to be of the same width. We have earlier mentioned the inlaying of shapes (shells, fan corners, etc., are typical examples). Both these and inlaid bands should be glued in and then pressed home with the hammer, as in laying a veneer, and there is a great temptation to scrape all up level as soon as the gluing is completed. The desire to do this is perfectly natural, but the temptation must be steadfastly resisted, because the glue (and possibly the wetted wood) shrinks on drying, and unless the job is given time enough to dry out (say 24 hours) before scraping, the inlay is very likely to sink below the rest of the work.

Fig. 223.—Record Router Plane No. 722.

Record Router Plane No. 722 is a small but very useful router which is provided with one cutter only $\frac{1}{4}$ in. wide. Its base measures approximately $2\frac{7}{8}$ in. $\times 1\frac{7}{8}$ in., and the cutter is very positively secured by means of a drawbolt. There is no need to screw this up more than finger-tight. The cutter can be arranged normally or as for bull-nosed work, and it will be set by sight as required, there being no screw adjustment to the cutter as in the larger 071. Where work of a small nature is encountered, as in small grooves and in the groundings of carved work and lettering, Router No. 722 will prove of inestimable value, and it has been noticed that with the increasing scarcity of timber and its consequent higher cost there has been a tendency to use thinner sections of wood, and the use of the router No. 722 has increased with this practice. As we have noticed with the larger router, a smoother surface is left when the router cutter is used on the skew, and this applies equally with the smaller router. Where the groove or recess is wider than the cutter, a skew cut is fairly simple; but if groove and cutter are the same width, a skew cut is impossible, and a straight cut and a light shaving will be called for.

Enough examples have been given to indicate the value of Record routers in overcoming not only those difficulties which gave rise to the Old Woman's Tooth, but also many others which the old lady's dental equipment is utterly incapable of tackling, and to show that the modern iron Router, with its screw adjustment, its cranked cutters of various sizes and shapes, its adjustable fence, its use for open or closed mouth, is indeed a precision tool of the highest grade, without which no woodworker's kit can be considered complete.

Chapter 17

Record Fibreboard Planes

When it was realised that throughout the world timber was being used up at a faster rate than it was being grown, various substitutes made their appearance. At first these were looked upon with suspicion by the craftsman, and it must be admitted that at first the substitutes left something to be desired, but as more experience was gained both by manufacturers and users, teething troubles were overcome, and these new materials have now a seemingly permanent place in the scheme of things. This is no place in which to sketch the development and uses of plywoods, built-up boards, fibreboards, hardboards and the various plastics which are being used in places where at one time only wood was used, or the relative advantages and disadvantages of the one over the other. Suffice it to say that new techniques have been, and are being, evolved to meet the newer circumstances, and new tools are called for to complete these techniques.

Hardboard and fibreboard are being increasingly used for covering comparatively large areas quickly and economically, and in response to the demand from the building trade and particularly the shop fitting section of it, two planes have now been designed for these materials, the Record Fibreboard Planes No. 730 and No. 735. In two respects these planes differ from the conventional plane—(a) they are "one cut" planes and not "shaving by shaving" planes; (b) they are provided with razor blade type expendable blades which are quickly and economically replaced as they become blunt. (For hard or tempered board, perspex and the like, as we shall see later, No. 735 has an additional thicker blade which is sharpened by normal methods.)

Record Soft and Hardboard Plane No. 735 can be used on all types of soft insulating board and on hard or tempered board. On soft insulating board it will bevel up to $\frac{3}{8}$ in. deep at 45°; using the grooving attachment it will groove up to $\frac{3}{8}$ in. deep; and it will slit up to $\frac{1}{2}$ in. thickness. On hard or tempered board it will bevel up to $\frac{3}{16}$ in. deep at 45°. Besides the grooving attachment it is supplied with a detachable fence, and six razor blade type cutters (for softboard), and one cutter for hardboard. The length of the tool is $10\frac{1}{4}$ in. and its weight $2\frac{7}{8}$ lbs.

Record Softboard Plane No. 730 is a simple dual purpose plane designed to slit and bevel all types of soft insulating boards, and its capacity in this respect is similar to No. 735, *i.e.* it will slit up to $\frac{1}{2}$ in. thick and bevel up to $\frac{3}{8}$ in. deep at 45° but it has no provision for grooving, and it is not provided with a special blade for hardboard, etc.

Fig. 224.—Record Soft and Hardboard Plane No. 735.
Showing hardboard cutter in position and (*right*) grooving attachment.

Fig. 225.—Record Softboard Plane No. 730.

In length it is rather shorter than No. 735, being $8\frac{1}{4}$ in. long, and its weight is approximately $1\frac{1}{2}$ lbs. It is provided with a fence.

Spare cutters for both planes are readily available, the razor blade type (suitable for both No. 730 and No. 735) being packed in half dozens, and the hardboard cutters, which are suitable for No. 735 only, being packed singly.

In both planes the body carries two cutter stations, one holding the blade vertically for slitting, and the other holding the blade at 45° for bevelling. In either position the blade is secured by clamps (Figs. 226 and 227E).

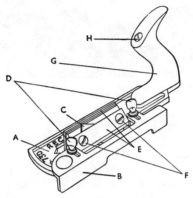

A Body, **B** Fence, **D** Thumb Screws with Washers for Fence (2), **E** Cutter Clamps (2), **F** Screws for Cutter Clamps (4), **G** Handle, **H** Bolt and Nut with Washer for Handle, **C** Cutters (6 razor blade type).

Fig. 226.—Record Softboard Plane No. 730, showing the parts.

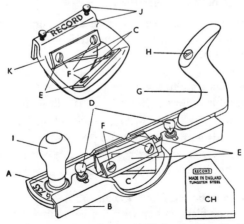

A Body, **B** Fence, **D** Thumb Screws with Washers for Fence (2), **E** Cutter Clamps (2), **F** Screws for Cutter Clamps (4), **G** Handle, **H** Bolt and Nut with Washer for Handle, **I** Knob with Screw, **C** Razor Blade Cutters, **CH** Hardboard Cutter. **Grooving Attachment**—**K** Body, **E** Cutter Clamps (2), **F** Screws for Cutter Clamps (4), **J** Depth Adjusting Screws (2).

Fig. 227.—Record Soft and Hardboard Plane No, 735, showing the parts.

Similarly, both planes are provided with a fence (Figs. 226 and 227B) which can be adjusted laterally and secured by the Thumb Screws (D) and washers.

The grooving attachment is supplied only with Record Plane No. 735 and is shown in Fig. 227.

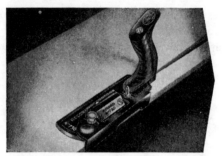

Fig. 228.—Record No. 730 slitting soft insulating board.

For Slitting Softboard (No. 730 and 735)

Insert razor blade cutter into the vertical or slitting station, as in bevelling allow as much "trail" on the cutter as possible (see Fig. 227C) in order that the maximum amount of edge will be cutting, and also adjust to correct depth. For removing narrow strips, adjust the fence as required and proceed to take a steady cut, keeping the fence up to the work with the left hand. When slitting away from the edge, remove the fence and secure a straight edge to the board to act as a guide. Always cut over a soft surface so as not to damage the cutter.

Another way of slitting when the cut is away from the edge calls for rather more skill but dispenses with the straight edge. Strike out the line cleanly with a pencil and then make the cut steadily, keeping the point of the V opening of the slot (see A, Fig. 226) always on the marked line. It is more accurate to use a straight edge; but for many purposes the visual method is quite satisfactory, and is a little quicker.

When first using the tool, make a point of putting slightly more pressure downwards with the right hand than with the left. Too much pressure on the nose may cause the front edge of the sole to dig in. Control of the tool is easy but a little practise is necessary.

For Bevelling Softboard (Nos. 730 and 735)

Insert the razor blade cutter with the larger bevel uppermost (*i.e.* with the word Record showing) into the bevelling station. Allow as much "trail" as possible (see Fig. 227C) in order that the maximum amount of edge will be cutting. Adjust the depth of cut. The angle of the bevel will remain constant at 45°. Move the fence laterally until the desired

Fig. 229.—Razor Blade type cutter in position bevelling soft board.

amount of bevel is obtained. The setting can be checked by taking a sight along the base of the plane when holding a piece of the material in position. Make a steady continuous cut, holding the fence well up to the edge all the time with the left hand.

Fig. 230.—Record Plane No. 735 bevelling hardboard.

For Bevelling Hardboard, etc. (No. 735 only)

Insert the thicker cutter in the bevelling station, set the depth and fence as with bevelling softboard, described above, and then proceed to cut.

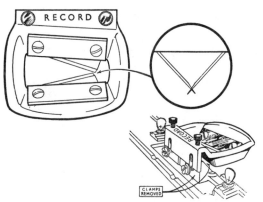

Fig. 231.—Grooving attachment for softboard for Record Plane No. 735.

191

For Grooving Softboard (No. 735 only)

Two cutters will be necessary, and one of these will be placed slightly in advance of the other, so that the tips of the cutters may overlap (see inset, Fig. 231) this resulting in a clean cut at the bottom of the groove. Both cutter clamps will now be removed from the plane and the grooving attachment fitted, using the long screws provided for this purpose.

The depth of the groove is determined by moving the attachment up or down by means of the knurled screws.

A straight edge is attached to the work to act as a guide, the sole of the plane is kept flat on the board, and keeping the tool close up to the straight edge, a steady continuous cut is made (Fig. 232).

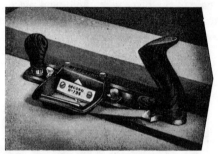

Fig. 232.—Record No. 735 making a groove.

So long as the sole of the plane is kept clean, it will not leave any marks on the work.

The softboard cutters can be replaced as they become blunt, but the hardboard cutters may be ground and sharpened as in the normal way, similarly to spokeshave cutters; and Record Edge Tool Honer No. 161 can be used advantageously for the honing. (See page 58.)

Chapter 18

Spokeshaves

Whilst the name spokeshave is sufficiently indicative of its original use, it is such a handy tool that it must have been used quite a long time ago for many other purposes than the making of wheel spokes in wood; and indeed, if its uses today were classified, the making of spokes would nowadays occupy a very lowly place insomuch as the wheelwright's craft has undergone many changes. The tool today will still be found of course in the wheelwright's shop, but the carpenter and joiner, the cabinet-maker and the patternmaker, and above all the chair-maker, probably use the tool more than the wheelwright. And surely the chair-maker must be born with a spokeshave in his hand—his skill with it is unsurpassable.

The older wooden stock of the spokeshave has largely given way today to its metal counterpart. The wooden stock, usually made of box or beech, is very subject to wear, the bearing surface being so small; and the constant in and out action of the tangs resulted in a slack fit which was often remedied by cutting a screw thread on them, the subsequent adjustment being made by nuts. As with the very early attempts to improve the plane, the effects of wear on the sole were often minimised by the screwing on of a brass sole.

Not until the advent of the iron spokeshave, however, were the disadvantages of the wooden spokeshave satisfactorily overcome. By casting the bodies in iron, production and consequently initial cost to the user, was relatively cheap. A sole, flat or round, could be easily machined, and then for the rest of the life of the tool, it would require no more thought or attention. The blades could be made in such a manner that sharpening on the grindstone and the oilstone were quite easy—which certainly could not be claimed for the cranked blades of the wooden spokeshaves. A fine (micrometer almost) screw adjustment of the cut was possible; and a firm yet easy to work attachment of the cutting unit to the stock was possible. The handles could be scientifically shaped so that hand and wrist action resulted in the minimum amount of fatigue; and finally, the tool could have a very long life. Initial disadvantage of the fragile nature of a cast iron body was then eliminated by the employment of malleable castings which are virtually unbreakable.

The range of Record Spokeshaves embraces both flat and round soles—the flat sole being used for working convex curves and the round sole for concave curves. Some spokeshaves are adjustable for thickness of shaving by screw adjustment, whilst others have no such adjustment and must be "set" by sight and experience. Some are made of cast iron (these are naturally somewhat fragile owing to the nature of the material) whilst others are of malleable iron—able to withstand with impunity any accidental fall without breaking. All have tungsten steel cutters which are easy to sharpen; they are not of course as long as a plane blade but no difficulty will arise from this source if a simple jig is made on the lines of Fig. 280, page 226. The veriest tyro (and many other more experienced workers too) will find Record 161 Edge Tool Honer of great assistance in the honing of these shorter cutters. Record Cast iron spokeshaves are designated with O to preface the number whilst unbreakable spokeshaves are prefaced with A; thus Record Spokeshave 0151 is a cast iron tool, painted blue, whilst Record Spokeshave A151 is unbreakable, and painted a bright red. The numbers, being identical, will indicate that the design is similar; the colour of the paint will indicate the material of which each is made.

Fig. 233.—Record A63 Round Face.   Fig. 234.—Record A64 Flat Face.

One of the simplest spokeshaves, light in weight (approx. half a pound) and very easy to handle even on long runs is the straight handled A63 which has a round face, and its counterpart A64 with a flat face. Both are of course unbreakable and not only are they good tools for **any** worker, they are eminently suited, by their design and weight for use in a school workshop. The cutters are held in place by a lever cap which is secured by a single thumb screw; and depth of cut may be set by sight or feel. A very useful way to "set" A64 spokeshave is to hold the sole flat on a plane surface—the wing of an 05 jack plane for instance,—and then, having the blade in place with the thumbscrew quite slack, let the edge just touch the plane surface, and then tighten the screw. Ninety-nine times out of a hundred the spokeshave will work nicely: if it doesn't, repeat from the start and it usually does. The round faced A63 can be set similarly; but you will have to experiment a time or two to know which part of the curve to rest on the plane surface. An experienced worker will have no difficulty in setting the cutter by sight or

Fig. 235.—Record spokeshave A51 Flat Face   Fig. 236.—Record spokeshave O51 Flat Face
and A51R Round Face (unbreakable)   and O51R Round Face (cast iron).

touch. (It is remarkable how much an experienced worker "sees" with his finger tips; the distaff side of the family has no monopoly of this skill!)

A larger, heavier (approx. 11 oz.) non-screw adjustable spokeshave is the 051, A51 series. The pattern may be obtained either in cast iron (051 flat, 051R round) or in unbreakable metal (A51 flat, A51R round) — the cast being recognisable by its blue colour, the unbreakable by its red colour. The cast iron is slightly cheaper in price, but the unbreakable is more strongly recommended. Whilst the handles of A63 and A64, which we considered earlier, are straight, the handles of the 051 and A51 are raised slightly. It is a pattern which is capable of very good work— the depth of cut must be set as we have noted for the A63 and A64.

Fig. 237.—Record Spokeshaves A151.   Fig. 238.—Record Spokeshaves O151
and A151R (unbreakable) and 0151R (cast iron).

One of the most popular spokeshaves in all parts of the world is the Record A151, A151R; and Record O151 and O151R. In basic design they are not very dissimilar to the A51 series we have just discussed; but they have a considerable advantage from many workers in their screw adjustment both vertically and laterally. This adjustment is effected as can be seen from Figs. 237 and 238 by means of two screws. It is advisable to slacken the lever cap thumbscrew slightly (a quarter turn, say) before making an adjustment, and then tighten it. Both screws will raise or lower the cutter, and more or less of either will bring the cutter parallel with the sole. It will be noticed that the lever cap has something of the effect of a cap iron as in a plane. The A series of these spokeshaves (A151, A151R) are unbreakable (painted red) whilst the O series (O151, O151R) are cast iron (painted blue)—the former although slightly more expensive are well worth their extra cost.

Fig. 239.—Record Spokeshave A65, unbreakable and fitted with adjustable wings for
chamfer and stop chamfer work.

Contemporary design has favoured the chamfer and the stopchamfer rather to the detrimf the note multi-membered mouldings, and this has called for a tool which will minimise such work. This tool, the Record Spokeshave No. A65 is shown in Fig. 239 where it will be seen that a straight handled round faced spokeshave, made of unbreakable metal is fitted with two adjustable wings which act as stops and secure a uniform depth of cut and consequent width of chamfer. The blade is not screw adjustable for thickness of shaving, but it is not difficult to set by sight or feel. The wings are quickly adjustable, and the temptation to use a pair of pliers on the adjusting screws must be stoutly resisted. Finger tight is enough to hold them, and when pliers or other mechanical aids are used to further "tighten" the screws, the end of the screw cannot go any deeper and the result is a damaged thread which will then never work satisfactorily. It is usually quicker to set the wings experimentally, trying the tool then on a bit of spare wood, rather than attempt to set them by measurement. A little practice with the tool will soon enable the worker to get good results. When making stopped chamfers a little practice of the wrist action will bring a quicker curve to the stopping which is more satisfying to the eye than a slower curve which is one's first effort. The shadows are more interesting.

Where there is a stopping at each end of the chamfer, the two stoppings may be made first, and then the chamfer worked out, watching the way of the grain; and when the wings have seated themselves on the work and the tool ceases to cut, the chamfer will be found to be pleasantly free from the objectionable waviness which so frequently accompanies such work when done by other methods.

The face of the tool is slightly rounded but this will not detract from its use on straight work, as the wings go a long way towards providing a bearing; and when the wings are removed the tool can be used as a normal round faced spokeshave.

It will have been noticed that a strong recommendation has been made for Record Malleable Iron unbreakable spokeshaves wherever there is a choice between them and their cast iron counterparts. They have been designed for shops where rough usage is prevalent. They will stand up to any knocks or dropping on the hardest floors, even concrete, without harm and they are confidently recommended for hard and lasting service under any conditions, deservedly popular with craftsmen and woodwork instructors all over the world.

USING THE SPOKESHAVE

When using the spokeshave (Fig. 240), if you bear in mind that the tool is a plane, and follow the general idea of planing, you will not have much trouble. In this way you will unconsciously acquire that light touch and wrist action which are essential to good, clean, easy working. Normally, the tool is pushed, but on occasion it may be pulled. Many

Fig. 240.

beginners stumble with spokeshaving because they omit to consider the direction of the grain. A study of Fig. 241, which illustrates a bread board, will show that the curves cannot be spokeshaved right through one way—the cuts must be made in the direction of the arrows, the work

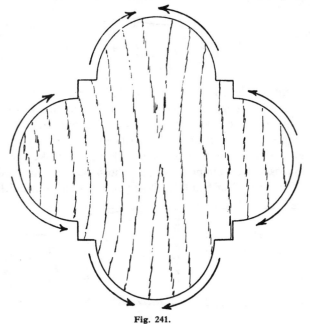

Fig. 241.

either being turned in the vice, or the spokeshave reversed, *i.e.*, pulled or pushed, as demanded by the grain. Another point to watch is one already indicated, *i.e.*, for a convex surface use a flat face; for a concave one, a round face. Thus, in Fig. 241 you want a flat face spokeshave, whereas in a shaping for a Bracket (Fig. 242) a flat face would prevent the cutter from coming into action, and the round face must be used. A

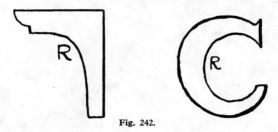

Fig. 242.

round face **can** be used **in a way** on a convexity, but as it has such a small surface in contact it cannot be recommended, a chattering being set up which does not allow for a good, clean cut.

Generally speaking, shapings in cabinet work are best when of a simple nature. Elaborate curves are more laborious to produce, and are not satisfying when they are done. A simple way of striking out a free curve to fit a particular space, say, an apron piece, is by folding a piece of brown paper (which, when opened is the size of the opening) in

Fig. 243.

half; striking out the half curve as indicated in Fig. 243 by the dotted line, and cutting through the folded paper on the line with scissors. On opening out, you have a symmetrical curve which you can try by placing the paper in position on the job. If satisfactory, use it as a template: if it does not satisfy, it is only a moment's work either to make a new scissor cut, or to make a new template. Using the same idea, but folding the paper in four instead of two (Fig. 244) you can strike out quickly and

Fig. 244.

198

easily, most pleasing and original shapes for occasional tables, etc., either from squares or rectangles.

Chamfers or rounds can be done with the spokeshave on curved edges. If it is desired to mould a curved edge, this is best done with a scratch tool after spokeshaving to outline.

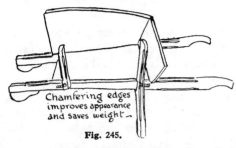

Chamfering edges improves appearance and saves weight.

Fig. 245.

Apart from curved edges, the spokeshave is called into use for reducing diameters as, for instance, the shaping of the handles of a wheelbarrow or bottle-neck shapes. An intelligent use of the spokeshave in chamfering and stop chamfering on a wheelbarrow will not only improve its appearance, but will reduce the dead weight to be pushed, without impairing the strength of the construction (Fig. 245). The spokeshave can be used for "wagon" moulding, where a drawknife is not available.

Fig. 246 shows a number of shapings which are typical spokeshave work:—

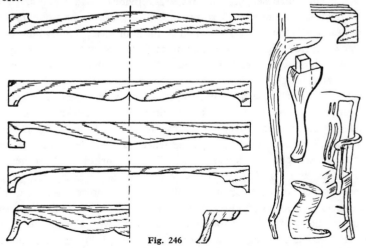

Fig. 246

Curved surfaces which are of too wide an area to be worked with a spokeshave are worked with an adjustable circular plane (see Chapter 15). Indeed, where the curve must be regular and geometrically accurate (as, for example, true circles for cart wheels), the circular plane is almost a necessity.

Chapter 19

Finishing

The greater attention which is being given to the finished surfaces of cabinet work, shop fitting, etc., calls for more consideration of the tools and processes by which this is accomplished. Work left from the plane, however well it may appear in "the white" is always apt to show variations of reflected light when highly polished; and plane strokes which show up in this manner indicate a lack of finish not consistent with the best workmanship. When articles have to be highly finished with shiny surfaces as with French polish, Cellulose, Varnish or Waxing, the surface must be scraped clean of all marks left by the plane, and every blemish of the grain, no matter how small and insignificant it may appear before polishing, must be smoothed out, for the process of polishing will intensify the character of the unevenness owing to the play of reflected light to such an extent as to mar the whole effect. The need for a scraper was felt from the very early times and its use is by no means a modern invention. The Romans knew it as the "radula"; in one form or another it has been used through the ages. A piece of glass has been used for this purpose, but this has very obvious disadvantages. The early Egyptians scoured their work after the fashion of the stone mason. Old-time craftsmen used a rectangular piece of steel, upon which they worked a burred edge; and up to a point this makes quite a good scraper. It is only those whose work has caused them to scrape for days—or even hours—at a stretch who really know how very uncomfortable this type of scraper can be; those who have used it for short spells have some indication. Thus many types of handle and other devices have been tried towards the improvement of the tool, and have as often been discarded. The worker finds by experience that in order to get the best results—to work out quickly and easily slight blemishes here and there—it is necessary to "spring" the blade to a curve; and the majority of the devices to lessen the labour of scraping have taken no cognisance of this fact—hence their relegation sooner or later. The "springing" of the blade in the old-fashioned tool is accomplished with the thumbs; and the very action of using the scraper creates enough heat at this spot to make the thumbs uncomfortably hot. The scraper blade moreover has always a tendency to follow irregularities, and leave a "waviness" unless a good deal of skill is employed in the application; and most of the handles which have appeared from time to time have intensified rather than eradicated this defect.

Fig. 247.—Record 080 Cabinet Scraper.

The Record 080 Scraper has been so designed that the very real disadvantages above discussed have been eliminated. The design of the handles is such that a firm hold may be taken without the least suspicion of cramp or fatigue. They are raised away from the tool so that a finger cut from a sharp arris—common enough with the old type —is an impossibility. The thumbs are not required to spring the blade, for this function is performed by a thumb screw, positive in action and untiring in effort. The pressure of the screw, and with it the variation of curvature, is fine in adjustment, and regular in action. It is practically impossible for the scraper to follow a wavy course (e.g., as after some machine planing) for the generous proportion of the sole of the tool acts in the same way as does the sole of a plane—and high spots are scraped off before the lower ones are touched when the tool is used with a long stroke. The character of the burr which forms the scraping edge being formed from a keen 45° edge, is considerably sharper in action than that formed in the old way from a 90° edge. Hence, with all these factors taken into consideration it is not at all surprising to find that the Record 080 Scraper works very easily and comfortably, and speeds up the operation of scraping to an almost unbelievable extent. The ease of operation indeed is one of the stumbling blocks of the old hand when confronted with this tool; he is accustomed with the old type to a laborious process, and is very apt to put an equal amount of work into the Record Scraper. This is neither advantageous nor necessary. So long as the tool is kept in contact with the work and propelled forward, the tool can be trusted to do its work provided that it is properly sharpened and set. The work with this tool is done best with a very minimum of effort on the part of the user.

The form of the tool is such that, with the changing of the blade for a toothing cutter, with either coarse or fine teeth, it is immediately converted into a very reliable toothing plane; very much ahead of the wooden variety of that tool which is in common use. In these days when veneering is so much to the fore and has every appearance of becoming more popular in the future, a toothing plane of some sort is fast becoming a necessary item of the tool kit of an ever-widening circle of woodworkers. The 080 Scraper, used with a toothing cutter, forms a most efficient toothing plane. For notes on toothing and veneering, see page 207.

Those unaccustomed to a 45° scraper edge may perhaps feel a little disconcerted at first in the sharpening of the tool; but they should not have any great difficulty. To the old hand who has been used to a 90° edge we would say: first get a keen honed edge at 45° (without any second bevel) and then burnish and turn that edge as with a 90° edge. That should be sufficient to put him on the right track. The edge cannot be too keenly honed on the oilstone. The beginner, or the man who finds difficulty in sharpening a scraper (and there are many such) should follow out the detail given here, step by step:—

TO REMOVE BLADE

Slacken all three screws and lift out blade.

TO SHARPEN A NEW BLADE

1.—The edge must be sharpened on the oilstone at the same bevel, *i.e.*, 45°, as it is ground. This edge must be as keen as possible, but there must be no second bevel as with a plane iron. Use a fine stone.

Fig. 248.—Honing to 45° bevel.

2.—When removing wire edge keep flat side of blade absolutely free from any bevel.

3.—Slightly rounding off the corners of the blade as with a smoothing plane blade is advantageous if not overdone.

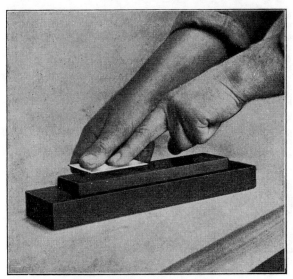

Fig. 249.—"Wiping-off" wire edge.

4.—Place blade flat on the bench, ground side downwards, and with a burnisher burnish to and fro (say 20 to 30 times) pressing quite

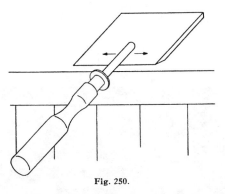

Fig. 250.

hard, but making sure all the time that the burnisher lies dead flat on the blade; *on no account must this burnishing turn the edge over*—it is done to consolidate the metal. If the edge is turned at this stage, the next operation will break the fine edge finally required.

5.—Set up the blade in a vice, ground edge towards the operator. Commencing with the burnisher directly on the 45° bevel, burnish to and fro, again bearing hard. As the burnishing proceeds, raise the handle by gentle stages until the burnisher makes an angle of 15° with the horizontal. Some 30 to 50 strokes may be needed, depending upon the amount of pressure put upon the strokes.

Fig. 251.—Burnishing Flat Side.

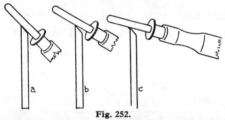

Fig. 252.

Fig. 253.—Burnishing Bevel Edge.

204

6.—The burnisher will work better and give better results if slightly lubricated.

The edge should now have a definite burr which can be felt with the tips of the fingers.

TO SHARPEN A BLADE WHICH HAS BEEN USED

First remove all burr from the flat side with a dead smooth file, taking care to keep this side perfectly flat and avoiding any suggestion of bevel.

Next, file with a similar file, or grind, the edge to 45°. This angle is important.

Fig. 254.—Filing to a 45° Bevel.

Then proceed as for sharpening a new blade.

Each time the blade is sharpened, the old burr must be removed, and a new keen edge honed and burnished.

TO ASSEMBLE AND USE

Place the body of the tool sole downwards on a flat surface. With all three screws quite slack insert the blade burred side to the front, *i.e.,* the same side as the *two* screws; bevelled side towards the single screw.

Tighten the two retaining screws, using a nail as a Tommy bar. *The back adjusting screw must be quite slack during this operation.*

The scraper may or may not give a cut now. If it does not cut, screw the adjusting screw until it just gets a "feel", and try a cut. The harder the adjusting screw is tightened, the coarser will be the shaving produced, and *vice versa*. The best surface is obtained naturally from a light cut.

HINTS FOR BEST RESULTS

1.—As with all iron tools, slight lubrication of the sole improves the working; and the tool itself improves with use. Oil or paraffin wax (a wax candle) may be used as a lubricant.

Fig. 255.—Using the 080 Record Scraper.

2.—The best way to use the tool is diagonally to the grain.

3.—Use the tool *lightly*. It requires considerably less effort than ordinary scrapers, and hard work with this tool is neither advantageous nor necessary.

4.—The tool properly sharpened and used gives a definite shaving. If dust only comes away the blade wants sharpening. Thin, silky, long and wide shavings indicate proper sharpening and working.

5.—When honing, aim at a very keen edge; when burnishing hold firmly and make firm, deliberate strokes.

6.—Record 080 Scraper will give a perfectly clean finish to any hardwood, however curly the grain may be; if you are not getting such results, read the instructions and carry them out step by step. When properly sharpened, it will clean up a panel straight from the saw if need be.

7.—Burnisher should be harder than the Scraper Iron so that it will turn the edge. The burnisher should be kept polished and free from rust and scratches.

TOOTHING CUTTERS

The object of toothing is twofold—first to remove any irregularity left by the plane on the ground which might result in unwanted high lights on the veneer after the polishing; second, to give a better "bite" to the glue.

Fig. 256.—Toothing Blade.

The toothing cutter requires an occasional rub on the oilstone, bevelled side only, keeping the same angle. Setting and using are similar to the operations for scraping. The ground should be toothed diagonally both ways. Thin knife cut veneers require no toothing; thicker saw cut veneers may be toothed if desirable in the same way as the ground. Remove dust before applying glue.

The worker using a Record 080 Scraper will find added advantage in the character of the surface which is left by the tool when he applies stain, polish, etc., because the lightness of the operation does not "push down" the grain to the same extent as with a scraper on which considerable pressure is used. In the latter case much trouble is frequently encountered in subsequent stages by the grain rising, necessitating further careful sanding. The processes of polishing by various methods do not fall within the province of this book, but space enough might be found, perhaps, to indicate one sound and durable finish for oak, walnut, etc., in its natural colour:—

i. Scrape clean and free from blemish with Record 080 Scraper.

ii. Burnish the surfaces first with clean shavings, second with a piece of clean hessian, until a dull shine covers them.

iii. (Optional, but labour saving). Give a rubbing all over with white French polish, using a fairly wet rubber and working in the main across the grain. Leave overnight; and then lightly wipe over with a piece of worn No. 0 glass paper to ease any ridges of shellac.

iv. Finely shred a piece of beeswax, cover it with petrol, stir it with a stick until it is like "warm weather" butter (about 10-15 minutes). Rub this all over the surfaces with a piece of hessian.

v. After 15-20 minutes polish off with a soft duster free from fluff, holding it loosely and lightly, but rubbing rapidly.

If a perfectly smooth surface is desired, with the pores of the grain filled, after burnishing with the hessian the grain should be filled with a colourless grain filler—best bought ready made and used according to the directions given with it. After the grain filler has set it is wise then to use the white polish prior to the waxing. The character of oak is such that it looks best if the grain is not filled.

THE BOX SCRAPER

Fig. 257.—Record 070 Box Scraper.

This is a tool which has a great use in removing stencil marks, etc., from packing-cases and the like, and will be found of service in removing knotty unevenness of floors. It is handily constructed with a long hinged handle, and the cutter and bottom being slightly curved, the Scraper is able to cut on uneven surfaces.

The blade is sharpened on an oilstone, retaining the original curve, preferably keeping to the one bevel which eliminates the need for grinding. There is no need to burr the edge as with the 080 Cabinet Scraper.

Chapter 20

The Bench and the Vice

Every craftsman has his own ideas on the design of benches, and their variety is great, so much depending upon the general nature of the work to be done on them. A bench that is eminently suitable in a carpenter's shop might not be so in a skilled amateur's shop; a cabinet maker's bench would often be found awkward by a joiner; the wheelwright's bench would suit neither of them. But all craftsmen would agree on certain points. Any bench must have a firm and sturdy frame; have a top free from any suggestion of springiness; be of suitable height so that unnecessary stooping or reaching is avoided; the bench vice must be up to its work; after that, individuals begin to differ. One will prefer a flat top to one that has a well; another will have a cupboard; another drawers; yet others will prefer to have the space under the bench free from either; and so on. It would not be possible to meet everyone's ideas, and the bench we show here is put forward as a suggestion, incorporating the results of many years' experience, and it may be varied considerably by the maker and user according to his own fancy, experience and needs. Nothing less than 3 in. × 3 in. is sturdy enough for the legs; and $3\frac{1}{2}$ in. × $3\frac{1}{2}$ in. is better, especially for the front legs (for unlike the majority of legs, these are to prevent movement, not to accelerate it!) 3 in. × 3 in. should be used for the end rails, top and bottom, but the side rails may be reduced to 3 in. × $2\frac{1}{2}$ in. Red or good white deal may be used for this framing. As the back legs are splayed, the best way to approach the setting out is to make a full sized drawing, preferably on a sheet of plywood, and from it take sizes and bevels for the mortise and tenon joints, which should be through and wedged. The height of the bench will vary as the stroke of the worker, but it may be taken as somewhere between 2 ft. 6 in. and 2 ft. 8 in. The top front board should be not less than 2 in. thick, and this thickness must be allowed for in setting out the frame. Width from back to front will vary according to the work to be done, and the room available. Two feet is a very scant minimum; 2 ft. 9 in. is a useful width. The bench should be as long as possible, four feet being taken as a minimum useful length, six feet being better. The side rails are through tenoned and wedged to the end frames, leaving sufficient room at the top to accommodate the vice, and enough room at the bottom for the toes of the worker.

(If a portable bench is under construction, the end frames should be made up, glued and wedged, and the rails can be tenoned and dove-tailed as in Fig. 258. Whilst the wedge is in, the tenon cannot move, and to dismantle, the wedge is removed and the tenon drawn up and out.)

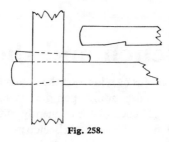

Fig. 258.

The front board of the top should be of 2 in. or $2\frac{1}{2}$ in. well seasoned birch or beech, clamped at both ends as indicated, and 12 in. or so in width, though 9 in. will do if the wider board is not available, or if it is not desired to join boards together. If birch is not available, the top may be of good red deal, with a slip of hardwood about 2 in. wide as a facing on the front edge. In any case it must be planed dead true, as if in winding or in warp it will be difficult to do much planing on it. The back part of the top, which forms the well, can be of red deal an inch thick. The spline at the back is screwed to the back of the top, and serves to prevent tools, etc. from rolling off and also gives a level base for a wide carcase under construction. The top is secured to the frame by coach screws inserted from the underside.

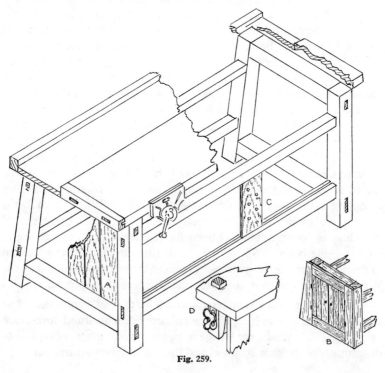

Fig. 259.

210

Having chosen the vice to be fitted to the bench, and preferably one of ample size to suit the work contemplated, and also bearing in mind that wood faces must be fitted to the gripping faces of the jaws, the craftsman must decide whether the wood face of the back jaw is to stand proud of the front edge of the bench, or whether he prefers the face to be level with the front edge. In either case the same method of fitting can be adopted.

The wood faces should be prepared, being of sound hardwood such as well seasoned beech, planed true and parallel, not less than $\frac{1}{2}$ in. thick and the grain set vertically. If the faces stand $\frac{3}{8}$ in. or $\frac{1}{2}$ in. above the top edge of the iron jaws they will save much damage to saws and plane irons. The necessary holes for fixing the wood faces to the vice are tapped ready for $\frac{5}{16}$ in. Whitworth screws, which should have counter-sunk heads so that the inner faces are flush. The faces being screwed in place, it will be evident how much the front edge of the bench will have to be recessed, this depending upon the amount of forward projection desired. Packing pieces may then be required between the underside of the bench top and the body of the vice, the size of these depending upon the thickness of the bench top. When these packing pieces have been fitted the vice can be attached either by coach screws entered from underneath, or by bolts and nuts passing through the bench top. In the latter case the bolt head should preferably be sunk below the level of the bench top, the recess thus made being filled with a wood plug, glued and planed flush. Unless the bench top is very thin coach screws are quite satisfactory.

Many craftsmen prefer a bench which is fitted with a face board, usually about $1\frac{1}{4}$ in. or $1\frac{1}{2}$ in. thick. The face board runs the length of the bench, and may rest underneath the top or be fitted flush as in Fig. 260, and is secured to the front legs by stout screws or bolts. The front of the bench is thus braced up and the whole assembly is very rigid. Fixing a Record vice to this type of bench may be done in several

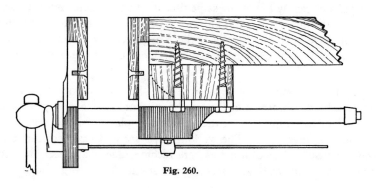

Fig. 260.

ways, but probably the best way is to fit the back jaw behind the face board. The method will be clear from Fig. 260 and description on page 212.

Fitting a Vice to Bench fitted with Face board

1. Prepare and fit hardwood face piece to front jaw of vice, preferably letting it project about $\frac{1}{2}$ in. above top of vice jaws (Fig. 260). Grain to run vertically.

2. Partially dismantle the vice. These instructions must be carefully followed. Extract the cotter pin from the end of the screw, depress the quick release trigger and tie it securely to the neck of the screw with string or tape. Remove the back bracket and draw out the whole of the sliding jaw. Leave the string or tape in place.

3. Place the back jaw in position on the inside of the face board, mark out and cut recess (mortise) in underside of bench top. This recess should be deep enough to leave about $\frac{1}{2}$ in. of wood between the top of the back jaw and the top of the bench.

4. Use the back jaw as a template for boring holes for the mainscrew and the steel runner guides, and for the quick release blade. Alternatively a cardboard template can be made from the back jaw and this can be used to mark the front of the face board—this is easier than working from the back.

5. The back jaw casting can now be placed in position on the bench, and it will be evident what packing pieces are required between it and the bench top. When these have been made and bored the casting can be secured with coach screws, making sure that the jaw fits closely to the back of the face board.

6. Re-assembling the vice. Allowing the string or tape (par. 2 above) to remain in place, insert the ends of the slides and screw through the holes in the face board into the holes in the Vice back jaw, pushing gently but at the same time guiding the quick release blade into the nut slot and nut guide. When the back bracket and cotter pin have been re-assembled, the string securing the quick release trigger to the screw neck can be removed, and the vice is ready for use.

By this method it will be noticed that the effective vice opening is reduced by the thickness of the face board, but if the vice is selected as advised, *i.e.*, of ample size for the work contemplated, this will not prove a serious disadvantage. The working parts are well screened from dirt and sawdust, and vices fitted as here recommended have been in hard service for many years with scarcely any attention.

When the top board is of soft wood, in the course of years of working, the constant pressure of the vice tends to make the part forming the back jaw hollow, and for that reason, if the tops cannot be of hardwood, they should have a slip of hardwood about 2 in. × 2 in. fitted to the front edge, which will minimise this wear. If this slip cannot go all the length of the bench (which is better) it should be fitted a little longer than the width of the vice, let in dovetail fashion.

The skeleton of the bench being complete, and work possible, the worker may improve on it to his own ideas. If prior to assembly plough grooves are run on the inner faces of the two front rails, a piece of wood, bored at intervals as indicated may be inserted. A peg of hardwood in one of the holes will support the free end of a long board whilst it is being planed on the edge. The board will slide along to suit varying lengths of work. If the upper groove is $\frac{1}{2}$ in. deep and the lower one $\frac{1}{4}$ in. deep, and the panel only $\frac{1}{2}$ in. longer than the distance between the rails, the panel may be removed easily by pushing upwards and outwards and withdrawing the bottom first. If at a later time it is desired to fit a floor and matchboard the sides, shutters can be fitted in the grooves in the same way.

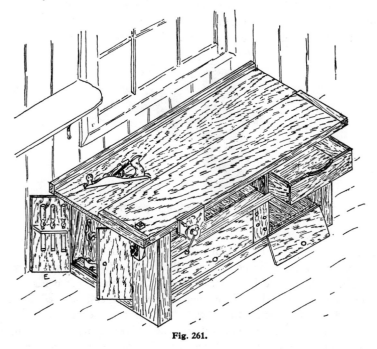

Fig. 261.

The ends may have matchboards nailed on from the inside as shown at A (Fig. 259) and a shallow cupboard can thus be completed for tools, etc., by hanging two doors on the outside. It would be better to do this by nailing a frame on the outside as at B (Fig. 259) for if the doors are hung as at E (Fig. 261) they will be inconvenient when the floor is covered with shavings. Toolracks may be fitted to the inner surfaces of these doors, and the tool rack may form the batten for the door Alternatively, the doors can be made of a single piece of $\frac{3}{8}$ in. or $\frac{1}{2}$ in. plywood, or of laminated wood.

There is no dearth of ideas for bench stops, most woodworkers having their own opinions on this subject. The roughest makeshift is a stout screw, the head of which projects sufficiently to steady the work in hand; somewhat better is a strip of wood nailed on the bench top crosswise, the nail heads being punched below the surface. Mechanical devices of many types have appeared for adjusting the height of the stop above the bench top, and of these, the worst from a practical point of view are those (however ingenious and perfect their mechanism) which have iron projections on the top of the bench. Apart from the injury they often inflict on the work, they are an ever-present source of danger to tool edges. The best pattern shows wood only above the bench, is easily and quickly adjusted, and remains rigid once an adjustment is made. The practical man will immediately appreciate the simple straightforward efficiency of Record Bench Stop No. 169. (Fig. 262) and it is sound advice to have one of these fitted to any good bench.

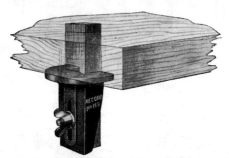

Fig. 262.—Record Bench Stop No. 169.

A mortise 1 in. × 1$\frac{1}{2}$ in., which is best marked out from the hardwood stop, is cut through the bench top. The fit should not be too slack, a nice sliding fit should be aimed at. The hardwood block being fitted in position, the metal guide is then offered to it and secured on the underside of the bench with screws. The wing nut secures the stop in any position. For maximum stiffness, the hardwood block should abut on the outer side of the bench leg; and for convenience, obstructions should be avoided so that the hand has ready access to the wing nut. The provision of a second stop 3 in. to 6 in. from the first, and in line at right angles to the face edge of the bench, is a convenience when planing and cleaning up wide boards. For the same purpose, a piece of $\frac{7}{16}$ in. hardwood (*e.g.*, birch) about 7 in. × 4 in., mortised so as to fit over the bench stop at one end, and provided at the other with a $\frac{3}{4}$ in. dowel which drops into a hole in the bench top, has been used with success. The 7 in. bearing will steady a very wide board, a table top, etc.

Many workers adopt a plan which considerably lengthens the life of a bench top, and keeps it always free from nails, chips from tools and other blemishes. On the top of the front board of the top they set a "panel" board, *i.e.*, one cut from the heart of the tree which will not warp, mortising a hole through it for the bench stop. Planing and other work is done on this, and nails and fillets can be put into it and fastened to it whilst leaving the true bench top always in good condition for special work, etc. A similar device will frequently give a new life to a very worn bench top.

The shaking and rattling to which tools are subjected when in a bench drawer is not good for their edges or appearance, but a drawer is a useful adjunct to a bench. If fitted as indicated, its front will be flush with the front of the bench, and a handle would be in the way. This can be overcome by spokeshaving a hollow at the top as shown, into which the hand fits so that the drawer can be withdrawn. For easy removal of the panels, finger holes may be bored.

In the choice of a vice, the craftsman has the benefit of the accumulated experience of many years of vice manufacture. Record vices are the original and genuine steel slide vices which are well known by woodworkers in every part of the world. The sliding bars are of solid steel, working in accurately machined housings, giving a perfect sliding motion, together with a firm and straight grip, entirely free from any side or cross motion. Thus, when working on accurate work there is a firm yet steady pressure. The craftsman's whole attention can be focused on the work in hand without any distraction from the vice—he uses it almost unconscious of its presence—it works so smoothly and in perfect harmony. By simply squeezing the trigger he may cause the jaw to slide in or out, and the work is held securely by a mere half turn of the lever—yet all is so gentle and free from "snatchiness" that a tightly fitting glued joint may be squeezed up smoothly into position. Record Vices stand up to the most arduous workshop conditions, and are guaranteed to do so; and after many years of hard work they can still be relied on to keep doing their work well.

There are three sizes:—

Width of Jaw	Opening	Weight
7 inches	8 inches	18 lbs.
9 ,,	13 ,,	32 ,,
10½ ,,	15 ,,	35 ,,

The 7 in. vice will take all ordinary work, and would be a suitable vice for the bench above described; but the 9 in. would be better, because it has a wider opening which is most useful for holding work for cleaning up (*e.g.*, a drawer) that the smaller vice could not take, and for cramping overnight. The 10½ in. vice is intended for the largest and heaviest work.

There is a choice of Plain Screw or Quick Grip. The Plain Screw must be screwed in or out all the way; but the Quick Grip has a trigger by means of which the half nut is released from the screw; thus the front jaw can be drawn straight out or in, or part way, instantaneously. As soon as the trigger is released, the nut comes into action again. This device is as useful to the craftsman as a free wheel is to a cyclist; the extra cost is very small, and is well worth while. For boys under instruction, where variations of dimensions of the work attempted are not significant, the plain screw is all right. School workshops may have a majority of plain screw vices, but for the usual run of a woodworker, the 9 in. Quick Grip is advised.

It is not every woodworker, however, who feels the need for a full size vice; for some workers a vice of smaller capacity is suitable, provided that it can be relied upon for service in an equal degree to that given by the larger vices; so that it would obviously be impossible to recommend a vice that would be universally acceptable to all and sundry workers in wood. So with just a reminder that it is good economy when acquiring a vice at any time to choose it so that it is a little over in capacity (rather than under) for the work likely to be attempted, it will probably be of most assistance to the reader of this chapter if a short summary of the principal types available is made. He will then be in a better position to choose the vice most suitable to his particular needs.

A Record No. 53 P., Plain Screw Vice is shown in Fig. 263. This is a solidly made vice with accurate parallel motion, without side play. The slides are of unbreakable steel, and the screw is of the square thread type, with a solid nut—a "screw-all-the-way" vice. For those who do

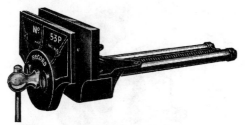

not use the Quick Grip, this is a sound general purpose vice, made in three sizes; 52P. having 7 in. jaws; 52½P., 9 in. jaws; and 53P., 10½ in. jaws.

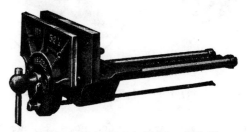

Fig. 264.—Record Quick Grip Woodworker's Vice.

Fig. 264 shows a standard vice, well known and used by woodworkers in every part of the world. It is solidly made, having unbreakable steel slides, even and parallel action, and stout buttress thread. It is fitted with Quick Grip mechanism and continuous screw action, and further important improvements have been incorporated. In order to prevent sawdust, grit, etc., from falling on to the working parts when the vice is fitted with the back jaw outside the bench (a fairly common experience, which may be due to incorrect fitting on the bench, or to natural shrinkage of the top board of the bench) a metal plate is fitted on to the vice body as shown in the upper part of Fig. 265. This is a great protection to the nut mechanism. Where much sawing is done in the vice, and particularly when there is an excess of oil on the screw, there is still a possibility that sawdust may be carried on the screw itself into the nut mechanism, and in course of time an accumulation there may cause uneven action. This may now be rapidly put right by simply removing the two screws of the half-nut bracket, which thus releases the half-nut for cleaning, and subsequent replacement. As will be seen from the lower part of Fig. 265, the operation of removing and replacing

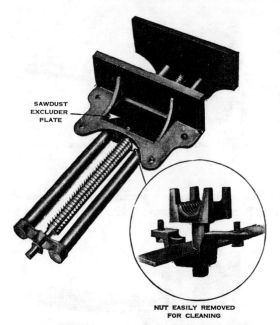

SAWDUST EXCLUDER PLATE

NUT EASILY REMOVED FOR CLEANING

Fig. 265.—Improvements to Record Quick Grip Vices.

the half-nut is simple and quick, and does not necessitate the removal of the vice from the bench. The half-nut should be cleaned occasionally, and lubricated slightly. An excess of oil tends to hold dust and grit. A spot of oil occasionally on the collar of the screw, where it bears on the front jaw is conducive to sweeter working. (The bearing where the end of the screw passes through the back bracket is always out of sight but that must not prevent it from having a little oil applied occasionally.) The two improvements will be greatly appreciated by the practical man, who may have this vice in the same three sizes as the Plain Screw type.

A still further improvement is incorporated in the Record Quick Grip Woodworkers' Vices Nos. 52A, 52½A, and 53A, which are of similar specification to the foregoing two vices, but to which in addition

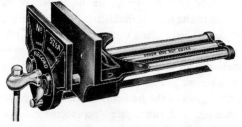

Fig. 266.—Record Quick Grip Vice with Screw and Nut Cover.

is added the Record Screw and Nut cover, extending the full length of the screw. This cover, in the form of a semi-circular hood (Fig. 266), protects both screw and nut from damage, and diverts any sawdust, grit or shavings from falling on to the thread, and thence into the nut mechanism, effectively preventing the choking of these parts. For long, hard and continuous service under any conditions this vice is specially recommended.

Fig. 267.—Record No. 55 Woodcraft Vice.

A vice which will commend itself to the woodworker whose work is of smaller dimensions than that of most professionals is shown in Fig. 267. This, the Record No. 55 Woodcraft Vice, has a similar stout construction to the other vices, but has jaws $6\frac{1}{2}$ in. wide, opening $6\frac{1}{8}$ in. There is perfect parallel action, a substantial square thread, and the slides are of unbreakable steel. Intended for permanent fixing on the bench, it is a screw-all-the-way vice, having no Quick Grip.

A yet smaller vice which may be readily screwed to bench or table, having slides, screw and handle of steel is shown in Fig. 268. It is just

Fig. 268.—Record No. 50 Amateur
Woodwork Vice.

Fig. 269.—Record No. 51 Junior
Woodwork Vice.

the right size for occasional work of small character where fuller facilities for woodworking are not available. The jaws are $6\frac{1}{2}$ in. wide and open $4\frac{1}{2}$ in.

Those who have need for a vice which can be instantly fastened to a table or bench will be interested in Record Junior Woodwork Vice No. 51 shown in Fig. 269. The jaws are 6 in. wide, and will open $4\frac{1}{2}$ in. Slides, screw and handle are of steel; and the vice will clamp on to any board, table, bench or trestle top which is from $\frac{3}{4}$ in. to $2\frac{1}{4}$ in. thick.

The illustration Fig. 270, shows the Record Junior Woodworkers' Vice No. 51 with Cramp attachment. It can be conveniently carried

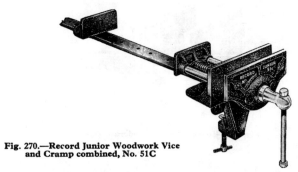

Fig. 270.—Record Junior Woodwork Vice and Cramp combined, No. 51C

in a tool bag, and the cramping bar is readily attached or detached; and if the vice is clamped to a support, there is no need to remove it for the manipulation of the cramping bar, which has a capacity of 32 in. Though smaller than the standard vices (the jaws are 6 in. wide and the opening $4\frac{1}{2}$ in.) there is the same perfectly parallel action and grip with no side movement. The cramping is accomplished with the aid of the vice screw itself, and the cramping attachment is only available with the Record Junior Vice.

There are few woodworkers who do not find the need on occasion for a vice in which metalwork of some kind can be done; and there are few who wish to use the woodworker's vice for this purpose as a makeshift. From the very wide range of the Record Metalworkers' vices available, three are here illustrated as being of utility for the odd jobs that crop up in the course of the woodworkers' round. The handyman will at once appreciate the value of No. 74 Vice (Fig. 271) whether he is a motorist or not. The jaws are 4 in. wide, and the vice opens $4\frac{1}{2}$ in. A pair of pipe grips which are incorporated will take and hold securely any pipe or cylindrical object up to $1\frac{1}{2}$ in. outside diameter. The offset jaws are designed so that long and wide work may be held vertically, a great convenience. On the lower part will be noticed a pipe and rod bender on which all kinds of bends on rods can be easily, speedily and satisfactorily done. The cylinder head holding plug, shown on the right, is threaded English and American plug threads, so that with its assistance, a cylinder head may be very conveniently held in the vice for cleaning purposes, leaving both hands free and the cylinder head firm and safe. A useful little anvil is readily accessible for riveting, etc., etc., and for delicate or highly finished work that would suffer in the hard steel jaws, a pair of fibre clams of special material selected for the purpose, which are readily detachable, is provided. These fibre grips will not damage the most delicate work, and in service they have a long life, whilst they are free from the objections attendant upon copper and lead clams. (Similar fibre jaws may be had for fitting to other metal working vices; in ordering them state the length of the jaw in inches.)

Fitting the Record No. 74 Vice to a bench is very simple. It should be fitted on the right hand side, as close as possible to the leg, and only one hole half inch diameter is bored through the bench top. The base stud is passed through this hole, and the strong wing nut underneath holds the vice securely in any one of several positions which are possible on the swivel base. When the bench is required for woodworking the Vice is quickly removed by unscrewing the wing nut and lifting the vice upwards.

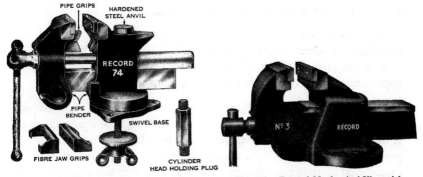

Fig. 271.—Record No. 74 Vice. Fig. 272.—Record Mechanics' Vice with Unbreakable Nut.

The type of Mechanic's Vice shown in Fig. 272 is as well known throughout the world as is the woodworker's vice—both are world standards. The Mechanic's Vice is made in ten sizes, ranging from $2\frac{1}{4}$ in. jaw opening $2\frac{1}{4}$ in. and weighing $5\frac{1}{2}$ lbs., to 8 in. jaw opening $9\frac{1}{4}$ in, and weighing 90 lbs. The one shown (No. 3) has 4 in. jaws which open $4\frac{3}{4}$ in. and has a lifetime's wear in it. Three coach screws or bolts will secure it to the bench. It would be best of course if it were fitted on a separate bench away from the woodwork bench, but a vice like No. 3 is so useful to the general woodworker that it would be well worth while to fit it to a bench such as we have discussed in the earlier part of this chapter with bolts and wing nuts. When not in use, it would be easily detachable, and could be stored in one of the cupboards under the bench. The only disfigurement to the bench would be the three bolt holes. In fitting a mechanic's vice to the bench, it should not be set too far in, as if

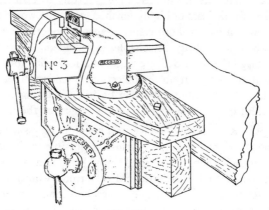

Fig. 273.

the vice is too far away from the edge of the bench it is not possible to work on a long rod which has to be set upright.

Some woodworkers bolt two pieces of hardwood together and to them bolt a mechanic's vice as shown in Fig. 273, gripping the combination in the jaws of the woodworker's vice. This may not be sound engineering practice, but it is a dodge that is useful at times.

No. 80 "Imp" (Fig. 274) Vice is really a miniature No. 74 Vice, having $2\frac{1}{4}$ in. jaws and opening $2\frac{1}{2}$ in., and in no way must it be confused with either toys or cheap and unsatisfactory vices. It is sturdily and compactly made; the screw is accurately made with a machine cut square thread, and there is a parallel grip which is free from any suggestion of looseness. The steel jaws are hardened and of high quality; there is a hardened anvil as in the No. 74 Vice, but of smaller dimensions of course. The slide is of steel. Small tubes and rods can be gripped in the

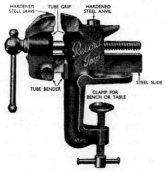

Fig. 274.—Record No. 80 Imp Table Vice.

222

specially designed jaws, and can be bent in the tube bender. It is fastened to the bench (or to any other support) with an exceptionally well designed and well-made clamp which is incorporated, which has a grip that is almost unbelievable until it is experienced. The vice weighs $4\frac{1}{4}$ lbs.

In selecting a vice, a good deal of thought should be applied to the character of the work that is to be done with it. It is very often found that a man has selected a vice that is smaller than is called for in the work that he demands of it. It is best to err on the large side rather than on the small side. Small work can be done quite conveniently in the larger vices, but it is not fair either to the vice or to the worker to expect heavy work from a light vice. No Record Vice has any suggestion of looseness that would unfit it for any type of work; they are made by craftsmen who know what a good vice should be and these craftsmen are conscientious in the work they turn out, and as proud of their products as are any other craftsmen.

Chapter 21

Workshop Hints

1. THE WORK of making buttons for a table top, etc., need not be a tedious process. The Multi-Plane or the Combination Plane should here be brought into service, and set as for cutting dados (see instructions under those planes, pages 144, 155). Trenches should be cut across a spare piece of wood so that the amount left is equal to the width of the grooves in the frame, the width of the trench being slightly more than the depth of the grooves. The trenches will be at a suitable distance apart as is desired for the screws. After the trenching is completed, the holes should be bored and countersunk, and a few rips down the board will sever the buttons.

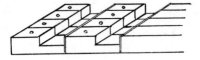

Fig. 275.

2. THE CRAMPING up of through tenons sometimes presents a little difficulty, especially when the tenons are required to show at the finish, projecting and bevelled off. Two pieces of scrap wood cut as shown in Fig. 276, will solve this problem, and one cramp only need be used, yet the joint will be kept quite square.

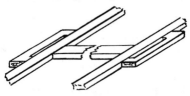

Fig. 276.

3. WHEN ENGAGED in a complicated bit of cramping, and it is essential to get the cramps on quickly before the glue has time to chill, it is astonishing how the cramps will tumble about at times. A pair of wood blocks as shown in Fig. 277, slotted for the reception of the tail end of the cramp will save all this bother.

Fig. 277.

4. IN GLUING up door frames, etc., which are mortised and tenoned and wedged, much valuable time can be saved if the frames are first assembled with the tenons entering about a third of the way only, and the cramps are arranged in position underneath ready. The exposed parts of the tenons are now quickly glued, and the cramps run up tightly. Squareness and lack of winding are now checked up, and the wedges inserted with a touch of glue.

5. IN TESTING for squareness of frames, etc., a rod as shown in Fig. 278 is very helpful. The broad end is chamfered off at 45° as shown so that the angle remaining is 90°. This end is now inserted in one of the inside corners, and the rod passes diagonally across the frame. A pencil mark is put where the opposite corner comes, and then the rod is tried diagonally across the other two corners. If the pencil mark coincides with the corner, the frame is square; if not, adjustment of the cramps must be made until the two diagonals are equal. This is much more satisfactory than using a try square at each corner as well as being speedier.

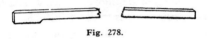

Fig. 278.

6. THE PROBLEM of boring a very long hole in a comparatively thin piece of material is a very real one. It is impossible for most workers when it takes the form of making a hole through an electric floor lamp standard, as even if it were possible to bore straight enough, bits of sufficient length are unavailable. The solution is to saw the spline lengthwise as shown in Fig. 279, and plane up the two surfaces true with a Record Jointer (No. 08). These two faces are now ploughed, (or one only may be ploughed if desired), and the two pieces are then glued up together as described under Butt Jointing. It is wise to put on a few G Cramps during the time the glue is drying. When cleaned up there is scarcely any trace of the joint. If it is desired that the hole should be circular instead of rectangular, this can be done by using a fluting cutter in the Multi-Plane, No. 405, cutting a semi-circular groove in each instead of the plough groove shown.

Fig. 279.

7. SOME WORKERS find a difficulty in holding small cutters, as for example spokeshave cutters when grinding and honing them. A holder shaped as shown in Fig. 289 will simplify this. The shape of

225

the piece is not material—it can be shaped to fit the worker's own fancy and comfort. The essential part is that the saw kerf at the end should be of such dimensions that the cutter stops in it while it is being used. If desired, the saw kerf can be made longer, and a bolt with a wing nut put in so that the two jaws can be nipped up when the blade is inserted.

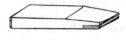

Fig. 280.

8. WHEN CRAMPING up the two ends of a carcase, as for instance the two ends of a sideboard, after the joints of both are cramped up, the two should be put together with the inner surfaces abutting. G cramps should now be put on to cramp the two together. This will ensure that when the next gluing up is done—the fitting of the rails—the whole carcase will go up fair and square.

9. THE GLUE that settles in the corner of a frame that is being glued up is often troublesome to remove, especially if there are mouldings present. The way to remove it is to dip a chisel in the hot water of the glue pot, and apply the chisel to the glue, holding the chisel in such a position that the glue can run down it. All the glue will melt on to the hot chisel, and there is no need to swamp the whole part in hot water as is sometimes done.

10. IN CLEANING up dovetailed constructions there is no better plane than a block plane, especially if it is one of the Record range with full adjustments. The low set of these plane cutters is ideal for this kind of work, as there is very little tendency, if the plane is properly sharpened and set, for the grain to break off at the end. When the work is small enough to be held in the vice for cleaning up, a piece of wood, end grain upwards may be put in the vice level with the joint being cleaned up.

11. SMALL WORK that does not readily lend itself to cramping with the usual cramps can often be satisfactorily cramped by winding a piece of string or tape round rather loosely and tying. Wedges can now be inserted between the string and the work so that the string is pulled up tight. If there is any danger of a corner being cut into by the string, it should be protected by a small fillet on each side of the corner.

12. WHEN CLEANING up with an iron plane a slight lubrication on the base is of great help. If a rag, or piece of cotton waste, slightly oily, is handy on the bench, the sole of the plane can be wiped over it without loss of time.

13. SCREWS ENTER with far less fatigue to the worker if they are lubricated. One of the handiest ways to do this is to have a hole about an inch or so in diameter bored a little way into the bench top, the hole being filled with Russian tallow. Before offering the screw, dip it into the tallow the length of the thread. If it is objectionable to bore the bench top, a cube of wood may be used similarly—but that is more easily lost when it is wanted than the hole in the bench.

14. IT IS heartbreaking to find that after a panel has been veneered it insists on curling. The remedy is to veneer on the heart side of the wood; or better still, to veneer both sides of it.

15. IN MAKING a corner cupboard, do not make the back corner exactly square—make it rather larger than a right angle. Then when the cupboard is fitted into the corner, both edges will fit up close to the wall. If the wall corner happens to be out of square, as it usually is, and the cupboard is exactly square, gaps may be left.

16. IN MAKING a wardrobe, or a tall cupboard, take a shaving or two off the bottom at the back, so that it will lean slightly towards the wall. That may prevent somebody pulling it over on top of them at some future time.

17. AWKWARD SHAPES to clean up can often be smoothed up by the use of glass paper files. These are fillets of wood, square, round, semi-circular, triangular, conical, etc., with a face of glass paper glued on. Glass paper blocks can readily be made by gluing cork mats cut to various shapes on to pieces of hardwood, and they wear better than solid cork does.

18. A SCREW has but little hold on end grain. Should it be necessary to screw into end grain, a dowel may be inserted across the path of the screw thread, and at right angles to it; the dowel being located at a suitable distance from the end of the wood. As the screw will then get a hold in the long grain of the dowel, a much more satisfactory fastening is assured.

REFERENCE LIST of PATTERNS and NUMBERS

of

RECORD TOOLS

PLANES

Type			Plane No.	Length	Width of Cutter
Smooth	...	...	03	8″	1¾″
,,	...	...	04	9¼″	2″
,,	...	...	04½	10″	2⅜″
Jack	...	...	05	14″	2″
,,	...	...	05½	15″	2⅜″
Fore	...	...	06	18″	2⅜″
Jointer	...	...	07	22″	2⅜″
,,	...	...	08	24″	2⅝″
School Jack	...	...	T5	13″	2″

Type			Plane No.	Length	Width of Cutter
Smooth			03C	8″	1¾″
,,			04C	9¼″	2″
,,			04½C	10″	2⅜″
Jack	With Corrugated Base		05C	14″	2″
,,			05½C	15″	2⅜″
Fore			06C	18″	2⅜″
Jointer			07C	22″	2⅜″
,,			08C	24″	2⅝″

Type			Plane No.	Length	Width of Cutter
Smooth			03SS	8″	1¾″
,,			04SS	9¼″	2″
,,			04½SS	10″	2⅜″
Jack	With STAY-SET Cap Iron		05SS	14″	2″
,,			05½SS	15″	2⅜″
Fore			06SS	18″	2⅜″
Jointer			07SS	22″	2⅜″
,,			08SS	24″	2⅝″
School Jack			T5SS	13″	2″

Type		Plane No.	Length	Width of Cutter
Smooth		03C-SS	8″	1¾″
,,	With	04C-SS	9¼″	2″
,,	Corrugated	04½C-SS	10″	2⅜″
Jack	Base	05C-SS	14″	2″
,,	and	05½C-SS	15″	2⅜″
Fore	STAY-SET	06C-SS	18″	2⅜″
Jointer	Cap Iron	07C-SS	22″	2⅜″
,,		08C-SS	24″	2⅝″
Smooth Rabbet		010½	9″	2⅛″
Jack Rabbet		010	13″	2⅛″
Duplex Rabbet and Fillister ...		078	8½″	1½″
Improved Rabbet		778	8½″	1½″
Bull-Nose Rabbet		075	4″	1″
,, ,, non-adjustable ...		076	4″	1⅛″
,, ,, Improved, adjustable		077A	4″	1⅛″
"3 in 1" Bull-Nose and Shoulder Rabbet		311	6″	1⅛″
Shoulder Rabbet		041	5″	⅝″
,, ,, ...		042	8″	¾″
,, ,, Improved		073	8⅛″	1¼″
Side Rabbet		2506		
Side Rabbet with Depth Stop		2506S		
Circular		020	10″	1¾″
Router		722		¼″
,, Improved		071	7½″	¼″, ½″ and smoothing
Plough Improved		043	5½″	3 cutters
,, ,, ...		044	8½″	8 ,,
Combination, Improved		050	9¼″	17 ,,
Multi-Plane		405		23 ,,
Additional Cutters (Sash, Fluting, Ovolo and Reeding)				
Hollow and Round Base ...		No. 6		½″
,, ,, ...		No. 8		⅝″
,, ,, ...		No. 10		¾″

Type				Plane No.	Length	Width of Cutter
Hollow and Round Base	...	...		No. 12		1″
Nosing Tool	...	...	...	No. 5		$1\frac{11}{16}$″
Block, Adjustable Mouth		...	...	09½	6″	$1\frac{5}{8}$″
,, ,,		...	...	018	6″	$1\frac{5}{8}$″
Block	...	...	...	0102	5½″	$1\frac{3}{8}$″
,,	...	...	...	0110	7″	$1\frac{5}{8}$″
,,	...	...	...	0120	7″	$1\frac{5}{8}$″
,, Double End	...	...	...	0130	8″	$1\frac{5}{8}$″
,,		...	...	0220	7″	$1\frac{5}{8}$″

SPOKESHAVES

Type			Plane No.	Length	Width of Cutter
Spokeshave (Flat)			A151	10″	$2\frac{1}{8}$″
,, (Round)			A151R	10″	$2\frac{1}{8}$″
,, (Flat)	Malleable		A51	10″	$2\frac{1}{8}$″
,, (Round)	Iron Body		A51R	10″	$2\frac{1}{8}$″
,, (Flat)	Unbreakable		A64	9″	$1\frac{3}{4}$″
,, (Round)			A63	9″	$1\frac{3}{4}$″
,, Chamfer			A65	10½″	$1\frac{1}{2}$″
Spokeshave (Flat)	...	... ...	0151	10″	$2\frac{1}{8}$″
,, (Round)	...	... ...	0151R	10″	$2\frac{1}{8}$″
,, (Flat)	...	... ...	051	10″	$2\frac{1}{8}$″
,, (Round)	...	... ...	051R	10″	$2\frac{1}{8}$″

SCRAPERS

Type				Plane No.	Length	Width of Cutter
Cabinet Scraper	...	...	...	080	11½″	$2\frac{3}{4}$″
Box Scraper	...	...	...	070	13″	2″

RECORD METALWORK VICES

Type				Vice No.	Width of Jaw	Opening
Mechanics' Plain Screw	...	...		00	$2\frac{1}{4}$″	$2\frac{1}{4}$″
,, ,,		...	...	0	$2\frac{1}{2}$″	$2\frac{1}{2}$″
,, ,,		...	...	1	3″	$3\frac{1}{4}$″
,, ,,		...	...	2	$3\frac{1}{2}$″	4″
,, ,,		...	...	3	4″	$4\frac{3}{4}$″
,, ,,		...	...	4	$4\frac{1}{2}$″	$5\frac{1}{2}$″
,, ,,		...	...	5	5″	$6\frac{1}{2}$″
,, ,,		...	...	6	6″	8″

				Vice No.	Width of Jaw	Opening
,,	,,	...	...	7	7″	9¼″
,,	,,	...	...	8	8″	9¼″

The above Vices are available with Swivel Base

					Vice No.	Width of Jaw	Opening
Fitters', Quick Grip		...	...	...	21	3¼″	4″
,,	,,	...	...	...	22	3¾″	5″
,,	,,	...	...	...	23	4¼″	6″
,,	,,	...	...	...	24	5¼″	7″
,,	,,	...	...	...	25	6″	8″

Vices Nos. 21 to 25 may be had with Swivel Base

				Vice No.	Width of Jaw	Opening
Record Auto Vice	...	...	...	74	4″	4½″
Record Garage Vice	...	...	...	75	5¼″	7″
Record "Imp" Table Vice	...	...		80	2¼″	2½″

For other heavy duty Vices, etc., see special lists

Fibre Grips for Metal-work Vices, 2¼″ to 6″. State width of Jaw of Vice.

RECORD WOODWORKERS' VICES

					Vice No.	Width of Jaw	Opening
Quick Grip		...	...	...	52	7″	8″
,,		...	...	...	52½	9″	13″
,,		...	...	...	53	10½″	15″
Plain (Screw-all-the-way)			...	...	52P	7″	8″
,,	,,		...	...	52½P	9″	13″
,,	,,		...	...	53P	10½″	15″
Quick Grip with Screw and Nut Cover					52A	7″	8″
,,	,,	,,		,,	52½A	9″	13″
,,	,,	,,		,,	53A	10½″	15″
Record Woodcraft Vice		...		...	55	6½″	6⅛″
Record Amateur Woodwork Vice				...	50	6″	4½″
Record Junior Woodwork Vice				...	51	6″	4½″
Record Bench Stop		...	...	...	160		

RECORD CRAMPS

Sash Cramps,	Fig. 133, Section	$1\frac{1}{2}'' \times \frac{5}{16}''$	...	24" to 60"	long
,,	Fig. 135, ,,	$1\frac{1}{4}'' \times \frac{1}{4}''$	...	24" to 48"	,,
T-Bar Cramps,	Fig. 136, Section	$1\frac{3}{4}'' \times \frac{3}{4}''$	...	24" to 72"	,,
,,	Fig. 138, ,,	$2\frac{5}{8}'' \times \frac{7}{8}''$	...	36" to 84"	,,

(Lengthening Bars also available)

Cramp Heads, No. 130, for use with 1" bar.
Junior "T" Cramps, Fig. 119, 3 sizes 2", $2\frac{1}{2}''$ and 3".
Ribbed "G" Cramps, Fig. 120, to take in 2" to 12".
Drop-Forged Steel "G" Cramps, Fig. 121 to take in 2" to 12".
Flooring Cramp, No. 153, to suit Joists $1\frac{1}{2}''$ to $3\frac{1}{2}''$.

———

The full range **of** RECORD TOOLS includes:

Metal Planes

Spoke Shaves

Carpenters' Cramps

Vices for Metal and Wood

Pipe Vices, Wrenches and Cutters

Bolt Clippers

Sheet Metal Cutters

———

GLOSSARY

ADZE—

A tool like an axe, but with a blade set at right angles to the handle, and curving towards it. It was used to smooth wood before the plane was used, and for coarser work for a long time after the plane was in general use. The pleasing texture of much mediaeval work is due to the use of the adze. Though not much used nowadays, the tool is still used dexterously by shipwrights and some of the old-time carpenters. The board is set on the floor, and the elbow rests on the knee when using the tool. A skilled man with an adze can leave a smooth surface well comparable with that left by a jack plane.

ALOXITE—

An abrasive made from the artificial aluminium oxide which is obtained by treating the mineral bauxite in an electric furnace. (See also Hone.)

APRON, APRON PIECE—

A board, shaped or otherwise decorated, stretching between two legs, the sides of a cabinet, etc., the function of which is to give a pleasing line; and frequently employed in the construction to help in keeping the corners square. Fig. 246 shows several apron pieces.

ARCHITRAVE—

A term borrowed from Architecture, where it indicates the chief beam which carries the super-structure, and rests immediately on the columns. Ordinarily it is the lowest of the three divisions, the other two being the frieze and the cornice. (Latin arcus, an arch; trabs, trabem, a beam.) In carpentry the term architrave is used collectively for the mouldings, jambs, lintels, etc., which surround a door or a window.

ASTRAGAL—

A term adapted from architecture; a small moulding of semi-circular section. Used widely for the bars of glazed cabinet doors, when it is made with a groove on the reverse side which carries a fillet, thus forming a rabbet for the glass on the inner side of the door. The glass is held in this rabbet by a bead. Narrow strips of canvas are usually glued in the crossings to strengthen the joints. Architecturally the astragal appears round the top and bottom of a column.

BALUSTER—

(Italian Balusta, balustra—the blossom of the wild pomegranate, which shape a baluster resembles. Corrupted in English to Banister, bannister.)
The upright which supports the handrail of a staircase. One of the units of a balustrade. A banister back chair has a back resembling a banister.

BANDING—

Strips of wood, parallel in length and thickness often built up in patterns, glued into grooves as inlaid decoration in furniture. When not built up usually known as stringing. Bandings can easily be made up by gluing strips of various coloured wood, such as box, ebony, walnut, etc., and then cutting "slices" from the end, in the manner of a chequered cake, about a sixteenth of an inch thick; but they are available commercially ready for inlaying at low prices. Strings o box, ebony, etc., for corners are usually square in section, and are called squares. These are also cheap to buy, but are cut off suitable coloured wood very quickly by taking two cuts with the small plough irons, one from the face side and one from the face edge. The plough is so set that the second cut releases the square. Apart from its decorative effect, a string of hard wood such as ebony tends to save a corner from wear. In the very best work, the string and the rabbet have each a saw cut, into which a veneer slip is placed as a key, thus strengthening the glued joint.

BARGE BOARD, VERGE BOARD—

A board suspended from the verge of a gable, frequently of ornate fashion, the ornament being in the main bow saw and spokeshave work, sometimes combined with boring and piercing.

BATTEN—

Properly a piece of squared timber not more than $7'' \times 2\frac{1}{2}''$, a scantling, but mostly referring to the strip which is nailed across parallel boards to hold them together and to prevent warping, as in a battened door. A ledge, a clamp.

BEAD—

A narrow semi-circular moulding. This may be so carved as to leave globular members of equal or unequal length. When a short one and a long one alternate, the Jacobean "Ball and Sausage" moulding is formed.

BENCH HOOK—

A battened board, hooked over the front of the bench to assist in sawing. For this purpose it is best if the battens are fixed with dowels rather than by nailing or screwing.

BENCH STOP—

A device, widely varying in pattern, which is set in the bench top, and against which the wood is held when planing (Fig. 262).

BEVEL—

An obtuse angle, a tool used in setting off this angle and the operation of making it.

BLISTER—

When veneering, it sometimes occurs that the veneer is not properly glued down in some part, forming a blister. To remove the blister, cut through with a very sharp chisel, insert glue with a shaving, and apply a hot iron. The object of cutting the blister is the removal of the air.

BLOCK PLANE—

A small plane, used chiefly in planing end grain (originally the end grain of butchers' blocks), having a single low set blade which is used bevel side upwards.

BOLECTION—

A moulding which projects before the face of the work decorated, *e.g.*, a raised panel moulding which projects above the frame.

BRINELL TEST

The best known method for the determination of the hardness of Steel and other metals is the Brinell Test which determines the resistance to penetration which the material offers when a hardened steel ball of given diameter placed upon it is subjected to a definite load.

The depth of the impression made is not measured direct, but the diameter of the cavity is accurately gauged by means of a microscope fitted with a millimetre scale, vernier, and cross hair.

From this the spherical area of the impression is calculated, and the maximum load in kilogrammes divided by the area gives a hardness number. This number denotes the degree of hardness of the steel or metal being tested.

Plane cutting irons are tested for hardness in a similar manner except that instead of a hardened steel ball a conical-shaped diamond with four flats on it is used.

The impression made by the diamond is very small and therefore does not damage the face of the cutting iron.

BROGUE—
A Bradawl (Scots).

BULL-NOSE PLANE—
A small plane used for planing close to projecting parts, the blade being set close to the nose of the plane.

BUTT JOINT—
The joint made when the two pieces are joined together without overlap.

"C" SCROLL—
A carved motif much used by Chippendale, so called from its resemblance to the letter "C"; said to have been introduced from the French.

CABINET—
(French *Cabinet*, Italian *gabinetto*, press, chest of drawers)—a piece of furniture, often ornamented, fitted with drawers, shelves, etc., for the display and preservation of specimens. Display cabinets became very popular with the wealthy classes during the later years of the seventeenth century, as trade with the East grew when, following the example of Queen Mary, there was a vogue for collecting choice pieces of china.

CAPPING—
A piece of wood generally moulded, topping some other, as on the post of a bed, etc. A capping plane was a plane that was used mainly for the upper surface of the balustrade of a staircase.

CARCASE—
The skeleton of a piece of work, as the framework of a chest of drawers, etc.; also the framework of a house which supports the floor or the roof. Also carcass.

CARPENTER—
An artificer in wood; one who does the framework of a house, etc., as opposed to a joiner, cabinet-maker who works at the bench.

CAST—
A board twisted in its length is said to be cast.

CAVETTO—
A quarter round concave moulding.

CELLARET—

A compartment of a sideboard for holding wine bottles, or a case of cabinet work for that purpose.

CHAMFER—

The surface produced by bevelling off a square edge or corner equally on both sides. Sometimes made concave when it is a hollow. (Possibly French chanfrein, chamfrain, perhaps from Latin *cantum frangere*—to break the edge or side.) Chamfers may be "through" or "stopped," and very effective edges can be made by working a second chamfer or a bevel (q.v.) on another one. Record A65 Spokeshave is useful for this work.

CHATTER—

The jumpiness or vibration of a plane, whereby it does not give a smooth, continuous cut. It can be traced to a variety of causes, lack of rigidity, badly-machined parts, wrong setting, slack screws, etc. The STAY-SET cap iron has eliminated chatter in smooth planes.

CHECK—

A Scots term for rabbet. Also used of decoration in squares, particularly inlay.

CHOKE—

If when using a plane the shavings stick in the mouth instead of escaping through the plane, the plane is said to choke. A frequent cause of choke is bad setting, or slack screwing of the cap iron screw, causing a shaving to stick between the cap iron and the cutting iron. Insufficient clearance between the blade and the front of the mouth will also cause choke, *i.e.*, when the frog is brought too far forward with the cap iron as near to the cutting edge as it will go.

CHOP INLAY—

An early form of inlay; the pieces were fitted into the solid surface. Later veneer was used.

CIRCULAR PLANE—COMPASS PLANE—RADIUS PLANE—

A plane so constructed that it has a convexity or a concavity in its sole, end to end, so that it can work on curved surfaces. Record Circular Planes are so constructed that they may be used on convex and concave surfaces, and the amount of curvature is adjustable at will.

CLAMP—

(Sometimes clam—the word has a cognate origin with clem, to pinch with hunger.)
1. The piece of wood used as a brace to keep one or more pieces together and to prevent warping. It may simply be a piece let into a plough groove or be slot-screwed on to the faces, but usually it is grooved and tenoned, as on a pastry-board, blackboard, etc. As a fastening it is inferior to panelling, as there is no provision for shrinkage, and for this reason is often discarded in favour of an iron bar which is let into a plough groove in the edge.
2. A cramp is sometimes called a clamp.

CLAP BOARD—

An American term for a lapping weather board.

CLAP POST—

The American term for slamming post—the upright post of a cupboard on which the door claps or closes.

CLASSICAL DETAIL, MOULDING, ETC.—

As in the architecture of the Ancient Romans and Greeks.

COCK BEAD—

A bead which projects above the ground work.

COLUMN—

A cylindrical or slightly tapering body, considerably greater in length than diameter, used vertically as a support. A pillar.

COMBINATION PLANE—

A plane capable of ploughing, rabbeting, beading, tonguing and grooving, dado cutting, and centre beading. No. 050.

CONCAVE—

Hollowed out; opposite of convex.

CONTOUR—

The profile or section of a moulding.

CONVEX—

Curving as the surface of a sphere.

CORD—

A pile of wood 4 ft. wide, 4 ft. high and 8 ft. long. Probably originally measured with a cord. Firewood.

CORRUGATED BASE—

The base of the "C" series of Record Smooth, Jack and Jointer Planes, in which a series of semi-circular grooves is machined longitudinally along the sole. It is sometimes found when planing thin and comparatively wide boards that, as the surface becomes true, a suction is created between the face of the board and the sole of the plane, due to a combination of an accurately machined and practically non-wearing sole and accurate work on the part of the user. The corrugations allow just enough air between the surfaces to break the vacuum and prevent the suction, which can be enough to lift the board with the plane under favourable circumstances. Hence, those who have much face side planing to do will find that a corrugated base plane will ease the work. The corrugations further assist by holding a little of the lubricant (oil, paraffin wax, etc.) which is applied to the sole of the plane when working.

CORNICE, CORNISH—

The horizontal moulding which crowns a building or part of a building (Lat. *Cornix*, crow)—and the similar moulding, running round the wall of a room, etc. To save timber, these mouldings are often planed from thin boards, the edges of which are planed at 45 degrees, one edge fitting the vertical and the other the horizontal faces.

COVE—

A large hollow cornice; a concave moulding.

CROSS-GRAIN—

A section of wood taken at right angles, or nearly so to the direction of the longitudinal fibres.

CROTCH—

A term sometimes used of the veneer which is cut from the limb crotch, or from twin trees which have joined together in growth, and having a characteristic grain.

CROWN MOULDING—

A moulding having a double curved face. The upper member of a closed cornice placed immediately below the roof proper.

CURL—

The characteristic grain of feather formation seen at its best in certain mahoganies.

DADO—

A groove cut across the grain—a Housing.

DEAL—

A slice sawn from a log of timber, 9 in. wide not more than 3 in. thick, and at least 6 ft. long. If shorter it is a deal end; if not more than 7 in. wide it is a batten.

The term deal is used of fir and pine wood loosely. White deal is the wood of the Norway Spruce, Red Deal that of the Scotch Pine, Yellow deal that of the yellow pine; but much depends on local custom, red and yellow deal often being the same wood, Pinus sylvestris.

A deal frame is a gang saw used for cutting deals.

DENTIL—

Each of the small rectangular blocks resembling a row of teeth, under the bed moulding of the cornice of the Ionic, Corinthian, Composite, and sometimes the Doric, orders. Hence, loosely a toothed moulding.

DIAPER WORK—

Decoration in squares or lozenges in which there is a repeat pattern.

DOWEL—

A headless pin, peg, or bolt of wood or metal serving to fasten two pieces of wood together. A round peg.

DROP—

A pendant ornament.

DUST BOARD—

A thin partition board between drawers, fitted in plough grooves in the runners. It is slipped in from the back after gluing up the carcase, and is itself not glued in. Usually nowadays of thin plywood.

END GRAIN—

The grain of wood which shows when the fibres are cut transversely.

ESCRITOIRE—

A writing desk; a bureau.

GLOSSARY—*continued*

FACE EDGE, Face Side—

The working faces of a piece of wood, guaranteed true and at right angles to each other, and from which squaring, measuring and gauging are done.

FASCES—

An ornament resembling a bundle of sticks with a projecting axe (though this is not always present). It may be carved on a bead in a running pattern. It had its origin in the Roman symbol of authority.

FEATHER EDGE—

The fine edge of a board that thins off to one side, so as to resemble a wedge in section.

FELLOE, FELLY—

The exterior rim, or part of it, of a wooden wheel, supported by the spokes. The central block, the hub, is called the nave.

FENCE—

A guide or gauge designed to regulate the movement of a tool, as on a plough plane, where the fence keeps the cutter at an even distance from the face of the work.

FIDDLEBACK—

1. A chair in which the back is so shaped as to resemble a fiddle.
2. A characteristic figuring of wood having a ripple pattern, caused by the overlapping of the fibres, much used on the backs of violins.

FIGURE—

The pattern formed by the grain of wood.

FILLET—

A narrow strip of wood fastened upon any surface to serve as a support, etc., or to strengthen an angle formed by two surfaces.

FILLISTER—FILLETSTER—

A rabbeting plane used in making sash windows.

FLUTE—

A concave channel, resembling the half of a musical flute cut lengthwise, used in the decoration of columns, balusters, friezes, etc. Many cutters for planing flutes are available as extras for the No. 405 Multi-Plane.

FORE PLANE—

A plane intermediate in size between a Jack Plane and a Jointer or Tryplane.

FRAME—

The woodwork of doors, windows, etc., minus the panels. The skeleton structure of furniture.

GAIN—

(American) A mortise or notch.

"G" CRAMP—

So called from its resemblance to the letter G.

GLOSSARY—*continued*

GEELLIM—GEELIM—
A shoulder plane (Scots).

GLAZED DOORS—
Doors fitted with glass panels, usually having a pattern formed by the bars between the glass panels. The glass may occupy all or only some of the panels. The beautiful patterns formed by the bars of cabinet doors, etc., are probably the natural outcome of the small size of glass that was at the time available—as only small panes were possible, the craftsman took advantage of that to introduce pleasing design. Had larger pieces of glass been available, it is possible that we should never have developed the technique of barred cabinet doors and multi-paned windows.

GRAIN—
The longitudinal arrangement of the fibres or particles of wood.

GREEN WOOD—
Unseasoned wood—that in which the sap has not been dried out.

GRIND—
To shapern by contact with a rotating abrasive wheel. See chapter on Grinding.

GROUNDING—
Removing the background of a design in carved work. 722 Router is admirably suited for this work.

HANDRAIL—
A rail as on a stairway placed for conveniently grasping by the hand.

HARDWOOD—
The wood of deciduous trees as opposed to that of firs and pines. In Australia, any timber resembling teak, especially *Backhousia Bancroftii*. Oak and Ash are typical hardwoods, though the softer bass or canary-wood is classed as a hardwood.

HAUFLIN—
Also Haughlin, Haflin—A Try Plane (Scots).

HAUNCH—
A sudden decrease in thickness, as in the outer portion of a tenon in a panelled construction.

HEARTWOOD—
The more durable wood from the heart of the tree and around it as opposed to the sapwood which lies immediately under the bark. The heartwood is mature the sapwood is living wood and of little use as timber.

HEAT TREATMENT—
The Heat Treatment of Steel is the whole of the thermal treatment and conditions to which the material is subjected from the time it is cast until it becomes the finished product ready for use, and includes Annealing, Hardening and Tempering. The great influence which heating to varying temperatures has upon the crystalline structure and physical properties of the metal is all important.

GLOSSARY—*continued*

Annealing.—Removes as far as possible the internal stresses in the metal induced by rolling or forging and brings the metal into the best state to resist fracture. It also produces the maximum degree of ductility and softness.

Hardening.—Is the process of heating the metal to a particular temperature and suddenly cooling it by quenching in water or other medium which will produce the maximum degree of hardness.

Tempering.—The degree of hardness produced in steel by the hardening process is often too hard for many purposes and has to be modified by tempering in order to suit a particular use. This is done by re-heating to a temperature which will give the required degree of hardness. Tempering reduces the hardness and brittleness and increases the ductility and toughness of the metal, therefore, by varying the conditions of heat treatment any degree of hardness within the capacity of the metal may be produced.

Temper.—The correct temper of a tool is the degree of hardness at which the tool will perform at its best.

To measure degree of hardness see Brinell Test.

HOGGING—

Taking very heavy cuts. For this purpose the plane cutter is rounded, as in No. 400½. Lighter hogging may be done with a jack plane by giving the plane a coarse set and adjusting the frog as far back as it will go. The improvements in machine saws in modern times have removed the necessity for hogging nowadays

HONE—HONING—(Old English, han)

A hone is a finely siliceous stone for sharpening instruments and honing is using the stone for this purpose. Other terms for the same thing are honestone, whet stone, oil stone, sharpening stone. The best form for sharpening plane irons, chisels, etc., is a rectangular block about 8 in. or 9 in. × 2 in. × 1 in. Hones for sharpening curved cutters, etc., may be pencil shaped, conical or other shapes. Straight edged cutters are usually sharpened by rubbing the cutter on the stone, but curved cutters are often sharpened by rubbing the stone on the cutter. The cutting action of the stone is due to the presence of quartz or silica, some being almost pure quartz. In others the siliceous matter is intimately mixed with aluminous or calcareous matter, these giving an extremely fine edge on the tool. Minute particles of garnet or magnetite are sometimes present, these assisting the cutting action.

German razor hones are made from slabs of a yellow vein from the slate mountains near Ratisbon. The slabs are cemented to slate for support.

Turkey stones come from Asia Minor via Smyrna. They are found only in small pieces, frequently flawed. Their analysis gives 70 to 75 per cent. fine silica intimately blended with 20 to 25 per cent. calcite. A hone of the finest character. Arkansas stone; found in small pieces in Garland and Saline Counties, Arkansas, U.S.A. 98 per cent. silica, with small proportions of alumina, potash, soda, and minute traces of iron, lime, magnesia and fluorine. White in colour, they are hard and keen in grit, not easily worn down. A "de luxe" stone for the woodworker.

Washita Stone; a second grade of Arkansas coming from the Washita River, U.S.A. More common than Arkansas, and probably the most popular of woodworkers' hones.

Charnley Forest or Whittle Hill Stone: a good substitute for Turkey Stone, but now difficult to obtain, possibly on account of the exhaustion of the quarry.

Water of Ayr, Scotch Stone, or Snake Stone: too soft for the woodworker's use. Used in polishing marble, copper, and in cleaning up silver work.

Greenstone from Snowdon: used in giving the last edge to lancets.

HORN—

The forward handle of mediaeval planes, and on continental planes in modern practice, serving the same function as the knob of Record Planes.

HOUSING—

A space excavated in one piece of wood for the reception of another, *e.g.*, a shallow groove for a shelf end. A Dado.

INLAY—

Decoration by setting pieces of wood, brass, ivory, mother-of-pearl, etc., forming a pattern into a ground of some other wood, the whole being left flush. Inserts are of veneer thickness as a rule.

INTARSIA—

A form of inlay, known from the 11th Century, probably at its best in Italian work of the 15th Century. Commencing with geometrical patterns, it gradually developed into representations of classical architecture, views, figures and drapery, and finally emerged as foliaceous scrolls as in modern marquetry. Many coloured woods were used, and further colour was obtained by scorching some of the woods to get shadow and other effects.

IRON—

A term generally used by the craftsman to denote the cutter or cutting blade of a plane. The term to give "too much iron" means to set the plane cutter too low. To give "less iron" is to draw the blade up.

JACK PLANE—

The term Jack is used in many other trades than that of the woodworker, *e.g.*, a motor jack, a jack knife, Jack of all Trades, etc. In connection with a plane it was in use before the close of the 18th century, and was doubtless adopted on account of the universality of the tool—it is the tool that is first picked up, that brings the wood to its approximate size, that does as it were, all the work ready for the special tools to follow.

JOINER—

A woodworker who makes joints, a shop worker. (As opposed to a carpenter, q.v.)

JOINTER, JOINTER PLANE—

A long plane used in the trueing of edges, etc., ready for jointing. A trying Plane, as No. 07, 08.

KEYING—

Strengthening, as in a joint, by the insertion of a slip of wood, which may be of various forms.

KIT—

An outfit of tools.

KNOT—

A hard mass in wood, rounded and cross-grained, formed at the juncture of a branch. A "live" knot cannot be knocked out; a "dead" knot is loose and can be separated.

LATH—

A thin, narrow, flat piece of wood as used in plaster work, tiling, lattice and trellis work, etc. A spline, a slat.

LENGTHENING BAR—

A bar which can be fitted to a sash cramp to extend its length. Also called an "EKE."

LOCKING STILE—

That part of a door to which the lock is attached, opposite from the hanging stile, to which the hinges are attached.

LOUVRE—

A slatted ventilating window, the slats being sloped to keep out the rain.

MALLEABLE IRON—

A form of iron which when cast to the desired shape is subjected to heat treatment causing partial decarburization, rendering its structure fibrous and ductile.

MATCHING, or Matched Boards—

Boards cut with a tongue on one edge and a groove on the opposite edge, their jointing being called a Match-Joint. The tongues and grooves are made parallel with the grain. On account of the inevitable shrinkage which occurs after assembly, the joint is frequently "broken" by a bead on the tongued edge; or by both edges being slightly chamfered, this improving the appearance. The effectiveness is often further enhanced by a centre bead stuck in the centre of each board. The Combination Plane and the Multi-Plane are both ideal for the planing of matched boards.

MEMBER—

Any part of an edifice, or any moulding in a collection of mouldings, as those in a cornice, capital, base, etc.

MITRE—

The joining together of two pieces of wood at an evenly-divided angle (not necessarily 45 degrees) as in a picture frame, bars in a glazed door, etc.

MOULDINGS, Stuck and Planted—

A Stuck Moulding is worked on the frame itself; whilst a Planted Moulding is worked separately and later affixed to the work by means of glue, nails, or screws. When planted, mouldings are put around a frame enclosing a panel, the nails should only go through moulding and frame, and should not hold the panel. If the panel is nailed, when shrinkage occurs, either the panel will split, or it will draw the moulding away from the frame, in either case leaving an unsightly gap. If the nails miss the panel the panel is free to shrink without leaving any gap.

MULTI-PLANE—

A plane capable of ploughing, dadoing, beading, centre beading, rabbeting and fillistering, match planing, sash planing, slitting, with the standard cutters supplied, and many other moulding operations with additional cutters. Number 405.

MUNTIN—

A central vertical member of a frame, between two panels.

NEATSFOOT OIL—

An oil obtained from the feet of neat (*i.e.*, ox) cattle. It is much used as a lubricant for the woodworker's oilstone, being slow in drying, and remaining longer than most oils on top of the stone. Old time craftsmen kept a bottle of it hanging near the bench, and applied it by means of a stick which remained in the bottle when not in use.

NEWEL—

A post at the top or bottom of a flight of stairs supporting the handrail.

NOSING—

The part of a stair tread which projects above the riser.

NULLING—

A Quadrant section moulding, carved or turned, seen at its best perhaps, in Jacobean work.

OGEE—

A term borrowed from Architecture, indicating a moulding of wave-like character, formed by a convex curve followed by a concave curve. The derivation is uncertain, but is usually considered an English corruption of French ogive, a diagonal groin rib, being a moulding commonly employed. The Latin equivalent is *cyma reversa*.

OILSTONE—

See HONE.

OILSTONE SLIP—

A small shaped oilstone for sharpening gouges and the moulding cutters of 050, 405, etc.

ONLAY—

A term sometimes used for ornament that is laid on the surface of the wood, as opposed to inlay, which is let into the surface.

ORMOLU—

Gilded metal used decoratively on furniture.

ORNAMENT—

Any addition or part so treated that it adds to the elegance or beauty of the object. Modern design in woodwork largely discards applied ornament, allowing the construction to become its own ornament, as in the careful planning of dovetails in rhythmical sequence, the chamfering of through tenons, etc., and relying on proportions and the natural grain of selected woods for major effects.

OVOLO—

A term borrowed from Architecture, indicating a moulding with the curved part composed of a quarter of a circle, or of an arc of an ellipse with the curve greatest at the top. The word comes from Latin *Ovum*, an egg, and may be compared with oval, egg-shaped. In carpentry a sash ovolo has a flatter curve than a common ovolo. The Ovolo is frequently further decorated with carving in the form of egg and dart, or egg and tongue.

GLOSSARY—*continued*

PANEL—
The board of a wainscot, door, shutter, etc., sunk below, raised above, or flush with the general level, which is set in a frame.

PANEL BOARD—
One which contains the heart of the tree. Such a board will not warp, though it may shrink in thickness at the two edges.

PARTING BEAD—
The bead used between two sliding doors or sashes to keep them apart.

PEDIMENT—
The triangular part, like a low gable, crowning the front of a building in the Grecian style; hence a similar part in later styles of furniture, though its shape may have varied, *e.g.*, on a wardrobe. The word is probably a workman's corruption of Pyramid.

PEG—
A wooden pin; a dowel. A mortise and tenon joint may be pegged by boring through the completed joint and inserting a round wooden pin. (A Trenail.)

PILASTER—
(Adapted from Architecture)—A right-angled columnar projection, frequently decorated with fluting, etc.

PLINTH—
(Adapted from Architecture)—The projecting part of a cupboard, etc., immediately above the floor. In modern design, the plinth is often seen as receding, thus not being subjected to accidental damage from (and to) toes, and providing an interesting shadow line. Further emphasis is often attained by veneering such a plinth with the grain vertically placed, contrasting with the horizontal grain of the covering frame.

PLOUGH—PLOW—
A plane for making grooves, usually parallel, with *i.e.*, along the grain

PLOUGH STRIP—
A strip of wood into which a plough groove has been stuck. Its principal use is in drawer making (see Figs. 115, 116).

QUIRK—
A term borrowed from Architecture, indicating an acute angle or recess, usually in connection with the narrow grooves forming part of a moulding. The derivation is uncertain, but is probably connected with an obsolete English word quirt, meaning to turn. (Welsh, *chwired*, a piece of craft; Gaelic, *cuireid*, a turn.)

RABBET, REBATE—Properly Rabbet—
The two terms are used to indicate a groove cut on the edge of a board in such a manner that the original corner is taken away. (A rabbet has one wall and a bottom; a plough groove has two walls and a bottom. See Fig. 136.) Both terms are used in this book.

GLOSSARY—*continued*

RAIL—

The horizontal member of a door frame or carcase. A door may have top rail, lock rail, bottom rail. The vertical members are, on the outside, stiles, in the centre, muntins.

RISER—

The board set on edge which connects the treads of a stair.

ROD—

A narrow board on which length, breadth and height of the object to be made are set out separately, full size, together with the details of panelling, doors, etc., etc. It is especially useful when such things as cupboards have to be repeated, and where drawings would be too large to be handy.

ROUTER—

The hand tool known as a Router is a two-handled tool used for cutting and smoothing depressed surfaces. An older form consisted of a chisel-like blade inserted in a block of wood, usually beech, secured by a wood wedge, and called by craftsmen "The Old Woman's Tooth."

SAPWOOD—

The young and living wood which is found immediately under the bark, and outside the heart wood. It is of little value in construction.

SASH—

A window frame.

SASH BARS—

The strips of a sash window which separates the panes.

SCANT—

Bare measure.

SCANTLING

Small sectioned timber such as 2 in. × 2 in., 3 in. × 2 in., etc. In the 17th century a carpenter's measuring rod was called by this name.

SCRATCH BLOCK (or Scratch Stock)—

A tool used by cabinet makers for inlaying strings and bands and less frequently for making small mouldings. It consists of a stock made of hardwood which is slotted lengthwise to carry a steel blade, the latter being secured by screws which tighten up the slot. The blade is filed to the desired section, the cutting edge being 90°. The stock is so shaped that it forms a bearing on the edge of the wood being worked, and the tool is moved backwards and forwards to allow the blade to scratch or scrape the desired groove or moulding, clearing the scrapings frequently. Another form of the tool has an iron body somewhat similar to a spokeshave, an adjustable fence being screwed to the sole. The blade works as in the wooden tool.

SET—

The adjustment of a plane blade and its cap iron to a desired setting.

SHAKE—

A split in timber due to seasoning, causing a separation of the wood between the annual rings. Sometimes the shake is annular, when it is called a Cup shake.

SINGLE IRON PLANE—

One with no cap iron.

SKEW—

Oblique. A skew plane has its cutter at an oblique angle to the side of the plane body.

SKIRTING BOARD—

The narrow board placed around the wall of a room covering the plastered wall where it meets the floor.

SLAMMING STYLE—

The vertical strip against which a door abuts when closed, and into which the lock shoots.

SLITTING CUTTER—

The cutter of 405 plane which is used to cut off narrow strips instead of sawing them off.

SPALT—

Wood that is brittle, short grained, breaking easily through dryness or decay, is said to be spalt.

SPLAT—

The broad, flat, vertical, central member of a chair back.

SPOKESHAVE—

A type of double-handed plane with a narrow face used for curved woodwork. It may have a flat sole for convex curves or a rounded sole for concave curves. Originally used for shaping or shaving spokes.

SPURS—

Used on Grooving and Rabbeting Planes when cutting wood across the grain. In the operative position the spur or spurs project below the bottom of the plane and act as a knife edge to cut a nick in the wood, which enables the cutting iron to make a clean cut without tearing or splintering the surface.

SQUARE—

At right angles.

STAFF BEAD—

The bead which holds a sash window in place.

STRING—

One of the inclined members of a staircase, into which the treads and risers are fitted.

STRINGING—

Strips of square or rectangular wood of small section which are used for inlaying. (See also Banding.)

STUB TENON—

A short tenon; one whose mortise does not go right through.

TAIL VICE—

A vice placed at the end of the bench. It is useful for holding long boards, and provides a handy cramp when pegs are fitted at intervals along the bench top.

TEMPER—

See Heat treatment.

TENON—

A projection at the end of a piece of wood inserted into the sockets or mortise of another to hold the two together, forming the familiar mortise and tenon joint. Its origin is lost in obscurity; the Egyptians used it as shown by its appearance in their wooden beds. Our words are from the French—tenon, tenir, to hold; and mortaise, but their ancestry is probably much more ancient than this.

TOAT—

A plane handle. It may be an open toat or a closed toat. The derivation is obscure.

TOOTHING—

Scoring the surface of the wood (ground) on which a veneer is to be laid. The toothing removes plane marks, and provides a better bite for the glue. It is done diagonally across the ground, both ways, and the operation is speedily worked with the toothing cutter of 080 Scraper (q.v.).

TORUS—

A convex moulding of approximately semi-circular section, much used as a base moulding.

TRENCH—

A housing; a dado. See Housing.

TUNGSTEN—

A metal found in certain minerals, chiefly wolframite. In colloidal form it is used in electric lamp filaments. As tungsten carbide, it is a constituent part of the steel used for making Record Plane Cutters. (See page 26.)

VENEER—

A thin layer of wood glued on to other wood for decorative effect. Rare woods are thus made to go farther, and grain effects that would weaken constructions are made available without affecting strength. Veneers may be saw cut or knife cut, the latter being much thinner. Saw cut veneer is more tedious to lay but it can be repaired and restored if need be, but many of the modern knife-cut veneers are so thin that repair is impossible, and they are so thin that they are very susceptible to damage. It is not good practice to lay veneer on to very inferior wood.

VICE CLAMPS—CLAMS—

Fibre grips fitted with steel lugs to fit the jaws of metal working vices so that delicate or highly polished articles may be gripped without damage.

WAINSCOT—

A lining of interior walls, usually panelled.

WARP—

The natural distortion of wood due to drying out.

WEATHER BOARDS—

Overlapping boards used as an outside covering to buildings, with a tapered end section. The thicker edge may be rabbeted to receive the thinner edge of the next board.

WIND—

A twist in a board or surface. To test for wind, winding strips are used. (See Fig. 72.) Many craftsmen take great pride in making their winding strips, planing them up from choice hardwood, and often inlaying strips or blocks of contrasting wood or ivory so that co-incidence is more clearly apparent.

INDEX